JUNE STEPHENSON
42 HAMILTON ROAD
OXFORD
OX2 7PZ

TEL (01865) 553680

Dervla Murphy

was born in County Waterford, Ireland, of Dublin parents. Since 1964 she has been regularly publishing descriptions of her journeys – by bicycle or foot – in the remoter areas of four continents. She has also written about the problems of Northern Ireland, the hazards of the nuclear power industry and race relations in Britain. She still lives in County Waterford.

Dervla Murphy is the author of many travel books, including *In Ethiopia with a Mule*, *Eight Feet in the Andes*, *Full Tilt*, *Muddling Through in Madagascar*, *The Ukimwi Road*, *South from the Limpopo*, *Cameroon with Egbert* and *Tibetan Foothold*.

KU-611-545

Other books by the same author

IN ETHIOPIA WITH A MULE
EIGHT FEET IN THE ANDES
WHERE THE INDUS IS YOUNG
ON A SHOESTRING TO COORG
FULL TILT
MUDDLING THROUGH IN MADAGASCAR
THE WAITING LAND
THE UKIMWI ROAD
SOUTH FROM THE LIMPOPO
CAMEROON WITH EGBERT
TIBETAN FOOTHOLD

DERVLA MURPHY

One Foot in Laos

'The mountains that surround it on every side fortify the land marvellously against the enterprises of foreigners ... Whole forests of full grown timber trees grow at the foot of these mountains seeming to have been planted intentionally to serve as a rampart against the great falls of rain which would cause great damage if there were not this natural obstacle. The Lao live at peace with all six neighbouring kingdoms, with the exception of the Pegu [the Shan States of Burma], with whom they have been at war for a number of years. But the unnavigable rivers, mountains and forests intervening mean they cannot do each other much harm.'

Gerrit van Wuysthoff, 1641

Flamingo
An Imprint of HarperCollinsPublishers

Flamingo
An Imprint of HarperCollinsPublishers
77–85 Fulham Palace Road,
Hammersmith, London W6 8JB

www.**fire**and**water**.com

Published by Flamingo 2000
9 8 7 6 5 4 3 2 1

First published in Great Britain by
John Murray 1999

Copyright © Dervla Murphy 1999

The Author asserts the moral right to
be identified as the author of this work

Author photograph by Michael Brophy

ISBN 0 00 655221 8

Set in New Baskerville

Printed and bound in Great Britain by
Clays Ltd, St Ives plc

All rights reserved. No part of this publication may be
reproduced, stored in a retrieval system, or transmitted,
in any form or by any means, electronic, mechanical,
photocopying, recording or otherwise, without the prior
permission of the publishers.

This book is sold subject to the condition that it shall not,
by way of trade or otherwise, be lent, re-sold, hired out or
otherwise circulated without the publisher's prior consent
in any form of binding or cover other than that in which it
is published and without a similar condition including this
condition being imposed on the subsequent purchaser.

For Caitriona, John and Ruairi

Contents

Preface

It is sensible to let oneself be pushed around by Fate. I had already bought a guidebook to Sri Lanka when Catherine called; since our last meeting, in Tanzania, she and her husband had spent three years working in Laos. We lunched outside, in bright August sunshine, while Catherine's boys – lucky lads, reared far from urban constraints – daringly climbed all over my roofs. And Catherine talked nostalgically of a mountainous country inhabited by gentle people, with a few tarred roads – a country as yet little touched, outside its two or three small cities, by consumerism and mass tourism. 'But,' she observed, 'things are about to change.' Already Thai television is watched along the western border – that is, on the left bank of the Mekong – many backpackers are arriving annually, motor traffic has increased since the opening of the so-called Friendship Bridge in April 1994 and developers are active. Soon the Laos she and Jan had known would be no more.

I heard then what I think of as my 'inner click', last heard before my Cameroonian trek in 1987. It happens when for some reason I am suddenly determined to visit a country previously unconsidered. Within an hour, Sri Lanka had been shelved.

Apart from Catherine's information and Norman Lewis's *A Dragon Apparent* – read soon after it was published, almost half a century ago – I then knew nothing of my next destination. A week later I was in London, buying a map and every available book on Laos; not many are available in English but quality makes up for quantity (see Bibliography). Settling down to a few months' serious homework, I felt shamed by my ignorance. I had not realized the extent to which this misfortunate little country (in area the size of Britain, population 4.5 million) suffered as a victim of both Cold Warriors during the Second Indochina War – otherwise known, misleadingly, as the Vietnam War.

Laos, the map revealed, is walking rather than cycling territory. As it is a hot country, even during its cool season, I packed three sleeveless shirts and three pairs of knee-length shorts before turning my mind to more taxing matters, like visa complications (formidable) and the appropriate malaria cure (elusive). Then someone warned me that bare shoulders and legs offend Lao sensibilities, as do grubby travellers. It didn't take long to replace the unsuitable garments but the Lao aversion to grubbiness might not be so easily dealt with at the end of a sweaty, dusty trekking day.

It seems odd that the wanderlust, unlike other lusts, does not diminish with age. As departure date approached my excitement level rose as uncontrollably as though I had never before left Ireland.

Historical Note

Francis Garnier, the French explorer, wrote during the 1860s, 'A sense of history is absolutely absent in the Lao, their imagination is fired by fables and extraordinary legends, with no precise date, making it impossible to appreciate their historical value.'

Not until the fourteenth century do verifiable characters and events emerge. In or about 1316 was born Fa Ngum, revered as the man who established the Kingdom of Lan Xang, from which the Lao People's Democratic Republic is tortuously descended. Fa Ngum was only a little fellow when his father, Phi Fa, disgraced himself. Phi Fa, eldest son and heir apparent to King Phaya Souvanna-Khampong of Muong Swa (now Luang Prabang), enraged the King by seducing a member of the royal household – possibly one of the royal wives. His punishment was permanent exile and he was told to take his first-born son with him. At the Khmer court at Angkor King Jayarvarman Paramesvara made the exiles welcome and here Fa Ngum grew up, in due course marrying the King's daughter. His father-in-law then put him in command of 10,000 men and he led them north, at the age of twenty-two, to assert his right to the throne of Muong Swa. A ten-year campaign secured him a far bigger kingdom, encompassing south-west Yunnan, north-east Laos, Xieng Khouang, most of the Korat plateau west of the Mekong and possibly Champasak to the south. During the siege of Muong Swa, Phi Fa died and in 1353 Fa Ngum deposed his grandfather and proclaimed himself King of Lan Xang. ('Land of a Million Elephants' – wars were fought with elephants so this naming of the new kingdom emphasized his power.) An administrator of genius, Fa Ngum established a civil infrastructure that lasted for more than three centuries. But it seems he eventually became too authoritarian, a quality deprecated by the Lao. At the age of fifty-seven he was deposed by a clique of noblemen and succeeded by his seventeen-year-old son, Oun Hueun Samsenthai. Five years later he died in exile.

King Samsenthai was gentle, peace-loving and deeply religious. During his forty-three-year reign the Kingdom of Lan Xang flourished, many wats (temples/monasteries) were built and Luang Prabang became one of the region's most renowned centres of Buddhist learning. Then began an enduring tradition. The Sangha (the Buddhist monks' 'Establishment') became an ally of the kingdom's secular rulers whose authority was reinforced by the Sangha's approbation – and in turn the Sangha gained respect as the spiritual mentors of the rulers. At intervals, Laos's chaotic history threatened this alliance, without ever destroying it. Garnier noted: 'The influence of the monks is very strong; religious and civil power live side by side peacefully. Neither trespasses on the rights of the other. The neutrality of the monks in all political matters seems absolute.'

A turbulent century followed King Samsenthai's death. Too often disunity among the nobles, brought about by the lack of any form of primogeniture, left the way open for more powerful neighbours to make trouble. The scene was constantly shifting; areas belonged to the kingdom, then splintered off and formed other alliances or became independent, then were reabsorbed into Lan Xang or replaced by other areas.

In 1563 King Xetthathirat, for reasons economic and strategic, moved his capital from Luang Prabang to Viang Chan (Vientiane), then a small fortified city with two wats – but a rich city, its wealth derived from the fertility of the surrounding plains and from taxes paid by traders going upstream. (Until very recently, the Mekong was this region's only highway.)

Under King Surinyavongsa, who won the throne in 1637 and reigned for fifty-seven years, the kingdom enjoyed a Golden Age of peace and prosperity, again becoming renowned both for Buddhist learning and for the secular arts of theatre, music and classical dancing. The monks who came from Burma and Cambodia to study in its well-endowed wats were 'more numerous than the soldiers of the Emperor of Germany'. That was the astonished comment of Gerritt van Wuysthoff, a Dutch East India Company merchant who arrived in the 1640s – as, coincidentally, did Giovanni-Maria Leria. This Italian Jesuit would-be missionary stayed for five years and learned the language before accepting that he would never be allowed to proselytize. He reported home: 'The population is a peaceable one and very little versed in the art of war. Hostility and quarrelling are banished from the land. Never has one of them spoken evil of another. They are of perfect sincerity, without deceit, humble and courteous, of unalterable trustworthiness, affable, accommodating and open to reason.' Perhaps he had realized, by the end of his stay, that proselytizing would do more harm than good.

Both those Europeans, the first to visit Laos, were astounded by the kingdom's wealth and both deplored the proportion donated to the Sangha. After their departures, no other Westerners visited Laos for more than half a century and, in Martin Stuart-Fox's words, 'the country was almost as remote and mysterious as Tibet'.

Sadly, the peaceable nature of the population did not protect them during the eighteenth and nineteenth centuries. At various times the Burmese, the Siamese (Thais), the Annamese (Vietnamese) and the Khmer (Cambodians) attacked Vientiane. Already the international arms traders, dealing in improved military technology, were active, strengthening those neighbouring kingdoms. In 1778 Vientiane submitted to Siamese suzerainty after a four-month siege – then was sacked. The famous Emerald Buddha and other deeply revered images were carted off to Bangkok – as was King Nanthasen. Thousands of Lao peasants were forcibly resettled in the north-east of Siam and reduced to serfdom – a regular occurrence, following Siamese victories, which is why many more ethnic Lao now live in Thailand than in Laos itself.

As Martin Stuart-Fox explains:

Siam remained a Southeast Asian mandala, not a modern state. There was no centrally appointed administration. The larger principalities were entirely autonomous. Even smaller muang that progressively transferred their allegiance, under pressure, from Viang Chan to Bangkok, could collect their own taxes and enforce their own justice. Only three matters had to be referred to Bangkok: permission to raise the necessary force to discipline a recalcitrant vassal; nomination of high officials to rule the muang; and sentences of capital punishment . . . King Nanthasen was permitted to return to Viang

Chan to rule as a tributary of Siam . . . Viang Chan was rebuilt and its population grew. In 1804 Anuvong succeeded his two elder brothers on the throne.

In 1826 Anuvong made the mistake of trying to re-establish an independent Lao kingdom. This provoked the total obliteration of Vientiane and its entire population was 'relocated' west of the Mekong. The Siamese soldiers who sacked the city in 1827 were US-armed – which sale of weapons to King Rama III marked the first US intervention in South-east Asia.

In the 1860s Louis de Carne described the ruins of Vientiane: 'The vegetation is like a veil drawn by nature over the weakness of man and the vanity of his works . . .'

In 1893 the French created an administrative unit named, by them, Laos – in area less than half the size of the former Kingdom of Lan Xang and with a far smaller population. They then rein-vented Vientiane as the 'capital' of the least profitable and access-ible of their Indochinese acquisitions.

For the next fifty years the kings were allowed to reign in Luang Prabang, performing their religious duties but having no admin-istrative power. The French treated Laos as a minor appendage of Vietnam, soon abandoning their ambitious development plans and leaving the Chinese and Vietnamese to continue controlling commerce and trade. During that period, a small French-edu-cated élite emerged from among the aristocracy, men who in the 1940s sowed the seed of Lao nationalism – if that is not too hard-edged a word for the mild Laotian requests to be granted independence.

In March 1945, towards the end of the Second World War, the Japanese took over from the French (pro-Vichy) administration. Within fourteen months de Gaulle's troops, backed by Britain and the US, had forcibly reoccupied Vientiane. Then came the First Indochina War (the French versus the Vietminh, 1946–54), during which various offers of partial independence failed to satisfy the Lao.

In January 1950 Ho Chi Minh's Democratic Republic of Vietnam was recognized by the People's Republic of China and the Soviet Union. The US was then urging the French to grant more substantial concessions to all the peoples of Indochina, to prevent their joining the anti-colonial Communist forces. On 6 February 1950 a formal transfer of certain powers to the Royal Lao Government was signed by the French but they retained control over the army, the administration of justice and the secret police.

On 22 October 1953 King Sisavangvong signed a Treaty of Friendship and Association with France, reaffirming Lao membership of the French Union in exchange for independence.

Martin Stuart-Fox explains that:

By establishing an extensive 'liberated zone' in Xam Neua and Phongsali under protection of the Vietminh, the offensive of April 1953 effectively divided Laos both administratively and politically [the Pathet Lao from the Royalists]. For the first time since its formation, the Pathet Lao possessed a consolidated territory to govern [most of northern Laos]. The Royal Lao government vehemently denounced these developments. For the government the offensive was a Vietnamese invasion, and the Pathet Lao were but Vietnamese puppets. For the Pathet Lao the invasion had been a joint operation 'in co-ordination with volunteer Vietnamese troops'. Neither version was accurate. The offensive of 1953 was a tactical episode in the First Indochina War between France and the Vietminh, a conflict from which the Lao could no more insulate themselves in 1953 than they could a decade later from the Second Indochina War between the Democratic Republic of (North) Vietnam and the United States.

The US funded up to three-quarters of the cost of the First Indochina War and the French military command remained confident that they could win – until the Vietminh victory at Dien Bien Phu. On 8 May 1954, the day after the French garrison surrendered (a piquant coincidence), international delegates, co-chaired by Britain and the Soviet Union, met in Geneva to negotiate a settlement. Cambodia was to remain intact, Vietnam was divided into two separate political entities. Within Laos, the US-backed Royal Lao Army and the Vietminh-backed Pathet Lao were to disengage and all foreign forces to withdraw from the country – apart from 5,000 French troops. The US refused to endorse the Final Declaration of this Geneva Conference. The then Secretary of State, John Foster Dulles, argued that it did not meet the conditions necessary to prevent the spread of Communism and President Eisenhower warned: 'The United States has not itself been party to or bound by the decisions taken by the Conference.' Part of the settlement included the Royal Lao Government's declaration that it would never allow its territory to be used by another power for aggressive purposes or itself pursue a policy of aggression. The Agreement also prohibited the introduction of munitions and armaments to Laos except for 'categories specified as necessary for the defence of Laos'.

Between 1953 and 1962 three main political movements existed. The Pathet Lao, led by Prince Souphanouvong, controlled much of northern Laos. The US-managed, Vientiane-based Royalist movement, led by General Phoumi Nosavan, controlled central and southern Laos. The neutralist Royalist movement led by Prince Souvanna Phouma, half-brother to Prince Souphanouvong, repeatedly tried to mediate between the other two. Dr Stuart-Fox has described this prince as 'a tragic figure in modern Lao history, a stubborn symbol of an alternative, neutral, "middle way"'.

In 1957, after internationally supervised democratic elections, those three groups formed a coalition government, soon sabotaged by the CIA; the US objected to the inclusion of the Pathet Lao. Prince Souphanouvong, who had won a higher popular vote than any other candidate, was then imprisoned with his fellow Pathet Lao political leaders. Two years later all those leaders escaped from prison, probably helped by sympathetic jailers, and joined their guerrilla army and their Vietnamese allies in the north.

In 1961 the Secret War began. The US, unwilling to commit ground troops to Laos, used the Royal Lao Army, and Thai and Hmong mercenaries, to fight on its behalf.

In 1962 a fourteen-country conference in Geneva led eventually to the Geneva Agreements which did no more than the 1954 Geneva Final Declaration to protect Laos from the Cold Warriors.

In 1964 the US launched its nine-year air war over Laos in a futile attempt to destroy the Ho Chi Minh Trail, part of which passed through eastern Laos. That country then became the most heavily bombarded in the history of the world, receiving more tonnage of ordnance than Germany did during the Second World War.

By 1973 it was clear the Americans could not win in Vietnam. During February a ceasefire was declared within Laos where a few months previously the Pathet Lao had announced the formation of the Lao People's Revolutionary Party (LPRP). In September a power-sharing protocol was signed between the Pathet Lao and the Royal Lao Government and led to another coalition.

In April 1975 the Americans were run out of South Vietnam and Cambodia. A month later they and their Royalist puppets left Laos abruptly and the LPRP became the party of government. On 2 December the Lao People's Democratic Republic (Lao PDR) was declared and the monarchy abolished.

In 1986 the government revealed its New Economic Mechanism (NEM), a first step towards the signing, three years later, of an agreement with the World Bank and IMF committing Laos to extensive economic reforms, 'liberal' policies on foreign investments and the privatization of state-owned firms.

People have asked me: is Laos another of those post-colonial 'pretend nations'? Superficially, yes; what the French designated as 'Laos' was not, and had never been, a nation-state in our terms. No such thing existed in South-east Asia, as Martin Stuart-Fox makes clear. However, a distinctive cultural unit did exist, 'where women wear *sins*, men make music on the *khene*, everyone eats sticky rice and fermented fish paste, houses are built on stilts and people prefer going to festivals than going into battle'. This definition of his kingdom is Fa Ngum's and in the fourteenth century it was accepted by all neighbouring rulers including the Emperor of Annam, when he and Fa Ngum were drawing up a treaty to mark the frontier between their kingdoms. Six hundred years later, the same criteria are valid. But they may not remain so for much longer, in our homogenizing age.

Significantly, the stabilizing influence of Buddhism was recognized by the Communist Pathet Lao. On coming to power in 1975 they engineered a typical Lao compromise – no suppression of Buddhism but a modification of its traditions to bring it into line (more or less) with socialist principles, thus enabling it to retain its historic role as an ally of the rulers. Some commentators describe this as a cynical ploy. Others see it as proof that the Pathet Lao were always Communists *manqué*, at heart respectful of Buddhism.

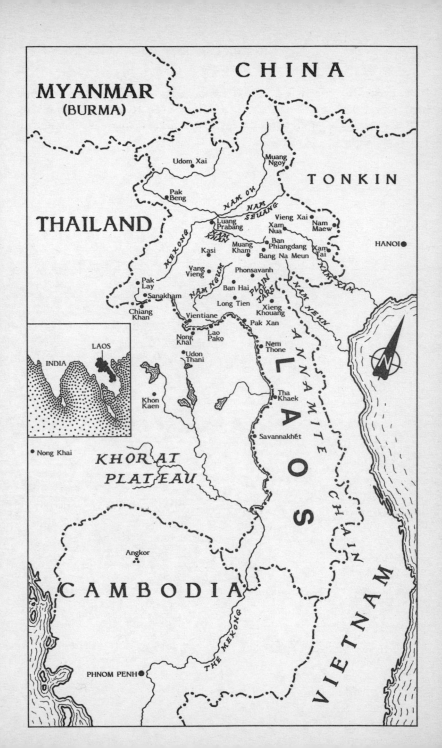

1

A Glimpse of Thailand

Emerging from the Underground at Heathrow, I shouldered a rucksack holding three months' luggage, walked briskly towards Departures – then registered a novel sensation of lightness and simplicity. Having spent the past fortnight with my daughter Rachel and two granddaughters (Rose aged two, Clodagh newly minted) I had become inured to much more taxing preparations for a three-hour journey. One had to assemble Rose's buggy, Rose's football in a large plastic bag, Rose's potty in another large plastic bag, spare trousers and knickers lest the potty might not be reached in time, Rose's teddy in his own buggy, a few changes of nappy for Clodagh, baby lotion, baby wipes, cotton wool, rubber pants, Vaseline, Sudocrem, a box of raisins lest hunger might strike, a bottle of milk lest thirst might strike, a loo roll to wipe small noses (permanently in need of wiping during December), stale bread to feed the ducks and geese in Peckham Rye park, waterproofs for everyone . . . No wonder I felt liberated at Heathrow.

On the Virgin Airways hop to Brussels most of my fellow-travellers were plump EU types wearing expensive suits and abstracted expressions. Brussels airport – unfamiliar to me – seemed even more crowded than Heathrow and the Sabena departure gate for Bangkok was invisible from afar. At the best of times, large airports fluster me. Now I approached a hard-faced Sabena-uniformed woman on duty at one gate and asked for directions. She treated me with breathtaking rudeness, ignoring my question. 'Get back to your place!' she snapped. 'Take your turn like everyone else!' Never, anywhere, have I been treated with such insolence. And the cabin staff were not much better: unsmiling and ungracious. As the tourist industry expands, and more and more 'operators' try to net more and more customers through lowering standards/prices, some airlines tend to process passengers as though they were goods in transit.

The Lao government, most guidebooks explain, has an ambivalent attitude towards tourists – especially backpackers. I can sympathize with its dilemma. Foreigners spend dollars; Laos needs (or has been persuaded that it needs) lots of dollars. However, the damage done globally by mass tourism so appals me that I would willingly – even joyfully – have forgone my Laotian journey had I found the country still closed to tourists, as it was until recently. An extreme attitude, you may (probably will) think. But a thriving tourist industry can rapidly undermine the cultures of hitherto isolated countries.

At 4.15 a.m. local time on 4 December I arrived in Bangkok – but my rucksack did not. I had had a premonition that this would be so, a premonition so strong I mentioned it to Rachel in London. As I was about to lose my cool (easily done after a sensationally turbulent eleven-hour flight) a young Thai woman materialized beside me and said in a soft soothing voice that my luggage was on a KLM flight due to land at 12.30 p.m. Disarmed by this first encounter with Thai charm, I forbore to complain about missing the 6.30 train for Nong Khai which departs from the station opposite the airport; now I would have to take a bus.

In search of a bus timetable I wandered wearily through an air-conditioned vastness, all glossy marble floors and harsh assertive colours and glaring lights. Tall plastic Christmas trees stood in corners, vulgarly loaded with 'snow' and simpering fairies and blinking psychedelic Santas. Escalators purred beneath strident signs directing one upwards to Kentucky Fried Chicken, Dunkin' Donuts, Burger King and the Cyber Café. Between these delights are several bureaux de change, and a glass-walled triangular protuberance called Internet Service, and unalluring souvenir shops and a prayer room for Muslims. Oil-rich tourists are valued and much in evidence, pushing mega-trolleys piled high with electronic goods. It was quite a relief to come upon the John Bull Pub, very authentic with 'Traditional Ales, Fine Wines & Spirits' in elegant golden script above a splendidly carved mahogany bar. Here were polished wooden tables, handsome chairs with velvetish green or crimson seats, an agreeably patterned carpet and dim lighting. Glancing at my watch, I did a swift calculation – 11.30 p.m. London time, not an improper hour for a beer.

The only other drinkers were three English businessmen with lap-top computers, mobile phones and an interest in Laos. I tried to eavesdrop but could hear no more than a phrase at a time. The TV, perched on a high shelf, was showing a BBC programme about the late Princess Diana's campaign against landmines. It soon switched to CNN, which proclaimed that if South Korea rejects IMF advice 'that will make a dangerous risk for US national security'. Then came many other scraps of sub-literate misinformation. No wonder the Poor World is confused and disempowered – increasingly exposed to CNN propaganda, never allowed to perceive the reality of its own position as victim of the Rich World.

The John Bull's cheapest pint costs US$4 so frugality restricted my intake. Moving on, I paused by a news-stand to read an item about global warming on the front page of the *International Herald Tribune*. How much energy is wasted in airports like Bangkok's, modelled on the American way of life? Another item dealt with the massive ecological damage being done to Jordan by mass tourism.

At the tourist information kiosk the young lady in charge knew nothing about buses to anywhere and spoke minimal English – which surprised me, since millions of English-speakers pass through this airport annually. However, in Thailand the tourist industry has not yet corroded human relations and most people seem well disposed towards foreigners. (Apart from the many notoriously skilful criminals who operate around the airport and elsewhere.) Soon I had been told that a No. 29 bus would take me the twenty miles or so to the Nong Khai bus terminus.

When the bureaux de change opened, my dollars proved to be worth 35 baht each. Some four months previously the Thai 'Miracle' had predictably ended in a 'Crash'. In Thailand, as Benedict Anderson has explained,

The Americans intervened politically, economically, militarily and culturally, on a massive scale. The notorious domino theory was invented specifically for South-East Asia. To shore up the line of teetering dominoes, Washington made every effort to create loyal, capitalistically prosperous, authoritarian and anti-Communist regimes – typically, but not invariably, dominated by the military. No world region received more 'aid' . . . The Washington–Peking coalition against Moscow, consolidated after the 'fall' of Indochina, meant that from the late Seventies to the collapse of the Soviet Union those countries of South-East Asia who so wished could continue to profit from Washington's Cold War largesse without facing any severe internal or external constraints . . . Thailand was a frontline state for the Americans virtually from the start.

So was Laos, and to understand that country's recent past one must remember this background.

In Nong Khai I was to meet a USAID educational consultant who deplored the misspending of Washington's largesse. 'It sure was a miracle era! But the Thai should have known it could not last – used it to prepare for a leaner future. Take a look at this country, never colonized so they can't blame the imperialists for the mess they're in. Just a few days before the Crash those World Bank guys were praising Thailand for maintaining a high rate of growth since 1970. All developing countries should follow Thailand's example – so they said. Bullshit! In '90 only 28 per cent of kids were getting any kind of secondary education and by the year 2000 70 per cent of the workforce will have had only bad primary schooling. The academic staff at state-owned universities get paid what you'd call pocket money and spend most of their time moonlighting – and who can blame them? Families with money send their kids to Bangkok's "international" schools [provided originally for the education of expats' children] – then off they go to universities in Australia, Canada, the States or the UK. The brightest graduates settle abroad – and wouldn't you! The bunch who return get into money-making and you don't make money teaching in the state system. When you get to Laos you'll find it's getting to be the same way there since the Commies lost their grip – more private schools opening, less funding for the state schools.'

The growth so admired by the World Bank was of course 'export oriented', as the jargon has it, and Thailand's domestic investors operated only within the sheltered sectors of the economy – dodgy banking, speculative real estate deals, the exploitation of natural resources (mainly irresponsible logging) and manic construction. At the time of the Crash, in July 1997, Bangkok's unoccupied office and housing units numbered a staggering 700,000 – and that is a conservative estimate.

Thailand sided with Japan in the Second World War but since 1947 its dictators (the majority military) have been America's willing puppets. During the Second Indochina War billions of us dollars were spent on building the network of roads and military bases necessary for the bludgeoning of Indochina by air, land and sea forces. Some 50,000 us servicemen were then stationed in Thailand, a country permanently culturally poisoned by that alliance. It created a newly wealthy and quite numerous Thai middle class, devoted to the American way of life. And the CIA helped to set up a horrifying number of heroin millionaires among the powerful élite who ruled the land. Something similar happened in Laos, on a lesser scale but with more obvious political consequences.

At 8.30 a.m. my body clock suddenly registered the fact that for me this was the middle of the night. In a quiet corner I lay on the cool marble floor and slept soundly until noon. An hour later, reunited with my rucksack, I stepped out into Bangkok's stifling midday humidity.

A high walkway, bridging the motorway's non-stop torrent, took me to the bus stop. In comparison with Bangkok, Central London's air seems Andean-pure; many Thai wear masks: the traffic police, bus and taxi drivers, building site workers, schoolchildren. In 1997 the number of cars on Bangkok's streets increased daily by 800. And each year, while vehicles wait at traffic lights, petrol to the value of us$500 million is (mis)used. In December 1993 a local paper complained: 'Our traffic congestion and pollution are the worst in the world – ever. Never in history have people had to live in the conditions we endure each day.' One wonders – why does anyone (apart from sex deviates) go to Bangkok for a holiday?

Across the road, outside the railway station, pye-dogs foraged between food stalls – some maimed and the majority mangy but none too thin. Beggars blind or crippled crouched in corners. For as far as the eye could see, in both directions, stretched a puzzling phenomenon: pairs of thirty-foot-high concrete pillars, ten yards apart, each sporting a cluster of rusty iron rods. This line of pillars continues for many miles, accompanying the highway and contributing significantly to the ugliness of Bangkok's outskirts. It is, I learned later, the residue of a failed scheme to construct an overhead railway.

The ramshackle No. 29 bus was overcrowded but a young woman immediately offered me her seat. The conductor wasn't interested in my baht: perhaps he had no change. Three tallish young soldiers, very slim, stood in the aisle; their trim brown uniforms, crisply laundered, revealed perfectly proportioned bodies. The classic statues seen in Laotian temples and museums are not idealized forms; such well-made bodies are usual in this part of the world.

At 2.30 I bought my ticket for the overnight bus to Nong Khai, departing at 8.40 p.m. All legends and signposts being in Thai, and English-speakers being scarce, it seemed prudent not to explore central Bangkok. Getting lost can be fun but were I to plunge into this city's maelstrom I might – probably would – miss my bus.

The Northern Bus Terminus, as big as two football pitches, was a diesel-hazy pullulation of people – the norm in Bangkok (population 11 million) I, at first, assumed. Then a friendly young English-speaking woman explained – tomorrow would be the King's seventieth birthday, a national holiday, providing a long weekend, therefore thousands (millions?) were going home to their towns and villages and every form of transport was overstretched and I was lucky to have got a bus seat . . . She gave me her card (Financial Consultant) and lent me the *Bangkok Post*. A quarter-page advertisement fascinated me; it showed the back view of a girl wearing only a pony-tail and proclaimed 'AMERICAN PLASTIC SURGERY NOW IN BANGKOK! Introducing an American Board Certified Plastic Surgeon with 15 years experience in California. Specializing in Facelifts, Eyelid Surgery, Nasal reshaping, Tumescent Liposuction, Breast enhancement, and a complete skin care line.' My companion couldn't tell me what Tumescent Liposuction is, nor has it yet found a place in my dictionary. But there must be someone out there who knows all about it and thinks it's worth the money.

An urban bus station makes a good observation post. This was not the sort of Asian scene I'm used to: where were the overloaded passengers, the begging children, the shouting competing porters, the hawkers, the cripples, the litter? Everyone carried conventional amounts of luggage in conventional containers, barefooted coolies moved through the crowds in an orderly fashion pushing handcarts of goods to weighing offices, no beggars or cripples were admitted, not so much as a grape pip or a matchstick defiled the ground. From high rafters depended several bilingual (Thai and English) notices warning people about an on-the-spot fine for littering – 2,000 baht. Burger King et al. fed the multitude and a mini-supermarket, facing the concourse, sold most of the things one might find in its twin back home. The many seats and benches were crowded – apart from rows of plastic chairs within a roped-off monks' enclosure at the base of a towering, glittering shrine dedicated to the King and surrounded by paper flowers and electric 'candles'. Above the shrine hung a life-size photograph of HM as a young man, wearing the sort of comic opera uniform universally beloved by senior military officers. In mid-afternoon a platoon of novice monks arrived, each carrying only an umbrella; possessing nothing, they travel without luggage. I saw few smokers – mostly coolies – but an alarming number of adults and obviously distressed children were using asthma inhalers.

At 8 p.m., when I began to look for my bus, a man with an antique loudspeaker and a hoarse voice had for hours been making non-stop incomprehensible announcements. Twenty frantic minutes later I was one of thousands unable to find fixed points from which services routinely depart. All around the concourse stood long lines of buses – some lacking destination inscriptions, others inscribed in Thai, all with their poisonous engines running. People stared blankly when I pleaded for information about the Nong Khai bus, showing my ticket. Many looked bewildered while struggling through this human whirlpool yet no one looked stressed, whatever they may have been feeling. And I saw none of the aggressive pushing and yelling that would mark a similar scene in India or some African countries. (Oddly, I was the only foreigner around.) Finally, a diminutive old man with a wizened face grabbed my ticket and dodged away through the throngs, yelling at me to follow. He was so elfin I soon lost sight of him, which did nothing to lower my anxiety level. Then he came

weaving back, seized my hand and pulled me through the conflict-
ing currents of bodies to a certain row of buses where, he indicated, Nong Khai passengers should stand, awaiting decisions.
Before I had time to thank him, he vanished.

Most of my companions in this non-queue were coughing
uncontrollably and mopping watering eyes. Eventually an
unmarked coach was designated as the Nong Khai service; fifteen
minutes later its door was unlocked and we boarded. Then came
another long delay, for a pleasing reason: one passenger was
missing and the driver rightly reckoned that people matter more
than punctuality.

For two and a half hours we moved at less than walking speed –
or did not move. Bangkok's normal rush-hour traffic averages 6
m.p.h. The city's many tangles of six-lane highways, on monstrous
concrete stilts, looked surreal from a distance under the glare of
orange lights – like magnified centipedes in their death throes.
For miles the ugliness of the aborted railway accompanied our
road, dwarfed by huge hoardings, many of them advertising
motor vehicles. Now I could understand why analysts refer to
Bangkok as an EMR – Extended Metropolitan Region. Its sprawl
covers 1,000 square miles.

Our plush air-conditioned coach provided Thai pop music
throughout the night – played rather too loudly but otherwise
agreeable enough, the instruments unfamiliar. Three well-
behaved toddlers gave the impression of thoroughly enjoying
long bus journeys. One, directly across the aisle from me,
repeated the final phrase in each sentence uttered by her mother.
The young man beside me slept until dawn, unaware of having his
head on my shoulder. I merely dozed, on and off; in a sitting position I never can sleep well.

The sun rose redly on a flat brownish landscape. Our straight
road – Route 2, now rather cloyingly renamed 'the Friendship
Highway' – was two-lane by this stage but still dominated by hoardings and very tall concrete electricity poles, their multiple cables
bringing power from Laos. The two towns *en route*, Khon Kaen and
Udon Thani, were important American bases during the Second
Indochina War; both have many new blocks of flats and office
buildings, much more attractively designed than their equivalents
in Britain and Ireland. Beyond Udon Thani the hoardings were

replaced by an increasing number of trees – low and scrawny, their leaves brown – and hereabouts a few water buffalo grazed on fawn expanses of paddy stubble. We arrived at Nong Khai four hours late, at 9.20 a.m.

I walked to the Meeting Place, a guesthouse recommended in guidebooks as a convenient source of Lao visas. This wooden two-storey Thai dwelling, pleasantly tree-surrounded, was rented in 1991 by Alan Patterson, an Australian who 'worked in tourism' for many years before moving to Thailand. He provided a visa form, to be accompanied by one photograph, US$50 for a fifteen-day tourist visa and US$11 to pay his agent's fee. Next morning, the agent would see me swiftly across the Lao border; without such an escort, I was assured, it took days to grope through the maze of Lao bureaucracy.

In fact this form was less bureaucratic than many I've known. Having completed it, I sat under the trees, writing my notes on a trestle table and enjoying the birdsong. Soon my host joined me and was informative. After the US retreat from Vietnam, many rich Vietnamese settled in Nong Khai and one such family built the Meeting Place. In 1980 they moved on to California (easily done as they came from a Catholic pro-US faction) where two genera-tions are now prospering in the medical profession. Alan offered 'more than a fair price' for the house but they wouldn't sell. 'And weren't they right!' exclaimed Alan. 'Look at the baht now!' He was making 'nice amounts' by importing indigenous Australian palm trees – an unlikely commerce, there being no shortage of palm trees in Thailand. It seems nowadays you can start a fashion for pretty well anything. Sadly, he recalled losing to another Australian a 2 million baht contract for the 'beautification' of the Australian-funded Friendship Bridge.

Then Ted arrived, a middle-aged Englishman resident for the past four years in Vientiane, employed as a mechanic by a road-construction company. His young Lao wife went to talk with Alan's young Thai wife before joining us. She spoke excellent English but seemed curiously subservient to her partner. When I ques-tioned her about life in Laos she looked at him anxiously, as though needing his permission before replying. Then Ted began to condemn the Lao as primitive, ignorant, lazy and stupid. The Thai, he asserted, are 'a much better sort, more Westernized'.

Many of the rich Lao who ran away from the Commies in '75 and '76 have recently returned to invest in the new capitalist Laos, 'but everyone hates them'. (An exaggeration, I later learned.)

This was one of those uncomfortable situations where to stay silent could seem like collusion with the barbarian yet to protest could make things even more painful for the person being insulted. I muttered something about 'jet lag' and withdrew.

My large, high-ceilinged room had two wide windows (not mosquito-proof, the netting torn) and two double plank beds with flock mattresses and dirty pillows. As I lay reading and sweating, cockroaches ran to and fro across the other mattress. Downstairs was a communal loo and hot shower – but who would want a hot shower in Nong Khai's climate?

Alan and Ted were continuing their conversation below my window. 'The way aid money's bucketing in now,' said the Brummie accent, 'only a fool couldn't get rich quick in Laos.'

When the worst of the heat had abated I became acquainted with Nong Khai – quite small, very friendly, architecturally still faintly flavoured by a French colonial seepage from across the Mekong. It was galvanized by the building of the Friendship Bridge and the opening up of Laos to tourists and investors. Three brash new hotels defile the riverbank – will two prove to be white elephants? Motor traffic, according to Alan, has increased by 300 per cent in three years, causing masks and asthma inhalers to appear. The shops are full of junk food, replacing the tasty, individually made titbits on offer from roadside stalls before the multinational food industry introduced bloated bright pink 'potato' crisps and a plethora of other unnatural comestibles garishly packaged to lure children. Fresh fruit juices and cane juice sold from barrows are now being replaced by you-know-what. And many children's teeth, as I first noticed in Bangkok and was to continue noticing in urban Laos, are falling out by the age of four, or have been reduced to black stumps. An independent study of the 'Free Market's' impact on nutrition in the Poor World is overdue. But who would fund it?

In a large eating-house with few tables (also the family living-room) I enjoyed, for the equivalent of 50 cents US, a wholesome supper of noodle soup containing slivers of tender chicken leg and chicken liver and bean sprouts and chopped lettuce. Across the room stood an illuminated Buddhist shrine, flanked by a four-foot-high music centre with shelves of tapes underneath and a large TV-cum-video-recorder. Three small daughters sat cross-legged on the floor only a yard from the screen, impassively watching a brutal gangster film. The frequent advertisements seemed even longer than ours: for detergents, shampoos, cars, motor-bikes, refrigerators, cameras, processed foods, Nescafé, cosmetics with skin-lightening ingredients – all the ads as clumsy and naïve as Irish television's in the 1960s. Why do Thai woman imagine they need skin-lighteners? And why has no one told them about the immense damage these do? On my way back to base I visited three video rental shops mainly offering (to judge by the covers) sex and violence.

In hot climates the early hours are precious but at dawn I found myself locked into the Meeting Place, where I was the only guest. When released, two hours later, I realized that the Thai are not, despite their climate, early risers. Nong Khai had the air of a town that has just woken up. Outside eating-houses food was being cooked in cauldrons on the footpath (tar barrels the cookers, bamboo the fuel) but as yet only coffee was available.

Later I observed Thai of all ages and both sexes enjoying four-course breakfasts. As follows: large bowls of noodle soup incorpo-rating meat or fish, served with a heaped plate of crisp fresh greens to be torn up and scattered on the soup; two fried eggs drenched in soya sauce and served with several slices of toast; more greens embedded in a savoury jelly (cold bone stock) eaten with fresh red chillis; bread-and-jam sandwiches for pudding, devoured as though nothing had gone before. All this was accom-panied by large mugs of coffee and pint glass tankards of a pale yellow liquid (herbal tea) poured over chunky ice and drunk through a straw. Presumably these Thai don't lunch – how could they?

At ten o' clock, as part of my 'deal' with Alan, a tuk-tuk took me to the border. This three-wheeled vehicle is derived from the motorbike; its brightly painted rear – like a miniature covered truck – has seats along the sides and in Laos one shares with others going in the same direction. The slow six-mile ride allows one time not to appreciate Nong Khai's most recent 'developments'. At the bridge, imposing new Customs and Immigration offices are ready to deal with a volume of traffic not yet happening. Instantly my minder appeared, saw me through the relaxed Thai formalities and escorted me on a shuttle minibus across the wide brown Mekong to the Lao border checkpoint. There he told me exactly where to wait: ten yards from the 'Foreign Passports' guichet. How would he have reacted had I insisted on standing by his shoulder, observing the details of his negotiation? On the visa issue my guidebook was, I discovered in Vientiane, out of date – though published only a few months previously. The Lao government changes its tourism regulations quite often; had I acted independently my visa would have cost $45 and there would have been no 'agent's fee'.

2

Vientiane Vignettes

The Friendship Bridge 'frontier post' is disconcerting – a fragment of the Rich World tacked on to the edge of Laos. Beyond that complex of absurdly elaborate buildings the forecourt is an expanse of sterile concrete – empty, that morning, but for a group of tuk-tuks in a far corner, their drivers relaxing. As I walked towards them no one rushed to capture the only passenger in view. The half-dozen men were talking animatedly but quietly – their voices soft, their laughter rippling chuckles. Until I was beside them they ignored me, then everyone smiled, murmured greetings, waited for me to choose a vehicle. My choice of the oldest driver (also the most shabbily dressed) seemed to meet with general approval.

For forty minutes we bounced slowly over pot-holes. Already the famed Laotian friendliness was palpable; people standing in their doorways or speeding past on little mopeds waved cheerily at the *falang*. One falls in love with Laos at first feeling rather than at first sight; this approach to the capital looks like a plot to sabotage tourism. Wayside hoardings abound, several depicting giant bulldozers and cranes and shouting 'WELCOME TO VIENTIANE!' – which seems odd until, on arrival in the city, their relevance becomes only too apparent. International banks, motor manufacturers, disco-restaurants and purveyors of Information Age equipment contribute to this chorus of 'Welcomes!' Mega-pylons rise above flat dusty paddyfields like statements of contempt for subsistence farming. Between thatched dwellings and tin-roofed shack-shops rise factories new and half-built, mountains of litter-strewn builders' rubble, two Shell petrol stations and the embryonic National Ethnic Cultural Park in which concrete dinosaurs inexplicably decorate construction sites.

We had passed through the city centre before I was aware of having reached it; architecturally, wats still dominated Vientiane. In a small hotel near the Mekong embankment a young man lay on a battered settee beside the reception desk; there was no one else around. His hands were clasped behind his head, his eyes were closed and he looked unwell. I woke him gently and asked for the cheapest room (US$10). He sat up and seemed worried. Unlike 99 per cent of his compatriots, he spoke a little English. 'For $10 no air-cold, you too hot!' He consulted the register (an exercise book), then announced, 'For tonight we have little people, I give you cold room for cheapest rate.' Picking up my rucksack, he winced with pain. Six days previously he had had his appendix removed, yet it was difficult to persuade him that he must not haul a heavy weight up two steep flights of stairs. My room was clean, with a cold shower (the water supply fickle) and a squat-over loo. But the 'air-cold' was so loud I had to switch it off at night.

Impatient to explore, I defied the midday heat – about 80 degrees F – and strolled downstream on a high embankment in the shade of the riverside trees: bluegums, pipals, teak. Here thatched hut-bars and eating-houses stood on stilts above the Mekong in pleasing contrast to Thailand's multi-storeyed hotels and apartment blocks, visible on the far bank. At one of many little hawkers' stalls I bought a bottle of drinking water; crossing the Mekong had not caused me to be born again but the label appealed as a souvenir: DRINKING WATER TREATED, ULTRA-VIOLETED, OZONATED AND BOTTLED BY SISOUPHANTHAVONG CO. LTD. This product must be aimed at tourists, but how many crave ultravioleted water? Radiation, incidentally, does not kill the parasites which product giardiasis and amoebic cysts.

Below the embankment on my left ran one of Vientiane's 'streets', a rough dusty track. When the Mekong curved away out of sight my path joined this track and wound between maize fields dotted with mango trees and tall clumps of bamboo. Coming to an isolated, empty hut-bar, I ordered my first Beerlao (flavour excellent, 5 per cent alcohol) and sat in the shade of a magnolia tree. Across the track, under a round grass roof – bougainvillaea cascading over it – a policeman (quite a rare sight in Laos) was rocking himself in a hammock, a vague half-smile on his face. The shy small girl who served me – there seemed to be no adults around – quickly scuttled out of sight as I poured warm beer into a tankard half full of ice from a cooler-box.

I was diary-writing when a powerful motorbike shattered the siesta-time silence. Two young men dismounted and the pillion passenger stared at me, then swaggered over to sit at my table. 'You a journalist? I'm Australian, where you from?'

I told him, then added, 'You're Lao by origin?'

He scowled. 'I'm Australian, didn't you hear? I was born there, no way would I live in this country!' His parents had emigrated in 1976, father did well as a car dealer, son had been sent through NEM's Open Door to suss out the possibilities for profitable car dealing in Vientiane. 'But tomorrow I get back home, I'm counting hours! Life is real in Australia. These people here, they're brain-dead, got no push!' He jerked his head towards the policeman. 'Look at him, he's not even asleep, he's just brain-dead!'

Pointedly I picked up my pen and replaced my spectacles and the young man took the hint. Moments later he and his companion roared away in a cloud of dust, having berated the little girl for selling warm beer.

In December, the sun sets at 5.45-ish and rises at 6.15-ish. Tempted by the late afternoon drop in temperature, I roamed too far in the city centre and when darkness fell found myself lost amidst a tangle of shack-lined laneways. But in Vientiane that was no cause for alarm. Even American expats, the most jittery of the species, admitted that one could safely walk around any district of this city at any hour; Laos's crime rate was then one of the lowest in the world. Eventually I emerged on to a long, straight boulevard and hailed a tuk-tuk. As the driver had never heard of my hotel (not a conspicuous establishment) and couldn't understand my pronunciation of the street name (Fa Ngum) we drove around in circles for some thirty minutes until I recognized Wat Chanthabuli, not far from the hotel. That little tour showed me Vientiane in festive mode; every roadside tree was festooned with coloured lights and 'MERRY CHRISTMAS!' hung over many shop and office doorways, inscribed in English on frosted paper. Earlier, I had noticed some shops stuffed with tawdry Christmas decorations and wrapping-papers and plastic toys – being bought by the more affluent citizens, though Laos's Christian population is invisible to the naked eye. It can only be a matter of time before Westerners are persuaded to celebrate (by spending) the Hindus' Dussehra, the Muslims' Id and the Chinese New Year.

Many roadside food vendors operate in Vientiane, some also providing table service. Near my hotel, outside a bamboo-walled shack, I enjoyed a breakfast of sticky rice, home-made sausages and cardamom-flavoured spinach-like greens. Who knows what went into those sausages; making them kept Granny busy in the background, chopping and chopping, then deftly filling the skins. Although tasty, they did require vigorous mastication. Beside my table Dad was using a heavy knife to produce bamboo spits on which his wife would impale countless sausages, and four-inch-long fish, for grilling over charcoal in a tin box set atop a pile of old bricks. When the toddler daughter fell and howled, Granny at once hastened to pick her up and a moment later she was chuckling, sitting on a loving lap, listening to a very beautiful song while the soles of her feet were being gently clapped together.

'Sticky' rice (*kao niao*) is a misnomer; when correctly cooked *kao niao* sticks only to itself. The staple food of most Lao, it is served to individual customers in lidded straw baskets the size of a two-pound jam jar and is eaten with the fingers – rolled into a ball, then dipped in whatever may be available. I became an instant addict. Business was brisk that morning, many customers bringing their own rice baskets to be filled (some capacious, family sized) and taking away sausages or fish in those featherweight plastic bags which cover all Laos's urban environs like a skin disease. Until recently, banana fronds were used as wrappings: now city dwellers regard these as 'primitive'.

At the Immigration Office the good news was that a fifteen-day visa may be extended for thirty days at a cost of US$3 per diem – and then extended again. The bad news was that a visa can be extended only on the day it expires. And the worst news was that it can be extended only in Vientiane. This seriously restricts anyone planning a long trek. In Peru I dodged the same rule by simply disappearing from officialdom's view for a few months – easy, in the high Andes, where officialdom doesn't function. (Or didn't, in 1978.) However, one is advised not to play visa games with the Laotian authorities; recently two Germans had been gaoled for an indefinite period, having entered illegally from China. Local authorities wield considerable power, especially in the remoter provinces. And where there is no legal system, in our sense of the term, travellers are helpless if by ill-luck some atypical official chooses to pounce on an expired visa. I therefore decided to spend my first fifteen days in Vientiane, then take a bus across the hot plain to cool Vang Vieng and from there walk north on footpaths through the mountains. At the end of that extension I could think again; bridges are best crossed when you come to them.

Vientiane's charm is engendered by its population and its quirkiness. Of the pre-colonial city few traces remain and when I arrived the whole place was in a road-construction mess – and getting messier by the day. Scattered around are the universal symptoms of 'development': banks, office blocks, car showrooms and pretentious hotels newly built by over-optimistic (I suspect) entrepreneurs. The French contributed a few wide boulevards and many spacious villas, some now decrepit, others recently restored by or for expats. Vietnamese shophouses survive between the Soviet contributions to the commercial district – grim and grey, with flat roofs and façades dismally damp-mottled. In contrast, the numerous renovated wats are colourful: sometimes excessively so. Many old wooden houses on stilts – traditional Lao dwellings – are separated from the streets by dikes in which variegated scraps of litter float on stagnant green water. Malodorous open drains, crossed by wobbly plank footbridges, are to be smelt within yards of the wide Parisian Boulevard Lan Xang. After a few days, one realizes that this capital is in fact an amalgamation of villages – as is London – each centred on its wat.

Not long ago, Vientiane's traffic consisted almost entirely of bicycles, cycle-rickshaws and handcarts. An expat who shares my wavelength commented sadly, 'In '92 you could walk across any city street without looking left or right.' Since then scores of magnificent trees have been felled to make way for a sudden proliferation of motor vehicles. This disastrous UNDP-funded 'highway project' also involves the razing of people's homes and the concreting over of fish-filled canals and ponds which provided free protein for the poor. The loss of so many tall, wide-spreading trees rouses local anger for practical reasons. During the long hot dry season Vientiane's temperature can reach 104 degrees F and pedestrians need tree-shaded routes. Moreover, many hawkers trade in the shade, their tiny stalls often seeming an integral part of some gigantic root system. Will 'developed' Vientiane offer hundreds of displaced hawkers an alternative way of living? They doubt this.

On 8 December I was invited to stay with Sheila, a compatriot first met in Rwanda ten months previously, and her South African partner Colin. Their pleasantly hybrid home – modest French colonial crossed with middle-class urban Lao – had a spacious square balcony (the Lao influence) overlooking a lawn generously shaded by mango trees and coconut palms. In Africa such a garden would be bird-rich; in Vientiane all winged protein has long since been eaten. From a small private school next door came songs and laughter and happy shouts five days a week. Educational standards may be low – most learning is by rote – but those children were certainly enjoying their schooldays.

This attractive *ban* (village) – fifteen minutes' walk from the Mekong, centred on a large, poorish wat – had few other expat residents and was never visited by tourists. Its tall trees crowded greenly around colonial bungalows or overhung laneways lined with traditional homes on high stilts, their walls of woven split bamboo. Soon I was familiar with the neighbours' routines and was recognized and smiled upon by food vendors, shop owners, tuk-tuk drivers, grannies sitting on their balconies, children going to school – and was greeted with thumping tails by dogs lying on thresholds. Sometimes, at 4 a.m., I could hear the wat drums, a muffled, ghostly booming that marks the moon's phases. At dawn a procession of orange-robed monks – barefooted, shaven-headed, some novices as young as eight – collected their daily rice from a few elderly women and even fewer elderly men who knelt and stood, respectively, outside their homes, praying as they awaited the monks' arrival. After each donation the monks chanted a brief blessing in unison – automaton-like, in the style of routine prayers everywhere.

The term 'wat' describes all the monastery buildings found behind low walls in a large compound, often guarded by a sacred bodhi tree. The central building is the *sim* (temple) – always rectangular, with very beautiful tiered sloping roofs. The tiles may be orange, black, red or green but never a mixture of colours. Triangular gable boards depict the Lord Buddha, the Wheel of Life, Indra riding Erawan the three-headed elephant (my favourite) and/or various Hindu gods which arrived in Laos via Cambodia. The main door, opening to the east, is often a wat's most memorable feature; Lao craftsmen have always excelled – and still do – at carving wood panels of wondrous delicacy. In the lavishly painted interior (one large room) the wat's most revered statue of the Lord Buddha occupies an altar at the western end, usually surrounded by many smaller statues. Here the devout leave their offerings of fruit, flowers, rice, incense, money. On ceremonial occasions monks and worshippers gather in the *sim*; individuals visit at any time of day to gain merit or pray for help or comfort. As *sims* were built of wood, brick and plaster they needed repeated renovations, even if never sacked and burned. The aim always was/is to replicate the original but few contemporary artists are equal to this challenge. Dating wats is difficult; an institution founded 400 years ago can look, as a group of buildings, quite new.

Also within the wat compound are *kotis*, monks' spartan dormitories often used as schoolrooms during the day; *thats* (stupas) containing the remains of monks or pious laymen, and a roofed platform on high stilts for the drum – which can rival the Lambeg in size though it seems sacrilegious to mention both in the same sentence. Optional extras are huts to accommodate pilgrims and *oupmongs* (miniature chapels) holding either a small *that* or an image of the Lord Buddha. As a wat's wealth is concentrated on the *sim*, many *kotis* look neglected.

Laos's most sacred monument is the stupa known as That Luang, made into a national shrine and symbol by King Soulinga Vongsa during the Golden Age of Lan Xang. According to some ancient texts, Ashoka himself founded That Luang to hold either a hair of the Lord Buddha or a chip off his breastbone – a pleasing fancy, for which no hard evidence exists. Archaeologists surmise that a twelfth-century Khmer monastery existed on this site. In 1976 three Khmer statues were excavated nearby and restored; one of them, a phallus-wielding six-foot-tall 'Khmer Guardian', now guards the cloister – looking rather over-gilded and over-lacquered. King Fa Ngum, in the mid-fourteenth century, marked his creation of the Lan Xang kingdom by ordering a Khmer-style That Luang to be reconstructed in the Lao style. Some 200 years later King Settathirat gained merit by giving That Luang its present form and in 1641 Gerritt van Wuysthoff reported being 'overwhelmed by the enormous pyramid, the top of which was covered with gold leaf weighing about a thousand pounds'. Subsequently That Luang was repeatedly plundered by invaders, then abandoned in 1828. Before the ruins had completely disintegrated Louis Delaporte, a French explorer, discovered them and made detailed drawings on which M. Fabertaux based his 1930 restoration. In 1957, to commemorate the 2,500th anniversary of the Lord Buddha's birth, the stupa was re-covered in gold and reinaugurated amidst joyous celebrations still remembered by the older generation.

Seen from afar, That Luang on its low hill is quite striking. Many slender gilded *thats*, rising from three levels, surround the ninety-foot central spire, representing an elongated lotus bud. However, once within the square cloister, its walls high and thick, there is too much concrete in evidence and very little artistic talent. When I visited, Sunday crowds were drifting up and down the walkways between levels and making offerings in the four small 'chapels'. (Our Sabbath, though of no religious significance to Buddhists, is a non-working day in Westernizing Vientiane.) Unsuccessfully I attempted to decode the numerous metaphysical and allegorical messages which decorate the abundance of architectural 'features'. These no doubt edify and instruct the initiated, yet to me the ambience lacked that vibrancy one expects (and usually finds) on 'a most sacred site'. My few fellow-foreigners were looking as underwhelmed as I felt – perhaps That Luang has been reincarnated too often.

Other cities have public parks; Vientiane has wat compounds. On benches under trees students do their revision, office workers eat lunch, barrow boys (or girls) pause to rest, parents entertain children, friends sit chatting, elderly folk doze – but one never sees a courting couple. The Lao young, though pre-marital relationships have always been tolerated, do their courting discreetly. A few monks and novices wander about, sometimes sweeping up leaves or hanging robes out to dry on *koti* balconies, and during the forenoon the Pali chanting of novices may be heard from schoolrooms. Occasionally a worshipper enters the *sim* or a pedestrian takes a short cut; in the city centre certain wats occupy all the space between two main thoroughfares. Some rich wats have bred mythical hybrids, up to twenty feet tall, which mingle with the luxurious vegetation: green two-legged winged elephants, gold and scarlet eagle-headed four-legged monsters perhaps remotely related to dragons, black lions with blue peke tails and equine hooves, tiger-headed monkeys with tails wound around swords, gold and green and crimson guardian *nagas* (cobra deities) – some coiled, some thirty feet long – their jaws agape, showing off sharp white fangs. Amidst this surreal menagerie, vaguely Khmer deities appear, sporting lotus bud top-knots; these sit in curiously informal positions on high backless stone thrones, painted blue. In comic contrast, Wat Simuang has added two crude ten-foot plaster statues of contemporary Lao peasants; the young man wears Hmong tribal attire, the young woman a smock recalling the uniform of Soviet factory workers.

In Simuang, Vientiane's most popular wat, dwells the city's guardian spirit. Laotian Buddhism coexists with animist beliefs and when King Settathirat founded Simuang, as his new capital's centre, the essential guardian spirit was sought. A deep pit having been dug for the *sim*'s central column, gongs and drums summoned the populace: who would jump into the pit, above which the stone pillar was suspended on ropes? Suddenly a pregnant woman named Sao-Si raced to the site and flung herself into the hole. At once the ropes were released and thus Sao-Si became the guardian spirit and Simuang got its name: Si Muang, 'Si's Town'.

My favourite wats were Sisaket and Prakeo. The former, built in 1818 by King Anuvong, is surrounded by a square cloister in the Bangkok style and was spared by the Siamese army in 1828. Although Vientiane's most recent religious foundation, it is the oldest surviving wat and houses the biggest population of Buddha statues – 6,840, many of them 'refugees' found on the sites of razed wats. Wall niches around the cloister contain more than 2,000 images in bronze, wood or terracotta. Below these, 300 larger images, of stone or bronze, stand or sit on long shelves. And within the *sim* are thousands more, including a standing Buddha reputedly given King Anuvong's exact physical proportions. Fading murals on the interior walls tell the Lord Buddha's life story and UNESCO has promised to fund their restoration. Luckily no money had so far arrived; amidst Vientiane's assiduously restored wats it was soothing to come across something that has been allowed to fade.

Prakeo, founded in 1565 to house the Emerald Buddha, stands in a tranquil garden fringed by frangipani trees. Next door is the Presidential Residence, where once stood the royal palace, and Prakeo was never a monastery, being reserved for royal worship. Now this tall dignified *sim*, on a three-tiered base with a three-tiered roof, is an underfunded religious museum, its high rafters cobwebby, its ancient curator courtly. He is touching devoted to this eclectic and jumbled collection of Khmer steles, exceptionally fine Lao images, erotically carved wooden doors of Hindu inspiration, palm leaf Pali books stored in an antique wooden chest and a seventeenth-century bronze image said to be unique – the Lord Buddha sitting with his legs hanging down in 'the European pose'. But it was the austere beauty of the life-sized Buddha images on the veranda that repeatedly drew me back to Prakeo. In their presence, melancholy echoes of Lan Xang were audible.

Sheila's household was run by Keo, a woman of great charm, competence and courage. Aged thirty-eight, with two young sons, a toddler daughter and a dependent widowed mother, she had spent three years at Moscow university, then returned home to teach Russian. But suddenly she and her husband lost their jobs for the same reason – Russian was OUT and English IN. Having since worked for seven years in expat households, Keo spoke enough English to teach in a state school – where her income would be halved. (A wise 1994 law compels foreign employers to sign a contract guaranteeing minimum wages, fixed working hours, maternity and sick leave and official holidays.) She hoped eventually to become fluent enough to teach in a private school; meanwhile the family were getting by – just. Her husband worked as an expats' driver or gardener but he lacked Keo's linguistic adaptability so his choice of jobs was limited.

Keo showed me where to find draught beer, known as 'fresh' beer and both cheaper and more palatable than Beerlao. This eat-drink-shop-cum-family-home, some thirty feet square, was typical of many in the capital. Its outer wall consisted of metal gates, pulled across and padlocked at sunset. Cooking happened on the veranda under a crooked tin roof – sporting a frieze of Beerlao pennants – that looked likely to be dislodged by the next monsoon. Against one wall stood stacks of yellow plastic beer crates, a large battered refrigerator and a dresser decorated overall with silver paper. At the living-room end a small black-and-white TV faced two armchairs and a sofa, occupied by a shifting population of children, adolescents, parents, aunts, uncles, grand-parents – plus certain regular customers. At first the kind young woman who served me would rush to switch on some excruciating American pop singer for my entertainment, the tape competing with the TV. On Day Three I managed to convey – being careful not to seem ungrateful – that while writing I needed no entertainment. A pye-dog bitch (in pup again) usually slept beside me, and between dresser and fridge a mangy black cat nursed three piebald kittens. Often the cock was raping one of his harem under a table (why do hens always sound as though they are being raped?) while his half-grown progeny hoovered the earthen floor around customers' feet. Sometimes a six-month-old baby was being bottle-fed and played with by its besotted twenty-year-old father. In Vientiane one sees a multitude of babies but no public breastfeeding – so usual in Africa.

On the eve of my departure from London Rachel had cut my hair with more enthusiasm than skill and now this put me at an unexpected disadvantage. Soon I noticed that some women – especially young women – were not returning my smiles. The explanation, once pointed out, was obvious: elderly solo white males who smile at Lao women are assumed to be the enterprising overflow from Bangkok sexpeditions. (Many Lao worry that as a result of the free market's commercialization of everything their country will soon have its own sexpeditions.) I therefore had to emphasize my femaleness by tucking my shirt into my slacks and not wearing my 'diary-bag' around my neck. This I believe is known as 'making a cultural readjustment'.

According to the *Lonely Planet* guidebook,

Thailand and Laos are rather similar with regard to women's social status. One major difference is that prostitution is much less common in Laos where it is a very serious criminal offence. While a Thai woman who wants to preserve a 'proper' image usually won't associate with foreign males for fear of being perceived as a prostitute, in Laos this is not the case (though a Lao woman generally isn't seen alone with any male in public unless married). But Lao women drink beer and rice liquor, something 'proper' Thai females rarely do, even in Bangkok. Hence a foreign woman seen drinking in a cafe or restaurant isn't usually perceived as 'loose' or available as she might be in Thailand.

All the women backpackers I met in Laos remarked on how wonderful it was to be free of sexual harassment. Laotian reserve also contributes to the relaxing atmosphere. My diary-writing in a public place caused none of the usual excited curiosity and friendly clustering around; the Lao know how to keep the balance between welcoming a stranger and intruding. On being invited to join me, urban children often showed their pathetically inadequate textbooks and school exercises, while their elders smiled and bowed and tried to communicate.

Officially, French remains Laos's first European language though most of the educated class fled in 1974–6 – an estimated 90 per cent. (Now thousands are returning, some with children who can speak only American English.) Many '70s 'refugees' were members or supporters of the ineffably corrupt Royal Lao Government (RLG) and had collaborated with the CIA during the Secret War. It is often said that their departure left Laos with 'a weak human resource base'. Clearly this is a matter of definition and opinion; the moral fibre of those exiles does not suggest to me that they would be likely to strengthen any base. However, certain 'experts' see them as 'a huge reservoir of untapped know-how and invaluable international contacts' – to quote one 'refugee', Phuongpun Sananikone, a senior World Bank official. Heeding his (and others') advice, Saman Vignaket, President of the Lao National Assembly, in 1993 urged exiles to come home and help guide their country into the twenty-first century. Even before that, Deputy Prime Minister Khamphoui had sought the advice of such people while drafting the 1996–2000 Development Plan. His advisers included Mr Sananikone and Visai Sutaratane, an Asian Development Bank high official with much experience of private consultancy work in the Poor World. Both these men, and some of the high-powered exiles who have returned permanently, come of notorious families. The Sananikone clan contributed quite a few members to the 'Gang of Thirty-one' who in 1975 were rightly regarded as national traitors and sentenced *in absentia* either to death (six) or to many years in gaol (the rest).

The apostles of consumerism are now leaning heavily on Laos – or on those parts they can reach – but it cheered me to hear expats bewailing the Laotian disinclination to 'get with it'. This pleasing trait is much in evidence. When searching for detailed maps I visited the government bookshop, which also sells Beerlao T-shirts and sundry other unappealing souvenirs, and my presence was ignored by the two young women assistants sitting in the middle of the floor playing cards. Dusty, sun-bleached Russian textbooks and Marxist tracts loaded the shelves; English primers printed in Thailand and of doubtful pedagogic value were piled on the counter. In a nearby stationery shop a monk and I were both potentially good customers, eager to buy pens in bulk, but there was no one to serve us. We waited and waited – and waited. Finally the monk climbed over the counter with enviable agility – he was advanced in years – and returned some minutes later with a beaming young woman who seemed astonished by this rush of customers.

Vientiane's enormous Morning Market, built in the dollar-soaked 1960s, offers an ominous array of goods imported from Thailand, Japan, Taiwan, South Korea, Singapore, China, France, Britain, Holland and the USA. A large section is devoted to the incomparably beautiful Laotian weavings – some cotton, some pure silk, some a mixture, the colours and designs so varied one can spend hours simply admiring them. Scores of women, mostly young, with baby on back and/or toddler at foot, preside over these stalls. They all smiled at me – that distinctive Lao smile, at once warm and genuine, yet shy and slightly remote – and clearly were pleased by my taking such delight in their displays. But no one tried to sell me anything. Throughout Laos, most merchants are women. And in the Morning Market many are the wives of government employees so badly paid they could not possibly support a family unaided.

The market's upper floor, acres wide, is mainly occupied by

Chinese merchants selling nasty nylon garments in distressingly contrasting colours – very popular among the younger generation. These women are the antithesis of their Lao counterparts: they almost kidnap the passing *falang*. Here, too, are the shoe stalls and the silversmiths' locked glass cases showing belts, bracelets, necklets, ear-rings. For centuries Lao silversmiths have been famous and their artistry survives.

The sprawling fresh food market in Sheila's *ban* – part covered, part open-air – was my favourite. When the merchants had opened up their stalls and displayed their goods one heard from all sides the clicking of chopsticks as they breakfasted off big bowls of steaming noodles. Meanwhile long narrow handcarts with tinkling bells were being pushed briskly between the stalls by ragged coolies; some carried mixed loads, others only stacks of egg cartons – as many ducks' as hens' – or bleeding carcasses or mountains of fresh-picked vegetables. Most goods are now transported to the entrance in tuk-tuks or pick-ups which throng the adjacent laneway, causing serious air pollution. A few years ago only handcarts were used, providing many more jobs for porters.

In Laos fish are the main source of protein and one can buy them raw, dried, stewed, fried, grilled, marinated – of all shapes and sizes, including giants from the lower Mekong five feet long and two feet in circumference. These weigh who knows what and travel in barrels of water, being killed and sawn up on arrival. From the nearby Mekong come bewhiskered catfish, six inches to three feet long, contained in wide, high-sided basins of water; the seniors jump so vigorously they have to be recaptured quite often. In other basins squirm eels a yard long and minuscule live frogs for grilling or soup-flavouring. Huge toads squat in wicker baskets, looking as though aware of being doomed; these are for broiling or sun-drying as titbits – a much more wholesome nibble than Tayto's. From the Thai coast some mounds of small mussels – alive, alive-O!

Many basins of water contained something initially puzzling: identical chunks, one inch square, of what looked like dark chocolate. This is pig or buffalo blood, treated so that it can be cut into cubes for adding to various dishes. When an animal is killed nothing is discarded; the display of bones, innards and organs makes the meat section look like a dissecting room in a Victorian teaching hospital. The organs include boars' and bulls' penises, the former as long and thin as sjamboks – an expensive delicacy. Poultry feet are sold cheap in bundles bound with grass; dried buffalo hide, the long hairs still attached, is sold in strips – another delicacy. Keo could find no English words for the more baffling bits of unidentifiable animals. Others were only too identifiable: pretty red squirrels, seemingly uninjured so either trapped or killed by catapult, and small velvet-coated deer, graceful even in death. Once I watched a woman hacking the shell off a turtle; its flesh is exceptionally costly. One visualizes turtles as round or oval (at least I do) but this one – perhaps by now an endangered species – was square, some three feet by three. Getting through the shell was hard work; the woman used a mallet to bash a knife like a short sword. And I had a ghastly suspicion that the creature was still alive . . .

Lao food, as cooked by artists like Keo, is deliciously unique. No wonder, given the choice of animal, vegetable and mineral ingredients – the last being rocks with health-giving properties, ground to powder. From the munificent forest comes an unimaginable variety of herbs, barks, grasses, dried berries and roots and weirdly shaped multicoloured fungi. Amidst these goodies rise hillocks of 'betel nut' ingredients: the leaf or catkin of the betel vine, lime and the nut of the areca palm. As the nut is not chewed, 'betel wad' would be a more accurate term. This addiction has its origins in South-east Asia; quite a few Siamese and Burmese lacquer betel boxes have survived from the fifteenth century. Now the urban élite disdain such a disfiguring concoction and go for nicotine instead.

This market attracts a few regular beggars, not yet a usual sight in Vientiane. These worn-out women (aged fifty-five?) had heart-breakingly wistful smiles. Each was huddled in her own corner, making no sound or movement but being helped by most shoppers. The Lao – so very small-boned and slim – do not age well; in early middle age their faces tend to shrivel up and fifty-year-olds can look like septuagenarians.

One day Keo bought twenty tiny, delicately mottled quails' eggs – later hard-boiled and presented to me as a treat to go with my beer. They tasted no different from hens' eggs. To be ecologically correct, I shouldn't have eaten them. But they were a generous gift and one can't respond to such a gesture by giving a homily on conservation – or at least I can't, though perhaps one should? On a day-to-day basis, maintaining principles, however cherished, is easier said than done.

Vientiane's December climate is tolerable: the temperature in the late 70s Fahrenheit, no humidity, often a slight cool breeze – agreeable walking weather.

My favourite dander – following the Mekong upstream, on a path shaded by majestic trees – took me through an elongated *ban* of wooden houses, each one different, all quite large. This modestly prosperous *ban* felt far removed in spirit from any city. Most families cultivated a vegetable plot, poultry and pigs swarmed everywhere, several small hucksters' stores were to be found in the corners of living-rooms and the few eat-drink shops sold fresh beer. Occasionally a new luxury villa intruded, looking brash. Outside one such home the family's pup had been provided with an ingenious toy tied to a veranda pillar – a ball of nylon mesh which he was striving to unravel with many excited squeaks and attempts at growling. From within the house, a little girl watched him, laughing.

Given the happy relationship between most Lao and their domestic animals, the minority of deformed cats baffled me. Why had their tails been deliberately mutilated, either cropped Manx-short or broken and twisted most horribly? I'm told this is a common enough sight throughout South-east Asia. Is there a superstition involved? No one in Vientiane could explain.

One forenoon, on a stretch of path not overlooked by houses, loudly rustling leaves made me look upwards. Two small boys had climbed close to the top of an eighty-foot tree from where the drop to the Mekong, directly below, was 130 feet or more. With a long stick they were knocking curly pods to the ground where an even smaller boy slid down the almost sheer embankment to collect them. He, armed with a catapult, was aiming accurately at pods on the lowest branches. These pods contain sour but refreshing seeds; one often sees them being sold by the wayside for a tiny sum.

I sat on a tree root and watched. Serious injury or death must have followed any error of judgement and most young Western parents would panic if they saw their offspring taking such a risk. But an error of judgement seemed unlikely. Those boys climbed higher and higher – the branches getting thinner and thinner – with a confident agility that was beautiful to see. They were aged ten or eleven, masters of the art of tree climbing – as were many of my generation, though we didn't have trees of such magnitude in which to exercise our simian skills. Now, sadly, most children are restrained from developing such skills even if the opportunity is there – which usually it isn't, in cities. (Climbing frames in public parks, the ground beneath carefully rubberized, don't count.) Within a couple of generations we have become a timid race, neurotically over-protective, believing that physical risk (like physical discomfort) should, if possible, be completely excluded from everyday life. 'Safety' has almost been given the status of a virtue. It bothers me to see children being denied the freedom to use their bodies daringly, as individuals. Even the athletes among them must operate in a controlled environment, hedged about with rules and regulations and never far from an ambulance and a hospital. No wonder some teenage skateboarders, when free at last of parental supervision, display suicidal tendencies.

Later, in rural Laos, I often observed toddlers using heavy sharp knives (much like the Gurkha kukri) to split lengths of bamboo in imitation of Daddy – sometimes with an infant sibling crawling nearby. The parental assumption is that once a child can walk it can use such tools and should be left to practise their use. There must occasionally be horrible accidents, even permanent maimings and deaths, but that risk is taken. And of course the parents' laid-back attitude reinforces the child's self-confidence. By the age of five or six Lao children have acquired skills we never acquire – and never need, in a mechanized world where we are no longer expected to split logs for the fire or dig potatoes for lunch or gut fish and poultry.

Occupied by such thoughts, I went on my way – and met Marie. (Her real name was unpronounceable and unspellable; many urban Lao adopt European names for their foreign friends' convenience.) We had already noticed and smiled at one another during my earlier walks through her *ban*. Now, seeing me sitting under a pipal tree with a jug of fresh beer, curiosity got the better of Lao reserve and she addressed me in Canadian English. Three hours later we were still talking.

Marie's family had been closely associated with the RLG and in June 1975, weeks after the Americans' sudden departure from Laos, she and her mother and three younger sisters moved to Thailand *en route* for California and, ultimately, Canada. Marie was then aged thirty, but childless. In 1973 her husband and father had sought refuge in the United States among their many USAID and CIA friends.

In Vancouver Marie became a mature student and read anthropology. She also became a militant feminist: 'Very fanatical but now I've mellowed. That mix of anthropology and feminism made me think, comparatively, about my own culture. I realized Lao women are fortunate, in some ways. Then I wanted to go home. Canada was terrific, gave me a lot. But when I looked at my own country from outside I saw something special. Something I'd never seen before, the way the *rich* lived in a cocoon woven by outsiders. Friends in Canada couldn't understand why I didn't hate the new regime, but Lao people aren't into hating – what's the point?'

In 1987, when the Open Door was open only a chink, Marie returned to Laos, much to her mother's dismay. But she didn't return recklessly, on an impulse. First she made subtle enquiries and found that if she trod warily she could 'reintegrate' by investing in a rural development project. She admitted to having private means; families close to the RLG were extremely rich in a revolution-proof way. The exceptional thing about Marie was that she didn't want to get richer – didn't mind getting poorer. In 1989 she married a minor civil servant of peasant origin, a widower with four young children. 'I couldn't ever have my own so I thought I'd borrow Nuki's! Now they're all teenagers but it's still working well, they're not running wild – or not yet! Poor Nuki, there's nights he can't sleep he's in such a twist. It's hard to guide youngsters, the way things are going now in Vientiane.'

I suggested that a city where night-clubs have to close at 11.30 might be graded as one of the world's less pernicious capitals.

Marie smiled at my naïvety – a sad smile. 'Remember,' she said, 'I've seen it all before. In Laos we have an infinite capacity for being corrupted. I was six when the Americans arrived in '54, I grew up in a moral sewer. By the late '50s casinos were thriving all over Vientiane and beyond, one of the biggest owned by the Royal Lao Army Chief of Staff, Phumi Nosavan. We'd never had gambling before and people got infected like it was a plague – especially women. Some lost everything. A million kip debt drove an aunt of mine away to Thailand, and she wasn't alone. I remember a satirical pop song when I was in my twenties: "Father prefers the night-clubs, Mother prefers the gambling house." Peasants on the plain around here sold their land to gamble, then became paupers. Senior army officers and government officials were making millions of bucks on heroin trading, helped by Air America Inc., the CIA's disguised air force. Vientiane had the world's largest legal opium den, a converted theatre. Drugs were so cheap and plentiful half my age group were addicts, including my husband. He liked to hang out with the hippies who settled here in the '70s. The tidal wave of so-called "aid" dollars turned most of the population – every class – into parasites. The rest went off to fight with the Pathet Lao. It's silly, but sometimes I feel guilt about having run away. I could have joined the Pathet Lao instead, followed Prince Souphanouvong to Xam Nua.'

I asked, 'Is it true Nosavan was also into gold smuggling and prostitution?'

'Sure he was – big time! But hundreds were in the flesh trade. Those thousands of Americans stationed here made brothels as common as noodle-stands. They called them night-clubs and girlie bars – the "rest-room" syndrome! Flesh traders paid village parents two to four hundred bucks for girls just coming to puberty. The parents were told they'd be working in factories and the wages were being paid in advance. Girls who tried to escape and go home were captured by the police and dragged back to their "owners". I know all this because my mother used to work with a pressure group trying to have prostitution outlawed. But that only happened when the Party came to power. Now the sentence is six months to three years – of course for the women. Men are such good guys if only those bitches didn't lead them astray! In '76 thousands of young prostitutes and drug addicts were imprisoned on islands not far north of here – called Boy Island and Girl Island! Most got home safely after learning crafts so they could earn an honest living. I guess they also learned it's more comfortable to keep on good terms with the Party.'

By then we had moved to Marie's nearby home. Traditional in design and materials, it stood some way off the path amidst areca palms. A long ladder led to a wide balcony where we left our shoes before entering the airy living-room, its two large windows unglazed. 'Deliberately I've modernized nothing,' said Marie. 'As a rich returnee I've some influence – and I'm an evangelist! I want to persuade my neighbours, and anyone else within range, not to replace thatch with tin, bamboo with concrete, wickerwork with plastic, hand-woven *sins* with blue jeans.'

Almost everything in that home was Lao-made, of grass and palm fronds, wood and wicker, silver and silk. Nuki's sister had woven the cushion covers and wall hangings and one of his colleagues had made the chairs and cabinets. Said Marie, 'Even now after all the years of disruption we've so many talented craftsmen and women – but we won't for much longer if they're only turning out souvenirs for tourists. They need their own people to be loyal to them – not buying plastic chairs from Thailand!'

Great was my rejoicing when Marie invited me to lunch with the family next day – a Saturday and the eve of my departure from Vientiane.

The Lao lunch early; by 12.30 all eight of us were sitting on the floor around a straw mat spread with a plain white cloth. Nuki, who spoke no English, was even smaller and slimmer than his petite wife; the children – girls of thirteen and fifteen, boys of seventeen and eighteen – resembled him in both stature and features. Marie had taught them English but adolescent shyness limited our communications. However, they listened, fascinated, while the family help (Marie's ayah fifty years ago, who ate with us) closely cross-examined me about my personal life.

The food was memorable. ('Everyday dishes,' said Marie.) We began with *laap*, which can be made from any minced meat, fowl or fish, cooked or raw. 'This is pickled raw pork,' explained Marie, 'mixed with roasted and powdered sticky rice, lime juice, garlic, green onion, mint, coriander leaves and chillies.' Each mouthful of this gastronomic delight is wrapped in a lettuce leaf and eaten with a ball of rice. No implements are required. Then came fish and lemongrass soup with mushrooms, followed by more sticky rice and a green papaya salad. Into this go unripe papaya, ground peanuts, shrimp paste, lime juice, soya sauce and a mystifying assortment of herbs. 'A good Lao cook,' declared Marie, 'is inspired about blending and balancing herbs. Our best dishes depend on this art. Some cooks have their own secret blends, discovered over the years. They'll tell no one till they're dying, then a daughter learns the secret.' Pudding was a sweet cheese-like substance made from mangoes with lotus flowers soaked in coconut milk – not standard fare, Marie admitted, but served to honour guests. Tactfully, she made no comment on my eschewing *Pa dae*. There is no English word for this sauce made from decayed raw fish and sprinkled on every savoury dish. Its preparation is extremely complicated and long-drawn-out (the fish must be very decayed) and the Lao cherish it as an 'ethnic marker' – rather like women's *sins*.

After lunch the teenagers dispersed: the girls to weave on their looms under the house, the boys to fish in the Mekong. Then Nuki excused himself; he had promised to help a neighbour who was repairing a boat.

'I'm glad we live outside the city,' remarked Marie. 'Here it's easier to encourage children to do sensible things.'

Over glasses of excellent coffee we discussed what corporate employees refer to as 'The Hydropower Debate' and conservationists describe as 'The Dam Crimes' – an unsuitable post-prandial topic, likely to impede digestion. The government's sell-out to prospective dam developers had then become an international scandal. Environmental Impact Assessments, even if carried out, are usually circulated only among allies of the developers. Memorandums of Understanding (mark the opaque jargon) are signed between the government and construction companies – and then, before it has been established that funding for a particular dam will be available, loggers are allowed to clear the proposed inundation area. Dams are prodigiously costly items and quite often the funding does not materialize. But by the time the proposal has been turned down numerous tribal communities have been displaced and many square miles of immensely valuable primary forest, home to hundreds of rare species, have been destroyed for ever under false pretences.

'Seems we're half-way back to the sewer I grew up in,' said Marie. 'I get angry when people comment as though corruption were inevitable – "that's what Asians are like"! In fact our own culture was genuinely anti-materialism before outsiders came – a claim you can't make for many cultures! Then it proved too simple, too fragile, we'd no intellectual muscle to fight off challenges. But getting rich was never our way of gaining power and respect. Indifference to wealth gained respect. Families with a surplus were expected to donate it to the wat to gain merit or spend it on lavish hospitality – and for centuries they did. We never had a greedy landowning class. Peasants were free and independent, of course with certain obligations. Like contributing food to their local wat for festivals and fighting as foot-soldiers or with the elephant corps during conflicts. In the rice season they had to cultivate the land of the local hereditary ruling family – never more than the family needed to fulfil their own obligations. Otherwise, people only had to produce enough food for themselves: again, no surplus. When family numbers decreased, they produced less, when numbers increased, more. The government should have thought about that, about how things could be in this country, before they opened the door. It wasn't just an ideal, it worked. The early Europeans noticed – no poverty in Laos! OK, a few like Mouhot were irritated by our aversion to your work ethic' – and Marie broke off to fetch Henri Mouhot's *Travels in Indochina*. 'Listen: this was written in 1861. "Their poverty borders on misery, but it mainly results from excessive indolence, for they will only cultivate sufficient rice for their own support; this done, they pass the rest of their time in sleep, lounging about the woods, or paying visits to their friends." Can't you imagine his expression while he was writing that? But if you've enough to eat, why not relax? We're talking about peasants, ordinary people with simple needs. I suppose you've no more peasants in the West – not really. But you still have ordinary people and does competing as consumers give them contentment? Wouldn't they be better off getting enough to eat and visiting their friends?'

It was my turn to produce a quote – from John Berger, cited in Susan George's *Ill Fares the Land*. For Marie it had to be paraphrased; verbatim it goes like this:

> The peasantry as a class is the oldest in existence. It has shown remarkable powers of survival, powers which have puzzled

and confused most administrators and theorists. The essential character of the peasantry, despite all the important differences of climate, religion, economic and social history, actually derives from its being a class of survivors. It is often said that the majority of people in the world today are still peasants. Yet this fact masks a more significant one. For the first time ever, it is possible that the class of survivors may not survive.

Momentarily, I thought Marie was going to cry. Then she recovered herself and half whispered, 'Who can stop this? This juggernaut of TNCs and development agencies and entrepreneurs – and most Lao are still so innocent and credulous, it's like the rape of a virgin! And then the conception of an unwanted child called Consumerism . . .' Abruptly she stood up, went to the balcony and requested a neighbour's child to fetch a jug of fresh beer.

I changed the subject. 'How much did you know, during the Secret War, about Pathet Lao military victories? When did people realize they were also winning hearts and minds and it was only a matter of time?'

'We knew nothing – and so long as the dollars were sloshing around who cared what went on up in the mountains? I suppose some smart guys read Senator Symington's writing on the wall in '71. He set an annual limit of $350 million for future US aid – for a population of three million or so! Before Laos was a multibillion enterprise and no questions asked. Then came the ceasefire in February '73 and the power-sharing protocol signed seven months later. That I well remember, it proved the PL had won – but we still hoped power sharing might work. In '74 quite a capable coalition government started to function, victors and vanquished co-operating – the Lao way of doing things. An election was due in April '76, the whole country was in the mood for reconciliation. But as things developed, the temptation to go for all the power was too strong – and the Pathet Lao must have felt they'd earned it, after enduring so much. In April '75 the Americans quit Vietnam and our Party could have softened their Communist hard line then – except that would have put backs up in Hanoi and Moscow. They did dither for a while in the fall of '75, maybe a Hawks versus Doves situation but nobody knows. We'd got rid of the Americans in May '75 when hundreds of demonstrators took over the USAID compound – including some Lao employees. They simply refused to leave until Washington pulled out all USAID personnel. Which they soon did – within days, as I recall. That's when my mother decided we should move to Thailand and watch developments from there.'

I asked: 'The thousands who fled then, was it mass panic? Or were the Pathet Lao openly intent on punishing the bourgeoisie indiscriminately?'

'I don't know – I honestly don't. But for sure we were scared when our "protectors" went. By that June the US army and their Thai allies and Hmong mercenaries were all gone. And the RLG was a mirage, not even as solid as a façade! For years there'd been no relationship between them and the people. Except for the Pathet Lao's liberated zones, Laos was run by USAID on behalf of the CIA. They'd hijacked all administrative power, even openly running essential services. Junior Lao staff in USAID departments were paid more than senior officers in the Royal Ghost Government, as the Pathet Lao called it. The peasants couldn't know all this but felt no obligation to a government that didn't relate to them in any way. No taxes were demanded because the US wanted to keep people loyal to its puppet – so the RLG offered nothing. All money, for us or the peasants, came from Washington. Think how that weakened the state! Society disintegrated every way round. In this province the *nouveaux riches* started buying up the best agricultural land and we'd our first landlordism problem – peasants reduced to seasonal work or menial casual jobs in the city. And traditional co-operation in the villages was threatened by economic rivalry – what Mouhot wanted to see! The Party, once in power, did try hard to put Humpty-Dumpty together again – with some success but they gave up too soon. The mess we're in now comes of uneducated peasants running the show. Brave men, great soldiers, idealists who truly cared about their fellow-peasants and believed Communism could help them. But not people able to govern a country in such chaos. If only they'd had the wisdom to stick with the coalition! The middle class would have stayed to work with them and they could have hung on to their socialist principles – not too alien to Lao culture. During the Second World War the Pathet Lao emerged as a straightforward anti-colonial movement but the Cold War left no space for a little country like Laos to work out its own salvation. First we'd the French, then the Americans sitting on our necks. Not to mention the Vietcong needing to use us – and Ho Chi Minh was truly inspiring, a great and good leader. So the young Lao who'd started out as unaligned freedom fighters became old men rigidly committed to Marxism. Now those are being replaced by younger leaders trying to walk the tightrope between state control and the free market – not a pleasant sight. Here in the city tourists are buying drugs and children are gambling, something against the '89 Criminal Code. And no one believes the official story about prostitution being under control. You can't count the "hostesses" in the discos and night-clubs – at $15 from a Lao and $35 or more from a *falang*.'

'For how long can it go on?' I wondered. 'Walking this tightrope?'

'Who knows? Most are content with our government. They trust it, it's given them peace after thirty years of devastation. They don't resent its grip, they're not agitating for democracy. So we've a stable "investment environment" for predators. If the government OKs a damaging development, that's it. The people directly affected may object but they've no power. And no notion how to form alliances with other threatened groups. This is a fractured country, people are ignorant about others' problems, there's no uncensored information. Each victim community is standing – or falling – alone. A few outsiders try to protect them but get nowhere. It's a great scene for predators!'

Marie refilled our glasses. 'I never drank beer as a youngster, in our cocoon it was French wines or whisky. In Canada I took to beer – and this is much better than theirs!'

I said, 'If you'd followed the Red Prince into the mountains, could you ever have come to see Laos's problems so clearly? On the other hand, you might now be a government minister – yes?'

Marie laughed and shook her head. 'No! The Party doesn't encourage assertive women. Their politically correct rhetoric about gender equality doesn't translate into action. Anyway, let's be realistic – look at me! Marie as a Pathet Lao guerrilla living for years in caves wouldn't have worked. I'm too much of a cultural hybrid, educated in France like my parents and grandparents

before me. As a family, colonial lackeys. Genetically Lao, intellectually European, temperamentally and emotionally half and half
– education can't cancel out all those genes. A bad start in life!'

'But in your case, if I may say so, a good end result.'

Marie shrugged. 'You are kind. But this hybrid is not, as you see,
a person at ease in her own country. Or able to forget it and be at
ease elsewhere. But at least I'm my own woman now. Back in '75
I'd no identity, I was just a terrified tangle, husband and father
gone without warning – one evening they didn't come home.
Nobody then told me anything about the background. Years
passed before my mother admitted my father was not a mere
passive collaborator but into serious CIA rackets, and using my
husband to run around taking the big risks. My mother is a great
woman, you'd love her. She has such integrity, all her adult life she
suffered hell in Laos, seeing how things really were. She doesn't
have my problem; she's only glad to forget the past and be a good
Canadian citizen.'

When I stood up to go, Marie suggested my visiting Nuki's home
village, a few miles from Vang Vieng. She gave me a letter of introduction to her sister-in-law and the name of a niece, Vang Vieng's
only English-speaker. 'Phomma isn't fluent but she'll be a help –
and thrilled to practise with you. Nuki's is a guinea-pig village,
though you may not realize that. People don't show their emo-
tions in Laos, especially not anger.'

On the balcony we stood together for some moments in silence.
The Mekong was reflecting the sunset and nearby trees stood out
blackly against a crimson sky: magnolia, teak and frangipani trees,
papaya, areca palms and banana plants, their contrasting and
overlapping leaf shapes creating patterns of great beauty.

As I fastened my shoes Marie said, 'On this journey you'll be
riding an emotional roller-coaster. My country is so magnificent –
but so vulnerable . . .'

3

Erratically to Kasi

The first bus for Vang Vieng departs, I had been told, at 6 a.m. The only people around, in the pre-dawn darkness of the small bus station, were a few food vendors – just arrived with their mobile stalls (adaptations of the tuk-tuk) and busy lighting charcoal fires. Many Laotian place names sound similar – or, to me, identical – and anyway the majority of Lao look blank when their language is attempted with a brogue. However, by 5.30 someone had advised me to board quite a smart little bus – 'A Gift from Japan for the Improvement of Vientiane's Public Transport', said a notice in English over the windscreen.

Clouds of mosquitoes were tormenting the four passengers already aboard and I hastily applied repellent to my bare parts before passing the bottle around. But it is a fallacy that clothes protect one; soon this swarm was feasting off my thighs and buttocks. Happily Vientiane is not malarial, at least in winter; dengue fever, borne by a soundless daytime mosquito, is more of a hazard. It kills many children and 'break-bone' fever debilitates adults for weeks, causing agonizing pain; there is neither a prophylactic nor a cure. Perhaps its worst symptom – certainly the most alarming, from the patient's associates' point of view – is psychological: dengue violence. A mild-mannered elderly expat told me that while fevered she hit her gardener over the head with a trowel. When she had fully recovered the young man suggested their going to the wat together, to sit in silence in front of the Lord Buddha and be reconciled. In our world, he'd have sued her.

As the sun rose the half-full bus moved off, all its windows open, and the ravenous cloud vanished. At irregular intervals we took on another few passengers – Vientiane has no bus stops, you simply step into the vehicle's path, waving vigorously. Because road-works necessitated many detours we were beyond the built-up area before I realized that this bus was going south instead of north. The Laotians' propensity to laugh is part of their charm; having been reassured that my error left me unworried, they found it hugely amusing.

Beside me sat two Ministry of Education inspectors, wearing quasi-military grey-blue shirts (the government officers' uniform) and cheap Chinese jeans. Both had been studying English for a year ('it is the rule now') but their never meeting English-speakers limited progress. In Laos all education is free, they asserted. There are no private schools and the average class size is twenty-five – each of which statements I knew to be false. They had spent three years at Kiev university, studying telecommunications, and biology and chemistry, and I wondered how productive those years had been. Many such students never did master Russian and came home equipped only with handsome certificates.

Soon we were bouncing along a pink-tinged track, its fine dust deep enough to camouflage pot-holes and erosion channels. So close to Vientiane, it surprised me to see miles of uncultivated bush and even a few patches of surviving forest. We paused briefly at two tiny *bans*, clusters of one-room dwellings on stilts where the sight of a *falang* brought small children scampering from all directions, to stand close to their adults while viewing me. The track ended at our destination, a large *ban* where all who came aboard were loaded with goods for Vientiane's markets. Three women carried rolls of their own exquisite weavings. A teenage girl struggled with ten vociferous hens tied by the feet and held upside down; they at once went quiet when pushed under her seat. A youth looked worried because his four buffalo legs were still dripping blood. A betel-stained granny – minute but astonishingly strong – gave me a toothless crimson smile when I helped her with a basin of catfish which could only be placed where everyone must step over it. Many layers of egg-boxes were also stacked in the aisle but no one complained. Most women held on their laps enormous baskets of vegetables and/or forest produce. The school inspectors took half an hour to load the roof with bales of firewood which their wives would sell outside the Morning Market, opposite the bus station. Meanwhile I observed five jolly toddlers frolicking in the dust with six puppies and ten piebald bonhams.

By 10.30 we were back in Vientiane. One pays at journey's end, perhaps because so many vehicles break down *en route*, but the driver laughingly declined my kip – then carried my rucksack across the concourse to a geriatric and extremely battered Soviet donation, full of shabby, ill-washed peasants from mountain villages; the contrast with the Mystery Tour passengers was quite startling. These people seemed somewhat dispirited (though friendly) and most had coarser features than the Lao Lum. The latter (also known as Lowland Lao, about 55 per cent of the population) live along the Mekong valley, and by the banks of some tributaries, and have always been the dominant group – though less markedly so since the Pathet Lao took over.

I never did get Laos's minorities sorted out in my mind. According to Dr James Chamberlain, an anthropologist, more than 200 distinct ethnic groups have been identified. Some may be numbered only in hundreds, occupying near-inaccessible heights and now endangered by forced resettlement (which can mean extinction) as 'development' renders their heights accessible to megadam-builders and foreign commercial loggers. The government has ruthless homogenizing ambitions; it wants everyone to feel, simply, Lao – rather than Lolo, Lisu, Lahu, Iko, Phu Noi or whatever.

On the outskirts of Vientiane a man sitting in front of me shouted to the driver to stop, then leaned from the window to converse at length with an elderly woman in a tuk-tuk coming from Vang Vieng. It had taken us an hour to get that far; four times we halted at shophouses to overload the roof with many large sacks of something very heavy. This vehicle was not designed to serve as a truck, and we had a sensible driver, so the 100-mile journey on a good tarred road took nearly six hours.

At noon we passed a torrent of schoolchildren – almost as many girls as boys – cycling home. Most rode brightly painted Thai bicycles, costing the equivalent of US$50, with long soft carrier cushions capable of carrying two or three siblings or offspring. Those girls keenest to avoid a suntan held parasols in one hand – blue, yellow, mauve, lime-green, pink, creating in the distance a 'swarm of butterflies' effect. Sitting bolt upright under their parasols, wearing long skirts, they looked comically Edwardian. Some rich boys were riding mountain bikes, 25 per cent dearer than the standard model.

In 1949 Norman Lewis observed:

... these girls, dressed as they were like princesses, came from shacks in the forest. Each one had a bicycle – infallibly fitted with dynamo lighting, and sometimes 3-speed gears. It seems that a bicycle for his daughter is one of the essentials for which a Laotian will work. It is considered ill-bred and irreligious in Laos to work more than is necessary ... There is no social insurance and there are no poor. The old and the sick are supported by the young, or, where they are left without able-bodied providers, by the community. The main difference, it seems, between Buddhism in Indochina and Christianity is that, whether we admire it or not, the former is largely put into practice.

When Norman Lewis drove to Luang Prabang with a French military convoy (lorries, jeeps and armoured cars, the Vietminh the enemy) he heard 'the mournful howling of monkeys' and saw many storks, ravens, vultures, parakeets, pheasants, peacocks. I saw no bird, large or small, never mind hearing a monkey. In 1949 much of the way was 'walled-in by monotonous forest'; now all the level land has been cleared for cultivation. Then Route 13 was passable only during the dry season and its condition restricted the convoy's speed to 8 m.p.h. Now it is a new, smooth highway, its occasional EU-style signposts – offensively incongruous: big, blue and brash – pointing to small invisible *bans* a few kilometres off the road. Sometimes the driver slowed as we approached a junction with a track or footpath and threw a few letters to waiting children.

Beyond the little town of Muang Phôn-Hông our long climb began, into the sort of mountains that give me an adrenalin surge. One high peak, when first seen, looked exactly like a sitting gorilla leaning back with his mouth wide open. On some steep upper slopes, amidst expanses of ochre grass, stood gaunt isolated tree skeletons – tall and fire-blackened, dismal victims of slash-and-burn farming.

We stopped at the next little town, not far from the wooded shore of a long, irregular lake only tantalizingly glimpsed between trees. The driver and several passengers spent half an hour in the open-air market, buying small chubby fish sold in dozens strung on grass. All such transactions take time because the Lao so enjoy chatting; to make a quick purchase would be to waste an opportunity. Vendors came aboard, cheerful girls and youths offering vile fizzy drinks, sinister-looking striped sweets, split coconuts, grilled banana strips, sweet over-packaged buns, cellophane bags of sticky rice and *Pa dae*, grilled half-chickens cleverly herbed. I indulged in the last: it was tough but juicy and tasted of chicken. (How many Rich World citizens know what a real chicken tastes like?) Over the market the hammer-and-sickle flew high, as it did in Vientiane over the bus station and elsewhere. Not everyone was listening in 1991, when the Fifth Party Congress decided to replace it with a silhouette of That Luang.

Approaching Vang Vieng, Route 13 follows a long narrow plain; all around is flatness. Then suddenly, the effect hallucinatory, karst mountains appear – sheer, stark, surreal, rising to 8,000 feet from the far bank of the Nam Xong, dominating the world, overwhelming the newcomer. Their harsh grandeur is unique, in my experience. A young American backpacker, met that evening, put it another way: 'Those mountains, they have attitude!'

Vang Vieng began as a French military post, semi-encircled by the river, where a few Chinese set up shop in the 1940s. During the American era it grew in a haphazard way to become, by Laotian standards, a biggish town with one winding mile-long 'street' (rough and dusty), many shophouses, a small market, a mix of traditional dwellings and mini-bungalows. The wat looks neglected and no monks process at dawn. On the outskirts are a CIA-built airstrip and a Chinese-built cement factory, both abandoned. The atmosphere even now is of a settlement created by outsiders.

Since the door opened to tourists Vang Vieng has become a popular stopover for backpackers. Of the three simple guesthouses I chose the least modernized, run by an ageing Lao woman not long returned from a twenty-year exile in France. Her two daughters cooked basic dishes on an outside mud stove which must have tested those returnees' adaptability.

Meals were served al fresco, under trellised vines, and coconut palms towered over the four-roomed sleeping-hut on stilts. Underneath, where the Lao keep their looms, were communal loos and DIY showers – 'dip and pour'. My clean though not mosquito-proof room (candle provided) cost the equivalent of £1. I booked in for two nights.

Because Marie had advised me not to reveal my trekking plans in Vang Vieng, and to leave the town before sunrise, it was essential to identify my track by daylight. Before retiring I studied five 1:500 000 maps acquired in Vientiane's imposing but mouldering state-run Geographical Institute. These cost less than US$2 and were 1986 edition marked 'En Secret' but no one questioned my need for them. They showed wide swamps, impenetrable forests, uncrossable ravines, high escarpments and various other exciting impediments to progress. But they were vague about footpaths and tracks. No wonder the Lao know so little about their own country; its terrain discouraged more travelling than was necessary – and for the majority still does so.

To find my track I set off at dawn, noticing that even the tiniest huts had exterior strip lighting over their doors – left on all night. Also, an alarming number of shiny blue TV aerials soared above thatched roofs. Only a few weeks previously, this region had been electrified.

From Vang Vieng several tracks wander away towards the north-east. One petered out after a few miles, having served a scattering of dwellings. Others soon turned southish or due east. Another ended outside a gigantic electricity transformer, razor-wire-surrounded. The next led to an old cemetery where scores of small stupas, their bright colours long since faded, had been half overgrown. Five enjoyable hours passed before I found what was almost certainly the right track, winding gradually upwards into an exhilarating jumble of mountains.

On the way back, I had a reassuring encounter with a group of villagers returning from market; their laughter was audible as they approached, before I could see them. One youth spoke enough English to pass on an invitation from a middle-aged woman who wanted me to accompany them to their *ban* and eat food – an invitation I looked forward to accepting next day. Continuing, I reflected that these are the happiest people I have ever travelled amongst.

By the Nam Xong I drank Beerlaos under the shaggy thatched roof of a bar-hut on stilts built out over the riverbank, some thirty feet below. Here is a busy dry-season ford and at intervals the clear water turned muddy as large trucks lurched across, loaded with rocks for some construction project. The traffic was constant, including several power tillers drawing carts piled with green bananas. (Power tillers are motorized mini-ploughs imported from China.) Two of these broke down in midstream and had to be hauled on to dry land after their drivers summoned helpers to hump the bananas. A very tall backpacker, wearing a scarlet bow on his long flaxen pony-tail, waded across carrying a guitar. Four straw-hatted young women, bearing formidable loads of thin bamboo poles, got the giggles when he had passed them. Young men, shouldering heavy sacks of rice, crossed cautiously; immersion in the Nam Xong would have done their precious loads no good. Three Toyota pick-ups were packed with passengers and pigs. Another power tiller appeared, pulling a shaded wagon full of women and children, the latter soothingly stroking the hens on their laps. An elderly man carried his bicycle across, taking care not to let it get wet. Then two slim canoes came speeding downstream, their outboard motors raucous; each carried four men, balancing on narrow slat seats. Below me suntanned boys were swimming gracefully with their dogs in a deep pool. (An unwary backpacker, a non-swimmer, had been drowned here a few weeks previously.) Upstream from the pool three young women, modestly draped in sarongs from armpits to calves, were bathing and hair-washing – then laundering garments while their hair dried before being vigorously brushed and swept up into chignons. (Nowadays some young women wear their long hair loose; previously this was considered indecorous.) When it comes to hair care, the Lao verge on the obsessional. Shampooing is a daily event for men, women and children and in all but the remotest villages sachets of imported shampoo are available; not long ago a shampoo equivalent was derived from forest plants. As I was leaving a mother wearing a garish nylon skirt (at the other end of the aesthetic scale from the *sin*) led her food-stained small son into the river for a post-prandial scouring.

By then it was 1.30 and very hot out of the shade. Marie's chit enabled me to find Phomma quite quickly – in a market stall, playing cards with three schoolchildren wearing neat bottle-green uniforms. At first she was disconcerted by my arrival on her scene. Aged twenty, slim and beautiful, she giggled uneasily in response to every question – a not uncommon reaction when young Lao, of either sex, are suddenly confronted by a *falang*. However, she soon relaxed and lost her inhibitions about 'my English not good!' I rode comfortably to Nuki's *ban* on her Honda's cushioned pillion, despite the track's extreme roughness. As a nonagenarian I may abandon my pedalling principles and buy a Honda.

Forty years ago this *ban* (population 1,200) did not exist. When it was established in 1959, by five extended families in need of land, its densely forested site had to be cleared by hand – and fire. Then, said Phomma, 'many big wild animals got killed or hunted away'. Lao houses weather fast and Na Thoua now looks as though it has been there for ever on the left bank of the Nam Xong. On the far bank, beyond a narrow strip of green garden plots, rise jagged grey walls of karst, partially wooded, and behind them tower other separate walls of various heights.

Vientiane's rapidly expanding market for weavings explains the different styles of homes in this *ban*; where subsistence farming prevails, no such disparities appear. Here are some concrete instead of tree-trunk stilts, some glazed windows, some brick-walled lower rooms below the original timber structure – an unwise substitute for that open space where people can take refuge from the summer heat. But no one had yet attempted to build an indoor stairway.

We found Nuki's sister and two of her teenage daughters weaving below the house; their three looms left little space for the sickly bull calf tethered in one corner. Mrs Achin, accustomed to trading in Vientiane, took the *falang* in her stride and asked anxiously, through Phomma, if I knew anything about bovine diseases. I admitted to total ignorance of the subject and a debate followed – whether or not to spend scarce kip on a vet's advice? It might be useless, kip wasted . . . On the other hand, a dead calf would be a big loss . . . Nothing had been decided when we climbed the ladder to drink herbal tea in a large, sparsely furnished room – uncomfortably hot, Mrs Achin being in the affluent tin-roof league.

Already I had recognized that here was a forceful lady, a natural leader of women – and probably of men, too. (Many outsiders remark on the Lao women's self-assurance; in an Asian country – and one supposedly exceptionally backward – this comes as a pleasant surprise.) Small and plump, but vigorous in her move-ments, Mrs Achin had keen eyes, a determined mouth and an enchanting chuckle. The next three hours were exhausting for poor Phomma as translator – and tiring enough for me, as I strove to express myself in the simplest possible words. (A challenge to which I am not unaccustomed, but this was a long session.) Mrs Achin, having been told that I was writing a book, wanted to explain something important. And here I must interrupt the nar-rative to give a little relevant information.

The Lao Lum's social organization is matrilinear and matrilo-cal. Descent can be traced through either the male or female line and usually the groom moves into his bride's home and cultivates her parents' land. After a few years, unless she is an only daughter or the youngest daughter, the couple construct their own house nearby, with the assistance of numerous relatives from both fami-lies, and another young husband moves in. So it goes on, down to the youngest daughter who inherits the home and land, together with the duty of caring for her parents in old age. Thus women have always enjoyed considerable decision-making power, includ-ing control of family resources, and the individual's place in society is determined by age and rank, rather than sex.

Even among Laos's other ethnic groups, who are not matri-linear, the Lao Lum – by osmosis? – seem to have encouraged women to seek economic independence and often to achieve it. They tend to operate within an informal 'women's solidarity' framework, a concept popular in Laos long before it entered any Western feminist's mind. The Lao being so flexible and easygoing, inter-group marriages are not taboo and most exogamic husbands accept the Lao Lum customs – proving that even Laos's patriar-chal groups are not too hung up on male dominance. However, the government's New Economic Mechanism (a euphemism for its conversion to the free market, privatization and foreign invest-ment) has already, in some communities, lowered the status of women.

Previously, women were in charge of irrigation; they under-stood and managed its complexities, which vary from place to place in accordance with topography, soil quality, local rainfall patterns and so on. In Mrs Achin's *ban*, an enormous traditional wooden weir was constructed in 1971, some three miles away on a tributary of the Nam Xong. The main canal was nearly 4,000 yards long and as time passed the dam was widened, to 170 yards. Communal work parties reinforced or rebuilt it annually and cleared the canal. Men, women and adolescents from every family contributed voluntary labour at regular intervals throughout the year and all was well until 1993. Then, by a cruel coincidence, a freak flood destroyed the dam and a freak drought followed. Less than 30 per cent of the normal crop was harvested and in '94 people had rice enough for only three or four months. They were left with no choice but to take out rice-bank loans at a crippling rate of interest: for each 100 kilos of rice borrowed, the bank demanded 200 kilos – unhusked – within a year. Cattle had to be sold and women and girls had to weave incessantly; Lao men have no comparable cash-earning skill but Mrs Achin commended their willingness, during this crisis, to take on all the chores normally done by women: cooking, cleaning, laundering, wood and water fetching. Some even participated in the weaving marathon by going to the forest to choose the appropriate bamboo sticks for ornamental designs and rolling silk thread for the shuttle.

We then came to the nitty-gritty and I remembered Marie's comment: 'Lao people don't show emotion, especially not anger.' Mrs Achin's expression remained serene and her voice calm, but I don't think I was imagining the anger that smouldered in her eyes.

In 1994 the villagers were surprised to learn that their irrigation scheme (by then the dam had been repaired) was to be incorporated into a Department of Irrigation Five-Year Planning and Design Programme, funded by a World Bank loan. To help the government repay this loan, water fees must be paid in rice or kip – 20 per cent to be retained by the villagers for maintenance. As happens in all such circumstances, the Department of Irrigation sent forth suckers. An NGO began to train a Water Users' Group (of course referred to in the rapidly proliferating documentation as a WUG) in how to consult with the District Irrigation Officer – a man the villagers had never before encountered. A Water Users' Committee Board (WUCB) was set up. So was a Water Users' Organization (WUO). WUOs had to be formed, following a ministerial resolution, to supervise the operation and maintenance of all government-supported irrigation schemes. The bureaucrats specified, in minute detail, the procedures to be followed by WUOS before, during and after the new dam construction plans were drawn up. They also specified the particular responsibilities of the WUCB. And women, despite their traditional role, were completely excluded from all these government-controlled 'bodies'. Here Mrs Achin's smouldering eyes almost burst into flames – and I don't wonder. Not surprisingly, the *ban* was still waiting for its new dam.

Next morning I woke unnecessarily early (4.20) in that mood of pleasurable suspense peculiar to the first day of a long trek. Joyfully I went through the loading-up ritual: money-belt under shirt, camera pouch around waist, rucksack on with water bottle attached, binoculars over right shoulder, cloth journal-bag (the most precious possession) around neck, torch, map and compass in bush-shirt pockets, umbrella-cum-walking-stick in hand. Then I left Vang Vieng by the light of a setting full moon – a splendidly distended globe, richly golden, seeming almost like a stage prop.

At 5.15 a few women were already astir, opening their shop-houses to reveal most of the family still asleep on straw mats under padded quilts. When the moon slid behind an oval karst peak I switched on my torch; these 'suburban' tracks are treacherously uneven.

Soon after, the local Party's public-address system swung caco-phonously into action; this was General Election Day. Hoarsely shouted exhortations to vote ravaged the dawn stillness, inter-spersed with excruciating American-Thai pop songs. Quickening my pace, I passed the previous day's turning-back point, crossed a ridge and left this desecrating din behind me.

To the east a faint pinkness was spreading above low mountains. As the light strengthened I wondered why sunrise retains the power, in certain surroundings, to awe human beings – to seem so wondrous despite being a daily event. Now I could see a blue-flow-ered weedy scrub covering the downward slope on my right: an untidy growth that commonly covers open spaces. On my left rose green cliffs or rocky ledges and clumps of feathery bamboo over-hung the track. Tall slender trees sported long scarlet blossoms, giving sustenance to the area's only visible birds – two-inch blue and pink humming-birds, not worth wasting shot on. Some miles away, banks of silver mist drifted between rounded hills. This terrain was untouched, uninhabited; only the distant whisper of a river, far below in a jungly chasm, broke the silence. Beyond the chasm precipitous mountains, rising to pointed summits, wore seamless garments of primary forest.

For four or five miles the track climbed gradually – then suddenly it dropped, very steeply, to river level. I lingered while fording; the clear shallow water was deliciously cool. Soon after came a stream, deeper and faster, and I gave up reshoeing myself, foreseeing more fordings on this level land – the edge of a wide valley. Near the fourth stream a few little vegetable gardens, bamboo-fenced, looked rather neglected. Then I glimpsed two small houses, tree-surrounded, and heard the thump of rice being husked. Where the track merged into raised bunds between paddyfields many thatched roofs could be seen on a long wooded ridge overlooked by high mountains, forested and rock-crested. Here, presumably, lived that kind woman who had invited me to eat.

Remembering Marie's coaching, I paused to survey the approach to this *ban*. Was there a conspicuous guardian tree decorated with balls of rice which I should not pass? Or displays of red flowers by the track, signifying the guardian *phi*'s wish to keep outsiders away for a few days? Or a white string laid across the track because of a recent violent death? Seeing no warning signs, I continued on to the ridgetop where large houses on tall stilts surrounded an expanse of beaten earth.

My sudden appearance caused consternation. Toddlers shrieked in terror, children fled, men and women going about their morning tasks stopped and stared apprehensively. No one smiled. This situation needed to be dealt with by my sitting, looking amiable and tired, in the middle of the open space; such displays of passive dependence rarely fail. But I was given no time to sit. Two Hmong soldiers hastened towards me, astonished and wary. Armed with rifles, revolvers and knives, they asked challenging questions – the challenge vaulted the language barrier. However, they were extremely polite, though when I signed my intention to walk on into the mountains it was made very plain that the *falang* must at once return to Vang Vieng; even had I spoken Lao, this would not have been a matter for negotiation. Then another young man appeared, this one Lao Lum, unarmed and wearing civvies and an ID badge – a local official, equally polite but equally emphatic that I must immediately turn back. Had I been foolish enough to defy this trio, they would certainly have arrested me. Yet I bore them no grudge; they were only obeying orders.

Retreating across the paddy, I observed something interesting within myself. Despite the depth of my disappointment, I was able to accept it calmly and genuinely to enjoy the return walk. Evidently Laotian laid-backness is infectious.

Near the river, five little girls emerged from the bushes carrying baskets on yokes. Seeing me, they stumbled in their haste to retreat. Then a young man approached on a Honda and stopped to question me, all friendly curiosity. As we communicated, the children ventured out of the undergrowth like so many shy fawns, poised to flee again – then clutched one another and ran past me towards the *ban*. For whatever reason, their fear was sadly genuine – not any sort of game.

Later, an old woman and a teenage girl came towards me, the woman unhealthy-looking and unkempt. Her antagonism was startling; she gestured angrily, seeming to tell me to get lost, and repeatedly shouted something abusive – my first and last experience of open rudeness in Laos. I wished I could understand the cause (or causes) of these various negative reactions. Had the villagers, the little girls and the old woman all seen me as a threat? If so, what sort of threat?

As Vang Vieng came into view at 10.40, an inevitable sense of anticlimax briefly afflicted me. In a roadside eat-drink shop, where four chairs stood around one unsteady table, I brunched – several glasses of herbal tea (free to all customers in Laos), two glasses of strong hot coffee with over-sweet condensed milk, a big bowl of noodle soup, lovage-flavoured and containing a few chicken bones. As I ate, future meals cruised around the floor seeking what they might peck – adolescent fowl at an unattractive half-naked stage. Several customers who work in the town came in for takeaway lunches: salads, soups, vegetables, all sold in small transparent plastic bags. The noon fill of sticky rice is taken from home in baskets slung over shoulders. A four-year-old girl sat on the chair beside me intently brushing the knee-length golden nylon hair of a revolting pink doll. When a large chunk fell off she burst into tears and her mother deserted four customers – who also rallied round, adding their condolences. Finally Grandad came on the scene with a tube of glue and ended the crisis. In Laos children's needs are usually given priority.

My new plan was to follow Route 13 to Kasi – a few days' walk – and from there attempt to take mountain paths to Luang Prabang. As I went on my way, along the base of those improbably shaped mountains, even I couldn't complain about the volume of traffic: one vehicle per hour. But after the perfection of that morning's track any main road had to seem dull and here the landscape is defaced by the alien, glittering angularity of very new, very high electricity pylons marching parallel to Route 13.

At noon Mr Tang overtook me on his antique bicycle; he was a 21-year-old farmer, gentle and kind and eager to practise spoken English. My spirits rose (the pylons had lowered them) when he invited me to stay with his family – at least for one night, better still for a week.

Around the next corner Mr Tang's *ban* came into view, set well back from the road – another newish *ban*, established in 1967 when American bombing drove this Pham community out of Houaphanh province. The majority, including Mr Tang's family, have by now added Buddhism to their original beliefs centred on guardian ancestors and the spirits of rocks, rivers, trees. They soon realized that when it comes to funerals, as it does for all of us, Buddhism makes economic sense. The Pham tradition involves expensive, week-long rituals – expensive in food for feasting and ornaments for the corpse and concluding with burial under an elaborate graveyard 'house'. The Buddhist ceremonies and cremation need take only one day. However, this was a *ban* without a wat; even the simplest wat is costly to build and sustain.

The forty or so houses – varying in size, a few tin-roofed – had been built every which way on an uneven dusty (or muddy) site amidst towering coconut palms. There was no semblance of a track or even a path. Families had no space of their own around a home – no garden equivalent – but each had its own livestock and, at some little distance, its own paddyfields. Mr Tang's parents were away in their fields when we arrived: 'All day they work hard, they rest only for two hot months.' Removing our shoes at the foot of the ladder we carried them up to the balcony: I wouldn't care to negotiate such a narrow flexible ladder after one too many Beerlaos. In the high-ceilinged main room, more than thirty feet long, thick swathes of cobwebs swung in the breeze between the rafters. The well-swept wooden floor was bare. Each gable end had a large unglazed window; shutters of finely woven split bamboo – hooked to the ceiling by day – were lowered at dusk. The plank walls looked solid; one, facing the entrance from the balcony, had been draped with white plastic sacks and decorated with empty packages sellotaped on at odd angles – Marlboro cigarettes, Lux soap, biscuits, detergents. To us a bizarre device, yet executed with such imagination that the overall effect was not displeasing. On other walls two vulgar posters of slinky white women advertised a Thai brandy and an American deodorant. The furniture was minimal: two small tables, covered with red-and-white cotton cloths, and nine wooden chairs only eighteen inches high but comfortable – the standard seating in better-off homes. Poor folk sit on the floor on grass mats on minuscule stools. Behind a woven partition were a small bedroom and smaller kitchen. The long-drop, shared with a neighbour, was outside, surrounded by a six-foot-high tube of matting and visually clean but rather smelly.

Mr Tang apologized for having no cold drink, then brought me a glass of warm water ('It was boiled') tinted orange-brown and faintly flavoured with some doubtless nutritious herb. As I sat at a window, enjoying the zephyr breeze, neighbours waved and smiled at me and called greetings from their windows or balconies. My host was the eldest of five sons; the teenagers were at high school in Vang Vieng (an eight-mile cycle each way), the nine- and six-year-olds attended the local primary school and could now be seen returning from the stream with buckets of water – their afternoon chore.

A glorious four-hour walk followed; Mr Tang wanted to show me his parents' 'farms' (small fields) and his own new field by the river in which he was planning to grow cucumbers for the Vang Vieng market. As we passed through the village many sows (white, or white with large black spots) trotted energetically to and fro followed by countless bonhams so tiny and mercurial I feared I might tread on one.

At first our path wound through vigorous secondary growth – a wood, in our terms, but dwarfed by the few surviving forest giants.

Mr Tang's parents were among those who cleared this land in 1967. All four of his grandparents were B-52 victims, killed in their fields near Vieng Xai, then the Pathet Lao headquarters.

As we emerged on to paddyland clouds came to the rescue – high and white and not many but enough to make the sun bearable. And soon an almost cool breeze arose. Here grazed scores of cows and calves (small-boned, short-horned) their shiny golden coats matching the stubble. During the dry season temporary bamboo fences confine each herd to its owner's land. Before planting begins all cattle are moved up to the forest and left to their own devices (tigers being almost extinct) until the harvest is in. They then come down to calve, to dispose of the stubble and to fertilize the fields. I had been told that many herds don't have to be fetched; the harvesting scents bring them down and they make their way to their owners' houses. This is true, Mr Tang confirmed, if they are within olfactory reach of home – which often they are not. But now a system effective for millennia is being threatened by 'development' – those power tillers. Undeniably it is less strenuous to plough with a machine rather than an animal. However, to buy that machine you must sell twelve or fifteen cattle and to fuel and maintain it you must sell more cattle. Soon not enough are left to fertilize the land and the rest must be sold to pay for chemical fertilizers. When your herd is gone you still need to fuel and maintain your machine and regularly buy fertilizer.

All this bothered Mr Tang. 'First I want a power tiller to make work easy. It is good for more than ploughing. It takes rice sacks and wood and water in a trailer, not carrying it. It takes children to school, not cycling. I ask my mother and father, they say "No!" In another village two families got power tillers – very proud! My mother says not proud now – no money, selling rice to buy fuel and fertilizer, their children hungry. I think about that, I see the children hungry, I think my mother is right. But when I am a rich man I should give to my parents a power tiller!'

Then we came upon Mr Tang's uncle and aunt sorting out an irrigation problem, Aunt making all the decisions while Uncle did the heaviest shovelling work. We could see them before they noticed us; obviously they were an affectionate couple who made a good team. Later we passed their two daughters and sons-in-law, tending their own 'farms' of 1.5 hectares each. Why do we associate subsistence farming with extreme poverty? Peasants who own enough fertile land should not be graded as 'poor' merely because they operate outside the cash economy. Subsistence farming means being self-sufficient (quite fashionable in the Rich World nowadays) using only local resources.

By 3 p.m. we were beside the Nam Xong and the sun had slid behind the serrated crest of a karst wall on the far bank. Here are many vast caves, gaping black holes in the white limestone. Mr Tang suggested visiting a few ('Very exciting!') but I could too vividly imagine the spiders within . . . Now we had to ford the river – about fifty yards wide, crotch-deep, the current very strong, the bed of slippery round stones mobile beneath the feet. Without a stick I could never have made it alone; Mr Tang, positioned on my downstream side, supported me. The locals of course cross with aplomb: they have the knack. We saw lines of children fording with the water up to their necks, holding hands. All are good swimmers, Mr Tang assured me when I made worried enquiries about the drowning rate. If swept away they can keep afloat until reaching a shallow stretch. We were now on a long stony islet where some savagely thorny ground-creeper made it necessary to replace footwear. At the next fording point – waist-deep – the current was less strong and the distance shorter. A little girl, sitting alone by the water's edge with four fish in her basket, was patiently awaiting an adult piggy-back. Mr Tang, having seen me safely over, returned to carry her.

The vague path to the parental farm meandered through thick bushes and woodland. On our way we met two men carrying over their shoulders home-made eighteenth-century-type muskets: a common sight throughout Laos's mountain regions. Soon we could see one of those shelters used as 'watch-towers' while the rice is growing, a platform on five-foot stilts under a thatched roof. Here Father was ineffectually trying to cook wild greens in a saucepan balanced on one end of a large smouldering log. A small man even by Lao standards, lean and muscular and wearing only shorts, he welcomed me politely though with some bewilderment.

Mountain walls were close on two sides, west and north. I sat on the platform's edge enjoying the silence and the beauty of this place while Mr Tang knelt by the log, blowing until it flamed.

Then two loud shots sent echoes reverberating weirdly around those rock walls – double, triple echoes. Sadly I thought, 'Two less of some endangered species!' Mr Tang pointed to the knife-crested summit of the highest mountain in sight and boasted that he and an older man, an experienced climber, had recently reached the top and shot for the pot two big birds – he didn't know the name in English – and a gibbon. I made no comment. If one wishes peasant cultures to survive, hunting for meat must be accepted. It is a much less off-putting activity than game-bird shooting and fox or stag hunting for fun – not to mention big game hunting. Mr Tang asked what animals people hunt in my country and looked puzzled on hearing that Ireland has no hunters who risk life and limb to feed the family.

In Laos the main threat to endangered species comes from commercial hunters, using modern weapons and sometimes helicopters; these merchants supply the insatiable Chinese demand for aphrodisiacs. (Perhaps the Worldwide Fund for Nature should distribute free Viagra throughout China?) Also, the border regions where ill-paid soldiers are posted amidst dense primary forest have been devastated. Hungry men sweep patches of forest with machine-gun fire, killing everything – including butterflies – then gather what is accessible and edible from amidst the general carnage. Unhappily there are many such army posts; Laotian border areas tend to be both politically and ecologically sensitive.

On the way back we took a different route, close to the river – here wide and deep, jade-green and smooth flowing. I glimpsed a yard-long water snake plopping into the stream to avoid us – the fifth live snake I had seen since dawn. The first was thin, two feet long with an orange back and pale lemon belly: poisonous. The other three appeared during our walk, all about eighteen inches long, silvery green or copper coloured. 'Very dangerous!' said Mr Tang – though not necessarily lethal, much depends on the site of the bite. Twice he was bitten on the thigh but that only made him feel ill for a few days; his mother used an effective traditional remedy. Much thicker, longer snakes inhabit the caves, he added. If not disturbed, these are less dangerous than the smaller jobs. Allegedly only 32 per cent of the world's snakes are poisonous; most of those seem to live in Laos.

Often Mr Tang paused to forage for supper, picking the small tender leaves from the tops of certain bushes, and the curly tips of bracken fronds, and shaking from a tall tree tiny beans in red-brown pods which are cooked whole. Two plants he identified as deadly poison, their juice highly valued by those small tribes who still use crossbows and arrows because 'They have no knowledge to make guns and no money to buy them.'

As we continued, Mr Tang confided in me. 'I am not happy. My mother and father need me now while brothers are at school. They need me to work, it would be bad to leave them. When others can work, I want to go. My English can be good and I know some French with it. In school my teacher said I am clever with languages, my English-speaking better than his. I can get an important job in the city, I have been there once in Vientiane. I have seen how life is comfortable there. Here is hard with no play for young people. Only work and worry about money. Before was no worry about money, my mother tells. Now we hear about new taxes for irrigation, for owning land. Why is this? Why docs our government want to take money from poor people? What will they do with our money?'

That lit my fuse: a short one in this context. But my answer to his sad question merely confused Mr Tang. The NEM's destructive potential was, naturally, beyond his comprehension – one reason why Laos is so vulnerable to predators.

After the river fordings I remained barefooted, remembering the two streams still to be crossed. But as we approached a field where women were repairing fences my host said, 'We come near people, please your shoes on!' Evidently going barefooted is a monk's prerogative. Most Lao wear plastic flip-flops.

When I suggested a Beerlao sundowner Mr Tang led me across Route 13 to a shack displaying on its veranda a few shelves of bottles – mostly soft drinks. The Grandad proprietor all the time dandled an eight-month-old boy on his knee: his first grandchild. My arrival prompted him to put a minute pair of shorts on the baby, a courteous gesture which struck me as a bit extreme – the sort of 'modesty' that afflicted Ireland in my youth. Since attaining grandmotherhood, it fascinates me to observe how similar is the behaviour of babies of all races; the differences come later.

The traffic was much heavier than during the forenoon. 'These people left Vientiane this morning,' explained Mr Tang. Many

Lao prefer to drive from Kasi to Luang Prabang by night, believing (surely mistakenly?) that bandits are less likely to shoot straight in the dark. No speed reduction was imposed for the villagers' benefit but all vehicles were forced to slow by livestock homeward bound via Route 13: buffaloes and pigs – hens fussing over broods of chicks – handsome, briskly waddling ducks and drakes of many hues, their plumage lustrous in the light of the setting sun – strutting turkey cocks in full display, their crimson and blue wattles swaying as they pursued bashful, pale brown turkey hens. (Turkeys abound in Laos; during the 1960s some NGO ran an unusually successful project to provide the country with more meat and bigger eggs.) When a toddler chased one turkey cock and grabbed at his quivering fan of tail feathers her agitated mother rushed to intervene although the bird – his mind on other things – was ignoring the attack.

After only one Beerlao, Mr Tang suddenly looked sickly green. Plaintively he exclaimed, 'I'm drunken!' – then admitted that never before had he tasted commercial beer. ('Too much kip.') It was my turn to lend a supportive arm as we returned to his home through the dusk. When he confessed to being not quite sober his parents laughed merrily and his brothers teased him.

My hostess took the *falang* guest in her stride – unlike diffident Father. Mother was a vivacious character, her witticisms lost on me but much appreciated by everyone else. She drew my attention to the six-year-old's calligraphy; he was in his first year at school and somehow a blackboard and chalk had been acquired so that he could practise writing under Mr Tang's supervision. His illiterate parents were glowingly proud of him, as well they might be. The Lao script is not simple yet already he wrote confidently and apparently quite accurately.

This was a happy, affectionate family. But also, I felt, a family under some stress, being in transition from their traditional way of life to an acceptance – albeit a questioning acceptance – of profound change. As orphaned youngsters the parents had been uprooted from their own remote place – remote even by Laotian standards. Now, living on the new Route 13, they were tenuously in touch with the NEM world and being subtly seduced by it, intuitively aware of its threat but not informed enough to defend themselves.

Before and after supper, all hands were washed in a communal basin of hot water and dried on a fraying towel. We ate sitting around two circular wicker tables, some eighteen inches high. Numerous sardine-sized fish, caught that afternoon by the nine-year-old, accompanied our forest harvest of greens and beans. Meanwhile the room was filling with neighbours of both sexes and all ages, eager to meet the *falang*. This was slightly awkward; a crate of beer provided for the family (Mother proved an enthusiastic drinking companion) was not enough to go round and the younger men had to share bottles. Several of those longed to work in Vientiane and were struggling to learn English from a Thai primer which depicted TV sets, fridges, washing-machines and three-piece suites as the average household's possessions. The printing was blurred and the text riddled with grammatical errors. But I ignored these and concentrated on pronunciation, a major problem for those who only hear English As She Is Spoken by American pop singers. Then the headman arrived, a most engaging septuagenarian bearing a tattered but treasured book of *Advanced Reading Exercises* (Longmans, 1938). Everyone looked puzzled by its illustrations of English families on seaside holidays (Laos has no coast) and English farmers' wives churning butter (the Lao eat no butter). Mr Yayongyia showed off his reading skill to the assembly, correctly pronouncing almost every word of this Standard VI text – yet he was unable to converse in English. He had been taught to read, he told Mr Tang, by an American mission doctor who lived in Vang Vieng many years ago.

By nine o'clock I could hardly control my yawns; it had been a long day. The six-year-old was already asleep, curled up in a corner under his small mosquito net. Normally his brothers shared that corner but now they moved their quilts into the bedroom. Unrolling my flea-bag, I placed it incorrectly – a major *faux pas*. My feet had to point towards the door, Mr Tang explained – something to do with *phi*. But despite having got myself auspiciously aligned, I slept badly. By then I was suffering from a delayed and extreme reaction to those mosquito bites on the bus. All night that itch tortured me – almost made me weep.

At 5.15 Mr Tang carried my rucksack down the ladder, while suggesting that I should return and stay longer next time.

For an hour I was walking by the light of the waning moon; stars gleamed between clouds sailing fast before a cool breeze from the north. On my left loomed those weird karst configurations, seeming even stranger in the half-darkness. Groups of cows and calves went wandering along the road; had they broken out, or were their owners as yet oblivious to the traffic hazards of the newly tarred Route 13?

At sunrise I stopped to nut-munch by the wayside, overlooking the Nam Xong. The sun's first rays burnished the pylons beyond the river and I thought about electricity. In Vang Vieng a few food vendors had begun to use imported rice-steamers instead of char-coal – the flexes running for yards and yards to some invisible socket. Allegedly this is beneficial for the forests – but is it? What did the building of dams to generate Laos's electricity do to thou-sands of hectares of trees? How many humans had to be forcibly 'relocated'? And how many creatures great and small were deprived of their natural habitat?

Ten more miles took me to a small *muang*, Phatang, standing on a high creeper-draped cliff at the very beautiful confluence of the Nam Xong and the Nam Noy. Here I breakfasted in a minute wayside stall run by a minute old woman – a natural comic, who entertained juvenile spectators by trying to put on my rucksack and pretending it was too heavy. When I arrived the combined weight of it and me had caused the bamboo pole floor, poised on thin stilts on the edge of a precipice, to wobble alarmingly.

That was a dire meal. Cold noodles, evidently cooked in the pro-prietress's distant home, were immersed in a repulsive lukewarm soup with fishes' eyes and intestines afloat on the surface. However, I devoured it all. By then I had realized how much energy one expends when serving as one's own pack animal; this was my first ever trek carrying a rucksack.

Route 13 swings west beyond Phatang and climbs steeply: ONE IN TEN warned a new blue sign. Forested mountains rose nearby on either side, then receded, leaving the road to form a causeway between impenetrable chasms brimming with subtropical vegeta-tion. Here the largest butterfly I have ever seen fluttered around me – and, when I stood still, alighted on my boot, displaying yellow lines and crimson dots against a black velvet background. Its wing-span was at least eight inches. The variety and brilliance of Laos's butterflies provide some compensation for the lack of birds.

Descending to flat paddyfields, I passed a *ban* dominated by a pylon, its wires stretching low and threatening over thirty homes – the inhabitants unaware of themselves and their livestock being at risk. All day those pylons were visible, their shiny multiple wires relentlessly intruding on every panorama – some depleting the cultivable land, some defiling mountainsides, dwarfing the stands of giant bamboo.

This region's signature tune is bamboo moving in the wind – creaking and squeaking, rustling and whispering, whining and groaning. Bamboo must surely be the most eloquent representative of the vegetable kingdom.

Around noon the breeze dropped and soon after I collapsed in the shade of a mango tree. Despite my outsize umbrella, bought in the Morning Market, I was heat-stricken. On the slope behind me, irrigated by a mountain stream, lettuce, lovage and spring onions were being gathered by a young woman. As I lunched, an elderly man came by, equipped with the usual large knife in a wicker sheath hanging from the back of his belt. Pausing to try to talk, he was curious about my form of sustenance. When I offered a handful of nuts (bought in Vientiane) he cautiously tried one, grimaced and spat it out – then laughingly returned the rest and went on his way.

Ten minutes later a youth appeared, cycling from the village. He too stopped to greet me – then we both turned towards the vegetable patch where the young woman was urgently yelling, sounding distressed. After a brief shouted exchange, which greatly amused the youth, he came to stand close to me, grinning broadly, whereupon the young woman rushed down the slope, giving me a scared sideways glance as she passed, and ran across the road. There she paused to shout 'Kopjai!' (thank you) to the youth before hurrying down a path to a far-away hut. Obviously the recent proliferation of backpackers, who travel by bus or truck and keep to their beaten track, has not yet accustomed the peasantry to *falangs*. But why such fear, I wondered again? Is it rooted in the recent past? By all accounts, early European travellers in Laos did not stimulate fear, though some aroused suspicion.

I slept soundly under that mango tree, making up for my itchy

night. By 3 p.m. spreading clouds – a regular afternoon phenomenon – allowed me to trek on enjoyably until six o'clock.
However, I was impatient to get off Route 13; predictable tarred
roads, even when the traffic is light, are not much fun – especially
when one's tender sensibilities are all the time being offended by
pylons.

Towards sunset no *ban* was visible – or audible in the unseen distance. It was time to look for a campsite and this terrain offered
little choice. The only level space was a ledge half-way up a mountain accommodating some twenty stupas, their inscriptions almost
illegible. Here was my oddest-ever campsite – though once, a very
long time ago, I slept by mistake in a Pyrenean graveyard, not
seeing my surroundings until dawn. Sexagenarians don't often
surprise themselves but now I did just that by finding myself at
ease amidst the dead. I think of myself (obviously wrongly) as a
rational being, a humanist who doesn't believe in any afterlife, to
whom human skeletons or ashes are irrelevant inert matter. Yet as
someone brought up in the Christian tradition, brainwashed
during childhood about Heaven and Hell, I suspect I would have
been slightly spooked had those stupas been graves, decorated
with crosses and angels and suchlike.

I wrote my journal by the light of a camping lantern hanging
from the lowest branch of a small tree. The Lao terror of nocturnal *phi* ensured that no one would use that path before dawn and
mercifully the itchy reaction had faded; for nine hours I slept
without stirring. My head was protected from the drenching dew
by a plastic bag – a Map Shop bag, which seemed appropriate.

Next morning I continued for six hours through this pylon-
flawed paradise of mountains, gorges and forests. Then, as the
heat was becoming intolerable, a large *ban* appeared, set amidst
miles of flat paddy where buffaloes wallowed blissfully in muddy
ponds. By then I was ravenous and a score of children, giggling
and wide-eyed, gathered to watch me consuming vast quantities of
sticky rice with a crisp salad of lettuce, spring onions and watercress. Sticky rice has a predictable effect, not corrected by all those
greens. Were I inclined to seek sponsorship, the manufacturers of
Senokot might have been requested to subsidize this journey.

I was planning a siesta beyond the *ban* but on the outskirts
bureaucracy struck. Under a palm tree sat a smartly uniformed

young policeman at a small table bearing a large ledger. He smiled and bowed and offered me his chair and indicated that I should write my 'details' in the ledger. It contained, I noticed, only *falangs*' details; seemingly passing foreigners were checked here. When I stood up and said 'Laa gawnder' (goodbye) it did not surprise me to be detained. As I unloaded, the policeman observed my sweat-soaked shirt and exclaimed sympathetically – then dispatched a little boy to buy a bottle of Fanta for his captive. Twenty minutes later he escorted me on to a battered minibus which took ninety minutes to cover the twenty miles to Kasi.

The driver stopped for my benefit outside Kasi's most conspicuous building, a new two-storey ten-room backpackers' guesthouse run by another returned exile, a former RLA officer – rather dour, a word rarely applicable to the Lao. His stout amiable wife, an excellent cook, was assisted by three adolescent offspring who appeared to lack job satisfaction. This entrepreneur may have misjudged the attraction of Kasi for backpackers. Their bible, the *Lonely Planet* guide, states flatly: 'There's really nothing to see in Kasi.' However, the former officer had other irons in the local foreign-funded 'development' fire.

I was the only guest that night. My mosquito-proof room (No. 207, US$2.30) had a comfortable double bed with ironed sheets, a free-standing electric fan and a waterless hand-basin for use when modern plumbing comes to Kasi. The stairs, all floors and the walls of the communal dip-and-pour bathroom were of shiny pale grey tiles. Half the bathroom's floor space was taken up by a square tiled tank, five feet high – filled at intervals, through a pipe in the wall, with clear water from a nearby stream. One ascended two steps to the squat-over in the corner; failure to place one's feet symmetrically on the footmarks could cause problems for *falangs*, their bodies being in general much larger than Lao bodies. Flushing was accomplished by pouring basins of water from on high.

Kasi, too, began as a French army post, the headquarters of a company of engineers. Their barracks is still in use and when I went walkabout I met some 200 young conscripts (unarmed) marching out of step – their uniforms slovenly, their expressions sullen, their two sergeants hectoring. This is the biggest (though not very big) town between Vientiane and Luang Prabang and at first glance it seems dreary: a mile or so of small shophouses and dwellings lining Route 13 at the base of a steep ridge, partially forested. On a ledge half-way up the ridge stand the ruins of a bombed wat and here the atmosphere is odd – uneasy. In general, the locals encountered along the main street – a considerable percentage Hmong – seemed less welcoming than their compatriots elsewhere. But I soon discovered the real Kasi, the friendly and attractive peripheral *bans* where most people live.

The map showed two paths to Luang Prabang, one much longer than the other, going west before turning north – my preferred option, for obvious reasons. At dawn I set out to identify it.

A dirt track led me through three *bans*, the first set amidst dense trees, its long, tall dwellings weathered to a uniform grey-brown. This, I learned later, was the original Kasi. Then came a wooden bridge over the Nam Lik, wide even in December. At 7 a.m. visibility was mist-restricted but on my way back I lingered here – the best vantage point from which to appreciate the wondrous beauty of this region. *The Lonely Planet*'s assertion is wrong – 'There's really nothing to see in Kasi.' But apparently backpackers need something specific to focus on: wats, waterfalls, caves, tribal villages. Natural beauty is not enough – which tells us a lot about the contemporary traveller's mindset.

The comparative newness of the other two *bans*, straggling along the track for a few miles, was betrayed by numerous palm tree stumps; most of the older residents had arrived as 'displaced persons' fleeing the Secret War. I couldn't understand, and no one could explain, why so many giant palms had been felled, leaving the place unshaded and naked-looking. Outside every home five-foot-high herb-beds were being watered before the sun reached them. During the dry season the ground becomes rock hard, hence these contrived mini-gardens – long wooden troughs, raised to protect them from livestock. Scores of children were cycling to school, some breakfasting as they pedalled, eating sticky rice from baskets hung around their necks. These special baskets – one side flat, to reduce bouncing – are also used when walking to the fields or the forest.

Beyond the *bans*, palms and banana plants lined the track as it descended gently to paddyfields. Here Mr Nuhak overtook me:

another 21-year-old on a decrepit bicycle yearning to talk English. After three years of studying the language he had made little progress – yet had recently been appointed to teach English at a primary school. He cycled slowly beside me, talking enthusiastically of his beautiful twenty-year-old wife who cost him 200,000 kip and his clever seven-month-old daughter. When we had forded the shallow Nam Kay, another two miles took us to Mr Nuhak's *ban*, its utterly unmodernized homes shaded by coconut palms, mango trees and banana groves. The newly built Nuhak hut was no more than fifteen feet square, its rattan walls frail, its floor of packed earth, its roof of rusty tin. A home-made double bed had been curtained off in one corner and the family's possessions were minimal: a few garments on a line of string, a few cooking and eating utensils on a small table. Mr Nuhak's story illustrated how matrilocality can go wrong; having moved into his bride's parents' home, he was exploited by his father-in-law. 'He want make me no teach, make me work in forest to get him money for sale trees to make houses.' A month after the baby's birth the young couple defiantly set up on their own and were now being punished by the withdrawal of all material support.

Shyly Mr Nuhak asked me to photograph his daughter – a common parental request – then hurried off to retrieve her from next door. His wife was far away in the forest, seeking bamboo shoots (free and nourishing) for supper. As Dad dressed his darling in her best clothes, and brushed her sparse hair, he drew my attention to the astonishing fact that six teeth were through and I registered an appropriate degree of wonder and admiration. Most Lao babies go into howling spasms when a camera appears but this chubby beauty remained calm.

Not far beyond Mr Nuhak's *ban* the significant junction appeared; on my right was the shorter route to Luang Prabang. I continued due west, across level paddyfields, towards the hazy blueness of a low ridge running the whole length of the horizon. For hours a high veil of milky cloud persisted and a cool wind blew strongly from the north – perfect walking weather. The only ban *en route* – a dozen dwellings – lay in a slight dip among palms and banana groves. The trees' swaying and rustling in the wind made them seem more animated than these impoverished villagers – the poorest Lao I was to see in three months. Malnourished, ragged and dirty, their only source of water was a sluggish opaque stream too shallow for the usual vigorous bathing and laundering. My arrival startled everyone, yet the elders showed much shy friendliness when I stopped at the 'shop' to buy one of its four bottles of Pepsi. Other imports on offer were a few tiny packets of viciously dyed sweets and biscuits hanging from a string above the one-plank counter. Sitting on a stool provided by the shopkeeper, I watched a woman and her two daughters lethargically hacking at coconuts with heavy knives, preparing them for sale in Kasi.

Then came the bad news. This path did not, according to the shopkeeper, go to Luang Prabang; his gestures indicated that it ended nearby. I was not greatly surprised; my faith in those maps had never been strong. However, curiosity prompted me to continue, to see where and why the path ended.

Half an hour later I was at the base of the ridge – which no longer looked low. The map showed the path winding around this obstacle but now dense bamboo jungle covers the whole area and no vestige of a path remains. Within twelve years a lot can happen, growth-wise, in the subtropics.

By then the wind had dropped, the sky was clear and on the return journey I became rather dehydrated. Luckily Mr Nuhak's *ban* also has a 'shop' offering Pepsi. Reclining there under a mango tree, I admired two men skilfully splitting bamboo poles into long thin strips. These are draped over a fence to dry before being woven into walls, a process requiring craftsmanship of the highest order. In all these *bans* the variety of self-designed homes is astounding – no two exactly alike. What a contrast to our thousands of identical council houses!

On the outskirts of Kasi I suddenly remembered that it was Christmas Eve. If you wish to escape from Christmas, as I always most fervently do, rural Laos is the place to be. In Kasi life went on as usual next day. No one had ever heard of Christmas – and why should they have, in a Buddhist/animist country? Yet two backpackers met that evening laughed at the locals for being so 'out of it'.

My hostess looked puzzled when I booked in for another night. Few *falangs* dawdle in Kasi and I was being furtive about my plans, not explaining that I needed an extra day to find the beginning of the short route to Luang Prabang.

That search took several hours. Turning north at the junction, I was in a well-watered region where narrow canals irrigated the golden paddyfields on my left. I paused to watch a man ploughing a flooded field with a buffalo. He wore a homburg hat and a thick purple sweater and underpants; he was up to his knees in mud. Ahead of me, and close by on my right, rose several karst peaks – dramatically naked, in contrast to their heavily wooded lower slopes.

When the track lost its identity I went astray; at various junctions paths branched off in slightly different directions, all soon petering out in hamlets of four or five dwellings. Eventually another track appeared, carpeted with yellow-brown dust soft to the feet; then I was carrying my shoes, so many streams had to be forded. This hilly land was uncultivated, covered with that weedy 'bluebush'. Here I met a young hunter – his smile heart-warming, his musket slung over a shoulder, his cloth bag full of feathered food.

The next *ban*, on a hilltop, was quite big and from afar one could hear the growling and throbbing of a diesel-powered rice-mill. (The pylons serve only motor road settlements.) Here a military post seemed a horrid possibility and I braced myself for another disappointment. The few visible inhabitants viewed me a trifle apprehensively as I strolled on between the houses, looking neither left nor right, pausing only where the path plunged into a ravine. Beneath a nearby house a man was swinging in a hammock. Seeing me, he jumped to his feet, pulled a policeman's jacket over his vest and hastened towards the *falang* – smiling, I was relieved to observe. He asked if I were going to Luang Prabang and clearly had no objection to my doing so. Eureka! I conveyed that I was not going '*moer nee*' (today) but '*moer eun*' (tomorrow). The policeman beamed and bowed and said '*Soke dee!*' (good luck). Then he returned to the hammock, removing his jacket.

On the way back I noted landmarks that could be seen next morning by torchlight. In Mr Nuhak's *ban* I stopped – feeling less furtive now that I had police approbation – to ask how long it took to walk to Luang Prabang. Mr Nuhak didn't know; his generation travels by bus (if at all) and he couldn't comprehend my not wanting to do likewise. Then a neighbour recalled taking five days to cover the distance, carrying quite a heavy load.

On the left bank of the Nam Kay I sat for an hour in the shade of overhanging shrubs – laden with pink and blue blossoms – observing the traffic. At this fording point the water is some two feet deep; a little way upstream are deeper pools. Schoolchildren, returning home, carried their bicycles across. Two young women, going to Kasi market, were pushing a long handcart piled with coconuts – so overloaded that it stuck on the stony riverbed. Soon a youth arrived and at once volunteered to help; he had come to wash four younger siblings and their clothes. An elderly woman, the wicker baskets on her bamboo yoke full of bananas, greeted me cheerfully as she hitched up her *sin* before crossing. Three young men, carrying clean garments, arrived to bathe in a pool; stripped to their underpants, they revealed not an ounce of fat but were unostentatiously muscular, their shoulders wide in relation to narrow waists, their legs shapely, their arms slender as a woman's. Presumably the female Lao physique – never revealed in public – is equally aesthetically pleasing. Before dressing, the young men washed their dirty garments with Lifebuoy soap; their parents would have used home-made soap. Meanwhile several groups of older children had arrived to fetch water for domestic use. They filled five-gallon plastic jerrycans – downstream from the Lifebuoy – then helped each other to heave them into small handcarts or secure them, pannier-wise, to bicycles. Three boys, aged no more than ten, proved unable to push their cart, holding eight jerrycans, up the slope from the river. They were helped by an elderly man transporting two sacks of rice on a bicycle. A young mother with baby on back, another in womb and a toddler at foot held the toddler's hand as they forded. He then scampered ahead, barefooted, up the steep stony slope and was expected to walk to Kasi, keeping pace with Mama. It depresses me to think of the mutations we are encouraging by refusing to recognize that toddlers can happily walk miles and only whinge to get into their buggies because foolish parents are willing to push them. I first saw the error of our ways in Ethiopia, in 1967, when a party of peasants walked with me over a fifteen-mile stretch. One of them was aged four. A few years later my daughter, aged three, uncomplainingly walked eleven miles in one day, thus proving that juvenile stamina is not race-related.

On the bridge over the Nam Lik two surly armed soldiers challenged me, an inconclusive encounter since we couldn't communicate. I beamed at them and said, 'Kasi!' Had they met me leaving the town, heading for the wide open spaces with a rucksack, they would certainly have turned me back. I resolved to start next morning at four instead of five.

On the guesthouse veranda eight backpackers of various nationalities, awaiting a bus to Luang Prabang, were studying their *Lonely Planet* guides and debating which 'tribal villages' would be best to target. In Vientiane I had been reliably informed that this obsession with 'tribals' soon antagonizes the tribes concerned. For centuries these people have proudly maintained their own distinctive cultures, sometimes at the expense of safety and/or prosperity. Naturally they resent groups of day trippers who treat them as quaint tourist attractions, their photographs to be displayed back home with other trophies.

The informality of Lao guesthouses, where guests share the domestic quarters, is very agreeable. Despite Kasi's new hostelry being so posh, the forty-foot-long restaurant was also the family's dining-cum-living-room and the teenagers' bedroom. Framed photographs of relatives and friends – dozens of pictures, enlarged – decorated the white walls. At one end stood a monster television set, plus video recorder and music centre – the most expensive models. Two capacious sofas (wine leatherette) at right angles to the TV with a glass-topped coffee table between them bearing a vase of paper flowers. The only beautiful object in the room was a rug from Yunnan where Father had business interests. From sunrise the TV offered Thai chat shows, American 'comedies', Australian soaps, boxing, billiards, soccer – all found equally enthralling by parents and children alike. The latter sprawled on the sofas in an oddly American (and very un-Lao) way, incessantly chewing bubble-gum.

4

A Circular Wander

There was no door between my room and the street; I only had to go downstairs and cross an open foyer giving access to the veranda – a short walk to freedom. When I hastened away at 4.10 a golden sliver of waning moon lay on its back between high masses of cloud and the air was cool. Soon I met a few women and girls carrying loads to the market; some held flaming torches of banana stems, their smoke incense-like. As I forded the Nam Kay a water snake was caught in my torchlight, his (her?) little head held high. Scared, s/he swerved sinuously away. In Mr Nuhak's *ban* cocks were crowing raucously on all sides but there was no one astir. Between chinks in some walls I could see candles or mini-oil-lamps flickering in front of ancestral shrines.

The cloudy dawn was slow and dim but when I reached the ridgetop *ban*, at 6.45, those women who couldn't afford to use the rice-mill were already working their foot-mills – long wooden contraptions – while simultaneously grinding spices in hardwood bowls with stone pestles. Beside some stood a small daughter, dextrously winnowing rice on a child-sized round straw tray.

Cautiously I descended the precipitous path into the ravine, using my umbrella as a walking-stick. Three girls were toiling up, carrying buckets of water on yokes, and they returned my greeting timidly, with downcast eyes. They were slim lasses, not much more than five feet tall – and water is heavy and that gradient is severe. Yet once safely past me they began to laugh and chatter excitedly and I marvelled at their strength.

The ravine's clear stream, overhung by massive, exposed tree roots and tangled vegetation, was quite deep but furnished with large stepping-stones. Here I felt exultant – then recalled also feeling exultant on leaving Vang Vieng . . .

The upward path, scarcely eighteen inches wide, led on to a high mountain covered either in bamboo or awesome primary forest. These ancient trees soaring up for 250 feet and more – never had I seen their equal – made me feel like kneeling and worshipping.

This was a neglected path, obviously little used nowadays. Sometimes, on my left, there was an almost sheer drop of several hundred feet to the Nam Kay – here, even in the dry season, a fast brown torrent, its foam golden where touched by the morning sun. I told myself that should the path collapse – or, where it had already collapsed, should I lose my nerve while crawling across a broken stretch – some tree would certainly stop my fall. On those stretches it was tempting to clutch at nearby vegetation but that might have disturbed a snoozing snake. Two crossed the path; I very nearly trod on the first. Fallen smallish trees thrice blocked my way where the mountain was much too steep to do a detour either above or below the obstacle. The only alternative was to break through the branches – during which process those trees seemed biggish. One had wine-coloured bark and pretty pink leaves, long and slender with arrow-point tips. Several adhered firmly to my arms and face and when I removed them my skin began slowly to ooze a little blood on areas the exact shape of the leaves. No punctures were visible and I felt only a slight soreness but the oozing continued for more than an hour. As for the vines, they demanded constant vigilance, especially the trip-trap species – lines of green 'twine' lying across the path and looking innocuous but potentially lethal above such drops because they don't snap when a foot catches on them. Such vines are greatly valued by the Lao, particularly for hut-building; even the thinnest is impossible to break with bare hands. Another variety, rope-thick, sometimes hung across the path just above my head; once it caught the top of the rucksack and I lost my balance, luckily where there was space to recover from a stumble.

For miles, after the initial climb, the path remained more or less level, twisting to and fro as it followed the mountains' contours. Sometimes the Nam Kay was lost sight of but always it reappeared, swift and sparkling in its narrow curving valley. On the far side, primary forest clothed high, steep, rounded mountains. Occasionally a gap revealed angular silver karst peaks – miles away, glittering against an intensely blue sky. This was a region unmarked by man apart from the path – which could have been made by large animals, in the good old days. (It is strange – and tragic – to think that those days were within my lifetime.) The silence was broken only by the falling, now and then, of huge dry leaves. All day I neither saw nor heard a single bird. Where giant bamboo prevailed, elaborate patterns were created by long fallen poles, supported on their still erect companions, lying in straight lines one above the other like builders' scaffolding – an extraordinary sight. Unfortunately my hands were by then so muddy I couldn't use my camera.

Beyond one bamboo forest, the path became a little wider, and rocky, before suddenly plunging down to river level – then at once climbing again. Here I was walking through a curious green-tinged twilight, so close to one another were the mighty trees. On this mountain several deep gullies presented minor problems. Their sides of soap-slippy red-brown earth were ladder-steep and I had to accomplish these descents on my bottom, clutching at vegetation as a brake regardless of snakes. There is something peculiarly undignified – with cowardly undertones – about proceeding on one's bottom; this is not the image people have of intrepid travellers confronting the unknown. However, it has to be admitted that sexagenarians who over the decades have broken many bones do lack the physical self-confidence, and therefore the agility, of the young. What I most dreaded was having to cross a gully by a single tree-trunk bridge, a device to which all mountain folk are inexplicably partial. Even when young, I balked at those. Within the next hour two such horrors challenged me. Mercifully both were avoidable by clambering down, sloshing through shallow water and mud, then pushing my way up through the low, dense vegetation that always grows near water. By this stage I had become fatalistic about snakes.

So far I had met no one. Then, as I was nut-munching by a gully stream, a handsome young Hmong – wearing a ragged Mutant Turtles T-shirt and psychedelic nylon shorts – came leaping down the slope above, going towards Kasi. His first reaction to the *falang* seemed a mixture of alarm and incredulity but when greeted and smiled upon he became shyly friendly. Sitting on a root, he wonderingly examined my rucksack, exclaiming at the padded straps and waistband and odd buckles. Then he peered into my box of nuts, judged them to be inadequate nourishment and took from the cloth bag around his neck a banana-leaf package, the size of a two-pound loaf, tied with grass. Carefully undoing the knot, he broke off a quarter of the solid mass of sticky rice and presented it to me. Gratefully I accepted this manna; though unsalted it was very palatable – still warm, strongly woodsmoke flavoured. Soon the last grain was gone – much energy had been expended since I breakfasted off bananas in my room – and the young man offered more, looking quite worried when I declined. As he went on his way I went on mine: two steps up, one step back, slithering and swearing. On that ascent there were no protruding roots or stones to help, which was unusual.

Clouds had been gathering, swiftly and darkly, during my rest stop. Now came a fifteen-minute downpour; the straight-falling rain drew a pale grey curtain along the valley, then splashed loudly on the foliage above me, without penetrating that canopy of leaves. Soon after, the path surprised me by emerging into dazzling sunshine. I found myself standing on the edge of a near-precipice, overlooking a golden expanse of paddyfields dotted with tiny watch-huts. This oval valley was perhaps two miles wide and five miles long, completely surrounded by forested mountains – some spurs extending far into the paddy. Its *bans* were as yet invisible. The Luang Prabang path presumably continued over the magnificent northern mountains.

That very long descent, extra-skiddy after the rain, dictated more bum-shuffling. On either side rose ten-foot-high elephant grass, its feathery tops pinkish brown; this provides the raw material for mats, baskets, window shutters. Here I had my second encounter, with a young hunter; having overcome his astonishment he looked amused, in a polite way, by my hyper-cautious approach to this gradient.

Back on level ground, the path became quite a wide track shaded by tall wild banana plants. Then it disappeared, as paths must do at the edge of paddyfields. To a stranger, the walked-on bunds look equally important – or unimportant – and one has to cruise around seeking what seems most likely to be the main path. But in this sort of terrain paths often have to deviate because of uncrossable rivers or mountain spur barriers.

I paused to consult the map; no *bans* were marked – had the cartographer become imaginative at this point? A spidery line prompted me to make for the west side of the valley before turning north. *En route* were three little rivers – thigh-deep, very fast, forty to fifty feet wide with mobile stones underfoot. Leaning on my umbrella, I forded them slowly.

Then, at the base of the western mountains, came a reunion with my old friend the Nam Kay – here not at all like the mild flow happily forded by the toddlers of Kasi. It was in fact a raging torrent, scarcely thirty yards wide but so turbulent one couldn't estimate its depth. Again I consulted the map; that spidery line continued on the far bank. Walking upstream, I came upon a feat of local engineering. Three slim palm trunks, with twelve-inch spaces between them, had been tied with vine ropes to trees overhanging the river on either side. This contraption, suspended some twenty feet above the water, was approached by climbing frail-looking bamboo stepladders. As I viewed it despairingly, a movement upstream caught my eye. Standing chest-deep in the racing water, a man was fishing with a hand-net. His very beautiful young wife, collecting berries on the bank, had already seen me. She beckoned, then pointed farther upstream to a dry-weather fording point. I would never have guessed that one could safely cross there. Smiling kindly, my guide led me to the precise point of entry, then was fascinated to see me securing my journal, camera, binoculars and money-belt in the rucksack's waterproof top pocket. The water came well above my waist and I longed for Mr Tang: the umbrella was a poor substitute. That crossing seemed to take for ever; I was too aware of the possible consequences of falling when heavily burdened. On the far side, while reorganizing things, I paused to watch two old women (probably great-grandmothers) fording quickly, supporting each other and cheerfully chatting as they went.

I rested briefly in the shade of a saraca tree; it was eighty or ninety feet tall and its smooth fluted trunk might have strayed from a Gothic cathedral. Soon a multitude of minuscule but painful black ants moved me on. A distinct path wound for half a mile through thin forest (many trees had been felled) and exuberant secondary growth. Then I was back on paddyland where newly flooded fields were being ploughed. A group of young people relaxing in a watch-hut, laughing and singing, abruptly fell silent on seeing the *falang*. Making an attempt to ask for directions, I gathered there was a choice of two routes to Luang Prabang; one led across the paddy, another along the wooded base of the mountain. I chose the latter and soon was fording a nameless (on the map) river, very wide but only ankle-deep. Ahead rose a grassy, hillocky slope where five squealing bonhams ran out of a blue-bush thicket towards their searching mother – so a *ban* was close.

I decided to avoid it, if possible, though my being thwarted so far from Kasi – now a ten-hour walk away – seemed unlikely. When the fifty or so thatched houses came into view, on a wide flat ridge-top, I paused to survey my environs and at once realized that a detour would be topographically impossible. The *ban* was fortified by a strong, five-foot-high fence of sharpened bamboo stakes and could only be entered via ladder-stiles. I climbed one and walked briskly between the houses feigning uninterest in my surroundings but smiling amiably when anyone crossed my path. Not many did. Approaching the exit stile, I became aware of being scrutinized by a group of ragged young men sitting under a large dwelling. When I called a greeting a few smiled uncertainly: others frowned. Then I was over the stile and hastening downhill through blue-bush – elated! But some moments later my heart sank (a graphic cliché: on such occasions one can feel it sinking) as running footsteps sounded behind me. A young man – one of the frowners – blocked my way, insisting that I must go no farther. I must sleep in the *ban*, otherwise I would be shot dead or have my throat slit – both fates easily conveyed through sign language. Bad men lived in the forests ahead . . . Effusively I thanked the young man and tried to explain that I would prefer to continue and camp out at sunset. He then became quite agitated, seized my arm and vigorously pulled me uphill. Whether or not those bad men existed, my minder believed in them.

Everyone smiled at me as I returned over the stile. Beneath the dwelling, a short unsteady bench was provided for the guest and we were joined by a feeble, betel-chewing elder who seemed grievously perplexed by my presence. No one looked remotely like an official of any sort but my minder took charge, sitting at my feet on a six-inch-high stool polished by generations of use. The elder also had a stool; the rest stood leaning against the stilts or squatted on the dusty ground. A small crowd quickly assembled – mostly male, the women being at work in fields or forest. This was a quiet crowd: the children fearful, the girls expressionless, the men uneasy.

As the intruder was being debated, I caught one adopted word – 'permit' – which inspired me to claim to have a police permit for my walk to Luang Prabang. Boldly I produced my passport and a 200 kip Wat Sisaket museum ticket. (I tend to keep such things as souvenirs.) For a full ten minutes my minder pored over the passport and turned the ticket every way round, muttering to himself. Anxiously he consulted his friends, several of whom had babies on their backs in cloth slings or were cuddling toddlers. When one dad realized that his daughter was missing I pointed in the relevant direction – having noticed the infant crawling purposefully away. Dad pursued her to the edge of a four-foot drop into a hollow where pigs are fed; she was peering down, entranced by something, but seemed in no danger of toppling in.

Photographs of my granddaughters caused great excitement and broke a lot of ice; in such *bans* photographs are as yet a rarity. Then a large party appeared, crossing the stile. Three hunters came first, their furred and feathered suppers in hide shoulder-bags. (The Lao can see monkeys and birds where I can't.) Twelve young women followed, carrying large sacks of rice on their backs, using Nepalese-style headbands. Some were the wives of the baby-carers; shedding their loads, they squatted down to suckle. The leading hunter, aged perhaps fifty, had an unmistakable air of authority: here was the chief, I guessed correctly. My minder handed him my passport and 'explained' me. Graciously he welcomed the *falang* and by 5.15 I had been installed in his son's house. My host's name sounded something like 'Thonglit'.

This was another long, high-ceilinged room, like Mr Tang's but even more minimally furnished; it contained only a bench – on which I sat by the window – a few straw mats and bedraggled quilts and a small padlocked cupboard from which a trannie was taken for my entertainment. Happily its batteries soon gave out. Mr Thonglit eagerly asked if I would like to buy *lau-lao* (home-distilled rice spirit, tasting remarkably like poteen) and when he returned with the bottle news got around that the *falang* was dispensing hospitality. Soon eighteen adults had joined the thirty-five children already sitting silently on the floor studying my every move.

I needed that *lau-lao*. Suspense about the morrow was building up – would the chief allow me to continue? Pouring a prudent measure into my mug, I presented the rest to my host and the bottle passed from mouth to mouth around the adult circle; there were no cups or glasses in evidence. I was not left long in suspense. The chief reappeared briefly, handed me my passport and made it plain I must return to Kasi – graphically he mimed the slitting of my throat or the shooting of me dead. I didn't try to argue. This was, after all, his territory. But then came an unexpected development.

The chief's two hunting companions were present, their muskets propped against the wall, and they offered to escort me to Luang Prabang for a fee of US$50 each. (They obviously had no notion of the kip value of $50.) Taken aback, I registered an ambivalent reaction. Proceeding under armed guard would certainly be preferable to returning to Kasi. But I detest being guided: that takes all the exciting unpredictability out of a trek. And, on another level, being alone is to me enormously important – the traveller and the place interacting, free of extraneous influences. Moreover, though not normally suspicious, I didn't entirely trust those particular men. They could rob me, push me over a precipice and say I had slipped . . . But quickly I banished that unduly melodramatic thought and began to negotiate. Explaining that I had no dollars, I suggested paying them 20,000 kip each (then about $10) on arrival in Luang Prabang. They happily settled for that and we planned to leave at 8 a.m. – any earlier would be too cold for my bodyguard. In retrospect, I'm always amazed at the complicated arrangements achievable through sign language; no one in that *ban* spoke a syllable of English.

Thus far Mr Thonglit had not intervened but now it became apparent that my new plan worried him. An argument started – low key, this being Laos, but serious. It seemed most of the men present were also worried and Mr Thonglit asked to see my passport again. When it was passed around some doubts were expressed about its validity – the photograph showed my hair longer and bushier. I could understand the apprehension in the air; Laos in transition makes many peasants apprehensive, as Mr

Tang had exemplified. Could I be some mysterious NGO rep planning to meddle with local irrigation systems? Or a foreign consultant advising the government on land registration and taxes? Or an ecological spy collecting statistics to be used against these swidden farmers?

While my companions argued – and a second bottle did the rounds – I observed the *ban*'s evening routines from my high window-seat. A section of the perimeter fence, on the river side, was a gate, now open to admit home-coming buffaloes and pigs. The former proceeded ponderously to their individual spaces beneath the dwellings where children tethered them to stilts. Sows were being fed rice husks and rice water in wooden troughs, women stirring the mixture as the pigs crowded around grunting and shoving and making nasty noises at each other. Growing piglets are fed separately. Here were no turkeys but countless hens and ducks. Teenage girls returning from the forest carried neatly cut loads of firewood, worn like rucksacks. A woman passed balancing a musket on her head, holding a baby on one hip, carrying a huge roll of banana fronds under the other arm. A small girl passed with a large tray of winnowed rice on her head, her upcurving arms stretched to their limit. Tantrums are unusual in Laos but on the opposite balcony a toddler lay kicking and screaming, his mother clearly exasperated but being commendably patient. Then, catching sight of me, she picked him up, held him standing on her lap and directed his attention to the *falang*. Instant silence. He was riveted – and, being in the maternal arms, not alarmed.

Several children wandered around eating cakes of sticky rice and followed by plump pups and dogs, hopefully wagging their tails. These hopes were always realized. Most children looked adequately fed but some had dirt diseases: open sores, ringworm, head lice, scabies. The little ones wore only vests and one girl, aged seven or eight, was stark naked but for the cloth in which she carried her infant sibling. While playing, the children were gentle with one another – and with their canine companions. An older sister severely chided one toddler for hitting a puppy. The variety of ingenious home-made toys made me sadly remember Mr Tang's *ban* where dozens of children crowded around recently acquired television sets for hours on end. Pre-electricity they would have been playing outside, doing their own inventive, energetic thing, developing their minds and bodies.

To the Lao their midwinter evenings seem very cold and at sunset small boys lit big bonfires with burning brands carried from their hearths. I watched men, children, dogs, pups, bonhams and a cat gather around a nearby bonfire. (One memorable vignette: a cross-legged man with a little girl on his lap and on her lap a kitten and a newborn bonham.) Soon several fires were burning crimson through the blue-grey dusk, their smoke aromatic. Then Mr Thonglit lowered the woven shutter as a daughter brought one of those pungent, minute kerosene lamps, with naked flickering wicks, common throughout the Poor World. Not long after, the guests dispersed, bowing to me as they left.

When supper was served we all sat on the floor around an enormous communal rice basket – Mr Thonglit, his wife, her mother, six children and two dogs with ears pricked, looking expectant but never begging. They knew they didn't have to: everyone gave them balls of rice. Our personal soup bowls were filled from a cauldron wherein floated pods and leaves from the forest, what seemed to be beetles (it was hard to tell in the half-darkness) and five small birds plucked but not gutted, complete with feet and beaks. I was offered one but declined. Protein is precious and all the birds were left for the older children who crunched them with relish, leaving not so much as a claw. The eldest son, aged twelve, had killed them with his catapult. During the meal there was much animated conversation between the older generations and between them and the children, whose many questions were answered patiently. I sensed a genuine equality between husband and wife and much affection between parents and children.

And so to bed. Unfortunately Mr Thonglit considered my space blanket and flea-bag too spartan (they don't look warm) and insisted on my using a filthy padded quilt which gave me a mild dose of scabies (easily cured in Luang Prabang by the application of a foul-smelling herbal ointment).

At dawn, after ten hours' sleep, I woke to hear a rhythmic thudding and creaking – my hostess husking rice at the foot of the ladder. Raising the shutter, I saw that all the nearby mountains were completely hidden by dense, slowly shifting cloud – silver grey, quite beautiful. If left to my own devices, I could have been on the path to Luang Prabang by 6.30, enjoying the cool of the morning. Again bonfires were lit and men and children hunkered around them while the womenfolk prepared breakfast: sticky rice. On neighbouring balconies, girls were vigorously brushing their hair, then tying it back with bands made of plaited grass. Small children released poultry from minature thatched huts, also on stilts, then collected eggs and carefully carried them up ladders. Older children untethered pigs and buffaloes and led the latter down to the river. I wondered why the men didn't stay warmly in bed till the sun came up, since they seemed to have no morning chores. But then I noticed that most did have paternal responsibilities, either tied to their back or sitting on their lap.

When I attempted a stroll around the *ban* Mr Thonglit would allow me to go no farther than the long-drop. Soon after, the chief appeared, looking stern, and embarked on a lengthy discussion with his son. Then my bodyguard arrived and seemed disconcerted to see the chief. The discussion widened; obviously the majority opposed my being escorted to Luang Prabang. Finally the chief cancelled the arrangement. I must return, at once, to Kasi.

Acute disappointment inspired me to try a long shot: my publisher's 'To Whom It May Concern' letter, written in English and French. Solemnly I unfolded both versions, smoothed them ceremoniously, handed them to the chief with a bow and asserted – trying to sound important and authoritative – that these gave me permission to walk from Kasi to Luang Prabang. Both were quite long letters, signed with a flourish, and on John Murray's headed paper they looked impressive. The chief gazed at them silently, passed them to his son – and for the first time seemed unsure of himself. During the next lengthy discussion I tried not to hope – this was such a very long shot! Then the chief turned to me, pointed to my rucksack, pointed towards Luang Prabang, indicated that I could proceed. With difficulty, I refrained from hugging him. But what about my armed guard? No, they need not accompany me; I had a strong hunch that the chief trusted them no more than I did. Joyously I loaded up, said my goodbyes and thank-yous and went on my way blessing John Murray.

Soon the path began to climb through primary forest, unmixed with bamboo. This was a mountain with a difference. At irregular but frequent intervals wide outcrops of grey rock, four or five feet high and water-worn into weird shapes, had to be surmounted. In between, massive tree-root extensions – equally high – served as 'gates' across the path. Never have I seen anything comparable to those root systems; they seemed to exist independently of their ancient trees, writhing around each other in a sort of witches' embrace. And they felt as steady and strong as the rocks.

All day it remained dusk-dim, the air laden with the odours of acrid fungi, bizarre swags of damp moss and arboreal decay. For hours the path ascended and sometimes I wondered if I had gone astray on leaving paddyland; it seemed improbable that this could ever have been a main track to Luang Prabang. As for bandits, no bandit in his right mind would operate hereabouts. Fifty years ago one might have met tigers, donkey-sized boars and black bears seven feet tall – but never bandits.

By mid-afternoon all those rocks and gates had quite exhausted me; climbing when loaded is something else. Then came what I had dreaded: an unavoidable single tree-trunk bridge. It spanned a deep dry gully with sheer sides, no more than thirty yards wide but with a fifty-foot drop on to boulders. I shuddered – unreasonably. That tree trunk was some five feet in circumference; any Lao peasant would have trotted across without even noticing it. I looked around in wild surmise, up and down the mountain, craving an alternative route. There was none. So I 'rode' across, sitting astride, inching my way forward, remembering an identical experience, more than thirty years ago, in Nepal. How did people contrive to put such a massive tree trunk in place? But I only wondered about that afterwards.

Two hours later a long, steep descent on an obstacle-free path took me to the edge of another valley, which looked benign and welcoming in the mellow evening light. On the far side, below a line of karst peaks, a *ban* occupied a ridge. I hesitated – more hassle? But then the chief appeared, musket over one shoulder, a recently deceased gibbon over the other. He was small and wiry and very self-confident – surprised, but not thrown, by my arrival on his patch. His entourage of five youths, firewood-laden, stared at me wide-eyed as he and I began another of those mentally strenuous sign-language exchanges. I soon realized that this chief did not view me with suspicion; he simply regarded me as a dotty old woman in need of shelter and advice. I was to be his guest for the night. He was a most endearing character, kind, shrewd and humorous.

This was a big *ban* of 127 houses – 'Neing loy sao-jet' said the chief, writing that number in my notebook. His own dwelling resembled Mr Tang's rather than Mr Thonglit's; there were chairs and a table and glasses for the *lau-lao* provided by my host. Hot boiled water, herb-flavoured, was offered from a Chinese mega-thermos-flask. A map of the region, identical to mine, adorned one wall and my host pointed out various bandit bases between this valley and Luang Prabang. His wife – equally impressive, fluent in sign language – joined in the 'conversation', using pen and paper to convey how many had been murdered in the past year: thirty-four, including two children when a truck-bus was ambushed near Kasi. (The government consistently suppresses such statistics.) I could see where our conversation was leading; no way would this chief allow me to walk on. When I half-heartedly tried the 'permit' trick it merely amused him: he dismissed John Murray with a wave of the hand and a twinkle in the eye. Then he advised me to secrete my binoculars in my rucksack; their brown leather case might be mistaken for a gun holster and certain men could react negatively to an armed stranger. At which point I began to suspect the real identity of these 'bandits'.

It transpired that I had indeed been on the wrong path all day but I rejoiced not to have missed that extraordinary forest. Next morning the chief courteously (or as a precaution against my rebelling?) led me to the start of the right path, at the southern end of his valley. Being on an unfamiliar path was some compensation for my defeat.

This route led up and down – or around – low spurs of varying bulks and gradients, some partially covered in the secondary growth that flourishes after swidden farmers have moved on, some bamboo jungle interwoven with groves of wild banana. (The banana is a native of these parts.) I was on level paddyland when a sudden half-hour downpour sent me scuttling to a watch-hut. This rain seemed to have the force of a waterfall and the thatch was leaking so I sat under the platform; many fish scales and the feathers of tiny birds were scattered around the cooking-stones. Then I noticed, hung on a stilt, the skull of a small monkey.

During the wee hours I had had a nightmare about the chief's gibbon – his expression was so innocent and his hands were so very human, even to the lines on the palms . . .

Continuing, I lost the path. On three sides dense forest enclosed this paddyland and on the fourth stretched secondary growth. For a long time I probed this way and that, slipping and scrambling across treacherous bunds, finding vestigial paths that soon vanished. Knowing that Kasi lay to the south-east was no help; in such terrain it may be necessary to walk for miles in the apparently wrong direction. I was beginning to feel slightly desperate when two bamboo-laden women emerged from the forest, paused to stare at me fearfully – then hurried away. My calling a greeting only made them trot faster. But they had provided guidance: their footsteps led me across a muddy expanse of half-cleared forest to what I hoped was the continuation of my track. Stopping to drink from a cliff-face stream veiled by vegetation, I found myself eyeball to eyeball with a smallish snake hanging from a branch. Most snakes try to evade humans but this one seemed otherwise inclined; I felt I was lucky to have seen him/her in time.

Two spurs later, on newly cleared paddyland, I passed several smouldering forest giants lying amidst the stubble. These can take up to four years to burn away, being extinguished each wet season, then reignited when November comes. Were such trees accessible, their cash value would be considerable. Here they are seen as a nuisance by peasants eager to cultivate the space they occupy and lacking the tools (or the will or the need?) to use them for fuel, furniture or building. It was distressing to witness their slow cremation; since they have to be killed, one would prefer them to be used, even by a logging company – if reincarnated as furniture, they could give pleasure for centuries. Or, if used as firewood, smaller trees would be spared. I felt that anything would be better than their futile smouldering away – though perhaps not entirely futile, if the ash is a good fertilizer.

By mid-afternoon Mr Thonglit's *ban* was visible on my right, far away across the valley – this path bypassed it. No other *ban* appeared all day though several must have been quite close, judging by the numbers of people ploughing, cutting firewood, gathering forest foods, hunting, collecting six-foot-long banana fronds and fishing in the little rivers.

Towards sunset I overtook two small girls leading the buffalo home; an even smaller girl rode on his broad back, her legs sticking out at right angles. The children giggled nervously when first they saw me, then relaxed and tried to question me as we walked together. Soon their *ban* was visible astride the track – more 'advanced' (nearer Kasi) than the other two, with a few tin roofs amidst the score of large thatched dwellings. A straw-walled 'shop' sold Fanta, biscuits, kerosene, soap, shampoo and packets of dried 'instant' noodles. Here I sensed none of the underlying tensions of Mr Thonglit's *ban*; everyone – post-astonishment – was outgoing and warmly welcoming.

Mr Somsak, the girls' father, looked so young I at first mistook him for an older brother. He, too, was a would-be English-speaker, elated at the prospect of entertaining a *falang*. Up-ladder, on a long wide balcony, I was introduced to his father-in-law – sitting on a mini-chair, aged about fifty, looking sorry for himself. He showed me a deep, infected axe wound in the middle of his swollen right foot and pleaded for medicine. Explaining that I had none, I offered nursing care instead. His immediate reaction was fear but Mr Somsak persuaded him to take advantage of *falang* expertise – then fetched a basin of very hot water. The patient was admirably stoical as I cleaned the gash and poulticed it before squeezing out a scary amount of pus. His eldest granddaughter (aged nine) deftly applied a bandage made of woven banana fibre and a few hours later he was happily walking on his heel.

In the living-room Mr Somsak seated me on a roll of quilts and his wife – yet another Lao beauty – came from the kitchen to be introduced. Would I eat sticky rice? she anxiously enquired. My enthusiastic response delighted her. Mr Somsak's query – would I drink *lao hai*? – elicited an even more enthusiastic response. Moment later a fat earthenware jar, some three feet high and containing fermented rice, was placed in front of me. From this everyone imbibes through yard-long, slightly curved bamboo 'straws'; the boiling water added at intervals seems – mysteriously – not to lower the alcohol content. As I sucked, nostalgia afflicted me; I last drank this brew when working with Tibetan refugees. As usual, several neighbours joined the party and my hostess occasionally left her cooking for long enough to imbibe deeply, using her husband's straw.

With our rice we had watercress and a spicy soup containing many slivers of an odd rubbery meat, its flavour extremely interesting. After the meal I sought to identify this. Mr Somsak didn't know the English name and his attempts to describe the creature through gestures and mime sent the older children into convulsions of laughter. Finally he picked up the oil wick and beckoned me to follow him to the kitchen. Something was confined in a wicker cage in a corner. Mr Somsak shook the cage to make it move and held the wick low. Peering close, I saw a monitor lizard. 'For tomorrow we have another,' said my host proudly. 'Today I get in trap.'

A restless night was had by all. The three-month-old baby was unwell – vomiting and crying – and the four-year-old boy had a bad cough and a slight fever. While Mum tried to soothe the former, Dad sat beside his wheezing and whimpering son making sympathetic noises, providing hot drinks and rubbing eucalyptus ointment (home-made) on the little fellow's chest. Sometimes one feels mean about not carrying basic medicines. Yet the arguments against doing so are strong, especially in countries like Laos with a surviving tradition of many effective local cures. Some travellers – their heads as soft as their hearts – lavish antibiotics on suffering peasants. But even the dispensing of aspirins, vitamin pills, throat lozenges or antiseptic ointment (something I've been guilty of in the past) is not really helpful. Sampling 'Western magic' can quickly undermine respect for what is accessible and affordable; this is our contemporary 'intervention dilemma' in microcosm. Within the foreseeable future, most Lao will have no access to Western medicines correctly administered: that's not what NEM is all about. But town dwellers have already acquired a taste for them and powerful antibiotics can be bought in any pharmacy without a prescription – and cheaply, compared to their price in the Rich World. People suffering from a sore throat, a touch of pinkeye or a twinge of lumbago habitually buy six or ten antibiotics – when forty is the course and anyway antibiotics are inappropriate. The dire consequences of this abuse, rampant throughout the Poor World for decades, are already apparent. Why do governments who ineffectually spend billions opposing 'recreational' drugs ('bad for the health') ignore those other drug barons, the pharmaceutical companies? Their uncontrolled activities are equally, if more insidiously, 'bad for the health'. We live in an ominously mad world: 'Those whom the gods wish to destroy, they first make mad.'

At dawn I set off in rather a subdued mood – partly lack of sleep, partly negative feelings about rejoining Route 13. From Mr Somsak's *ban* the track to Kasi was unmistakable, for the first few miles hacked out of sheer cliffs where swathes of vines half obscured miniature waterfalls. This was an easy day's walking, through tranquil beauty. Sometimes the track undulated between rustling bamboo – the tallest I had seen, rising to seventy or eighty feet. Then I was overlooking wide shallow valleys where small patches of paddy glowed golden amidst tangled subtropical vegetation. Hereabouts the butterflies seemed larger, more numerous and more gorgeously coloured than anywhere else in Laos – perhaps because of a particular local plant. During a long, gradual descent to a more arid area of low scrub and blue-bush I put up two pheasants. For the last hour I was crossing level paddyland – the peaks ahead familiar, surrounding Kasi.

5

Limping around Luang Prabang

The Luang Prabang bus departs from Kasi 'some time between 9 and 11'. Awaiting it on the veranda, I was diverted by the contents of a taxi tuk-tuk from Vang Vieng – a group of adolescent American backpackers being led, it seemed, by a middle-aged man. A memorable man: tall, pot-bellied, grey-haired, loud-mouthed, with auburn (dyed?) moustaches of such proportions – touching his shirt-front – one doubted their authenticity. Impatient at having to wait indefinitely for the onward bus, he tried to negotiate with three young men about to leave in an antique pick-up van. Its back was loaded with second-hand power tiller engines, lengths of lead piping and two new china lavatory bowls. When the trio refused to convenience him by unloading he became downright rude – then moved restlessly around the veranda, complaining about the delicious Lao coffee (not instant decaffeinated) and reiterating a wish to see a UN vehicle approaching. That would solve his transport problem – or so he assumed, probably correctly. The boys of his party were discussing American football and the girls gossiping about some sex scandal at their high school. A reasonable breakfast bill provoked everyone to haggle with the polite young waitress. At this point a local entrepreneur, scenting dollars, offered transport in his own new minibus. The youngsters looked terrified when an armed soldier – their bodyguard for the journey – hoisted himself on to the vehicle's roof. No one was sorry to see them go.

Meanwhile the trio had been adjusting their pick-up's wheels which seemed to have gone out of alignment. I rejoiced when they indicated space for one passenger in the back; 10,000 kip (3,000 more than the bus fare) would ensure me an unimpeded view of the landscape. But as I settled myself comfortably on the rucksack, using a lavatory bowl as arm-rest, it became apparent that there was another problem, this time with the steering wheel . . .

Twenty minutes later I asked myself, 'Do you really want to take a famously twisty mountain road in a vehicle with so many frail-ties?' The answer was 'No.' As I disembarked the trio protested plaintively; to them 10,000 kip was a substantial sum. It took eight men to push the van up the slight slope to Route 13 – where at last it started, after an inauspicious series of coughs and jerks.

At eleven o'clock the bus arrived, rattling, tattered and smelly – a Soviet truck converted to bus-hood by some ingenious black-smith-cum-carpenter. Only from a back corner seat, by the pas-sengers' doorless entrance, could one see anything of the landscape. Nobody objected when the only *falang* aboard bagged this seat. At 11.20 two soldiers, complete with rifles, side-arms and daggers, ascended the roof-ladder to recline amidst the baggage. Also on the roof were four cocks in specially designed, loosely woven travelling baskets. At every stop they crowed stridently and were given water. Since cocks abound all over Laos, why – I won-dered – take these to Luang Prabang? Later, in some wat com-pounds, I observed their like displayed for sale: very tall birds with long feathered legs and iridescent plumage. An English-speaking novice monk said they have some religious significance – to do with *phi* rather than Buddhism.

During our six-hour journey we passed only one town: Xiang Ngeun, fourteen miles from Luang Prabang. The traffic was minimal and outside of the occasional sad roadside settlement of 'relocated' people we saw no one. However, bald slopes were visible where the terrain permitted swidden cultivation (mostly it didn't) and my thwarted trek had made me aware of the many little *bans* lying hidden behind the mountains.

I have travelled through quite a few celebrated ranges but none – not even the Simiens – looks as improbable as the free-standing mountains beyond Kasi. And yet there was something oddly famil-iar about these eccentric peaks – some spear-sharp, others knobbly, one summit with twin rounded bumps like gigantic bal-loons poised above the forested slopes. Then suddenly I remem-bered. This landscape took me back to my early childhood when I used to mould Plasticine mountains, placing them at some little distance from each other, the heights and widths and formations irregular – a madness of mountains. I recalled my father explaining, in his kindly, earnestly didactic way, that real mountains are not like that: peaks don't stand isolated on flat land. But he was wrong. Real mountains are like that, in Laos.

At one settlement stop a couple boarded with a newborn infant on Mother's back and a toddler in Father's arms. On seeing me by the entrance the toddler freaked out, screaming as though he were being flayed, writhing and kicking in an attempt to escape. This caused considerable amusement – a rather heartless reaction, I thought. His parents looked anxiously embarrassed, imagining that I might take it personally, but to reassure them was not difficult. And by journey's end the same toddler was playing peek-aboo with the *falang*.

At another of our brief stops, when a few people got off and on (or the driver was put in charge of some load to be collected in Luang Prabang) an argument arose about two bonhams. The conductor reckoned these should go on the roof; their owner – a young woman carrying a beaming baby – thought otherwise. I signalled my support for the owner and the little creatures settled down happily in their basket on my rucksack, nuzzling each other and squeaking; they were too small to squeal. But at the next stop they had to be thrust under a seat – the squeaks becoming indignant – when a bent old woman struggled aboard with a massive load of forest produce: big furry brown pods, bundles of aromatic red leaves, large green berries packed in small wicker containers, long white roots resembling seriously deformed parsnips and sharp thin sticks bearing a bark much valued for dyeing. To accommodate all this merchandise, I put my feet on the metal seat in front of me: there was just enough space to insert them under an iron bar. The woman gave me a grateful, betel-red smile as she squatted on my rucksack; by then the aisle was packed with seatless passengers.

Half an hour later we rounded a hairpin bend and the driver braked so violently that my right foot, caught between the seat and that iron bar, was severely wrenched. Also, my left shin was cut by one of those precious sharp sticks. But at the time I scarcely registered my injuries as we all tried to see what had caused our abrupt stop.

Blocking the road was the trio's pick-up, its front smashed in and the lavatory bowls shattered by the wayside. One young man lay unconscious with blood seeping through his trousers. Another was half scalped – a stomach-turning sight. The third was holding a hand to his broken jaw to keep it in place. The rusty petrol tanker with which they had collided – perhaps because the steering had failed again – was not much damaged. Its driver and his passengers (five though the cab was small) stood on the verge looking shocked and helpless; none had been injured.

When we disembarked I did register the damage to my foot. Then I saw that our driver was bleeding from the teeth – not surprisingly, as his seat consisted of two up-ended beer crates. The pick-up was manhandled to the verge and we took the injured aboard and two hours later delivered them to Luang Prabang's provincial hospital, though the bus normally stops a few miles short of the city centre. Naturally I wondered about my own fate, had a well-developed instinct of self-preservation not propelled me out of that pick-up. Possibly – like the lavatory bowls – I would have been all over Route 13.

In 1995 Betty Gosling wrote: 'Even today, Luang Prabang remains remote, pristine and detached from the modern world . . .' Three years later, its outskirts gave a different impression. Looming over the bus 'terminus' – a patch of oil-stained wasteland – is a colossal hoarding: WELCOME TO LUANG PRABANG BY BEERLAO! Then comes a sports stadium, opened in 1996, its long high white wall plastered with Marlboro advertisements showing soccer players doing clever things. And nearby is a scattering of opulent villas recently built by local notables, some rumoured to be heroin barons – a plausible rumour, in this region.

The bus deposited me at a roundabout marked by a conspicuous Shell sign. Leaning heavily on my umbrella, I sought lodgings nearby but at the third fully booked guesthouse was advised to look no farther. During the Christmas/New Year season both backpackers and expats on local leave gather in comparatively cool Luang Prabang. However, Mr Somphavan promised a room for the morrow.

Back on the peripheral and utterly unpronounceable Xayacha-kaphatphanpheo Road, I reluctantly paid US$15 for one night in a newish, pretentious hotel, unwelcoming and ill-designed. From my cramped windowless room a plywood door led on to a concrete balcony overlooking a high block of Soviet-style apartments. The wc was w-less and the shower tried to behave like a water cannon. Both bar and restaurant were closed and it took me fifteen minutes to find someone to open the former. Then the receptionist-turned-barman asked how many Beerlao I needed, giggled when I said 'Four' and, having provided them, relocked the bar and disappeared for good.

After a shower, I plastered the gash on my shin and soaked the shoe into which it had bled copiously. By then my right foot was painful enough to prevent a food hunt but I knew it wasn't broken – that pain is unmistakable.

Mr Somphavan's guesthouse stands at the junction of three rough, dusty laneways shaded by magnolia, flame-of-the-forest, frangipani and palm trees. Close by are two of Luang Prabang's oldest wats, Manoram and That Luang, and this *ban*, less than ten minutes' walk from the 'city' centre, feels more rural than urban. As does the rest of Laos's ancient royal capital – population 16,000.

The guesthouse's atmosphere is best conveyed by a handwritten request displayed on the balcony door:

NOTICE

To all dear guests please. Who stay in my guests house. At night after 10.00 pm when you would like to talk with your friends. Please speak softly and be quiet because we have some guests that go to bed before. Thank you very much.

As Luang Prabang is Laos's main tourist attraction (its only one, say some), I paid $3 a night for a corner room; the double bed left no space for table or chair but two big windows allowed a splendid view of the neighbourhood. The communal bathrooms were downstairs and for a few hundred kip the Somphavan daughters washed and ironed clothes, returning them within hours.

On that first day the Foot restricted my sightseeing to nearby wats. In Manoram I met a fluent English-speaker from

Vientiane, an elderly Lao Lum who made some interesting comments on the security situation and was in a position to know what he was talking about. Certain regions, he explained, are unsafe because not under government control – so of course my treks were curtailed. Dead or disappeared tourists highlight a government's lack of control. And the problem, he asserted, was getting worse. Since the door opened, the Hmong bandits and their military allies have become bolder, believing that those 'friends' who recruited the Hmong to fight their Secret War are in the process of regaining power.

'And who,' I asked, 'are the bandits' military allies?'

'Drug-trafficking army officers,' replied Mr X. 'Here is the edge of the so-called Golden Triangle. Plenty of our provincial government officials and army officers are into the heroin trade, like the RLA was in past times – with CIA help. The US State Department accuses our central government of being involved too but they've never been able to prove it. I don't believe it myself. I'll tell you what I do believe: most "security problems" are to do with gang warfare about controlling that trade. And I can tell you something else – the way you were walking from Kasi, you might have had the bad luck to come to a heroin laboratory. And the people who run them don't like visitors.'

I was asleep as 1997 became 1998; I never can keep awake for New Year's Eve jollifications. Next morning, when it seemed that Time was not going to be the Great Healer, I limped to the provincial hospital at 7.15. This run-down colonial complex of one-storey units has many beds, a few nurses, a score of servants and several doctors most of whom tend to concentrate on their private practices. In one corner of the large grassy compound the TB unit was empty though TB is locally rampant. In the paediatric unit most beds were occupied and on the veranda stood many anxious parents carrying small patients too ill – I noticed with foreboding – to cry or fuss. Understandably, people come to this hospital only as a place of last resort.

A young woman doctor – elegant, sympathetic – spoke scraps of English and listened to me attentively. Having examined the swollen and inflamed ankle she wrote a prescription for two kinds of pills and a half-litre bottle of pale pink liquid made in Thailand. All that, and a bandage, cost 5,850 kip – about US$2.25 – in the hospital pharmacy. Then, inexplicably, I was led across the compound to the radiography department. Why an X-ray after treatment had been prescribed? In a dingy outbuilding the radiographer was still asleep on a mat, his blanket over his head. However, the equipment worked better than the Romanian machine which in 1990 X-rayed this same foot and found three broken bones. In another unit a teenage trainee nurse, advised by two older colleagues, clumsily bandaged the Foot. Eventually an older, male doctor arrived bearing two X-ray plates (no charge). All was 'normal', he confirmed – but then advised me not to walk for three days and to keep the Foot 'elevated'.

Back in the guesthouse, I read the tiny print on the bottle's label; this liquid was guaranteed to cure heartburn and flatulence, afflictions with which I am happily unacquainted. The pills may well have been for a kidney infection or some thyroid dysfunction so I discarded them. During three inactive days I was fortunate to have many congenial fellow-guests – from Argentina, Britain, Canada, Denmark, Ireland, Mexico, Zimbabwe, the USA.

Mr Somphavan's English also helped. It had been picked up many years ago from an American International Voluntary Service (IVS) worker, a CIA agent who in 1975 suddenly went home. 'And then,' said Mr Somphavan sadly, 'I could use not until 1990 so is much forgotten now.' The five Somphavan daughters and four sons ranged from twenty-seven to four years. A son and two daughters were already married but three remained at school. Mr Somphavan sighed. 'So many children are very costly, now outside people have made our government take money from students.' We soon became friends and my host confided his abhorrence of Communists; he had spent five years in a re-education camp, perhaps because of his close association with that IVS worker.

The Foot caused me to spend a fortnight in Luang Prabang, a week longer than planned. After its three non-curative days of rest and elevation, and one painful day of limping around the town, I realized that trekking was *out* for the foreseeable future – though not, oddly enough, cycling. New plan: back to Vientiane by boat – renew visa – buy bicycle – make for Xam Nua and adjacent tourist-free zones. Meanwhile I hired a male bicycle, quite a tolerable machine, a gearless, sit-up-and-beg Chinese model with a comfortable hermaphroditic saddle. It was well balanced and surprisingly speedy despite a heavy metal stand and a sturdy carrier capable of bearing at least two sacks of rice. I recognized it as the model most popular in Uganda and Tanzania; later, I had reason to regret not having bought it. The owner fretted about the saddle being much too high though I could see at a glance it was exactly right. Why, in Laos (Land of Ten Thousand Bicycles), does no one ride on a correctly adjusted saddle? It exasperated me to see men, women and children pedalling so inefficiently – legs never fully extended, ankles inflexible, knees often striking the handlebars. As in Vientiane, poor adults often rode expat children's discarded bikes – something possible only because most Lao are so small.

Even I couldn't get lost in Luang Prabang, confined as it is on a narrow peninsula between the Mekong and the Nam Khan. Three pot-holed streets run the length of the peninsula and are linked by shady laneways winding between stilted houses. Sadly, the centre is now defaced by a telecommunications mast ten times the height of any other local structure. And, inevitably, this has sired a large brood of satellite dishes. Otherwise, it is evident that Laos's royal and ancient capital has changed little in the past half-century.

Cycling around was a joy unconfined by traffic lights; even at the main roundabouts at 'rush hours' (an absurd concept in the Lao context) it was enough to slow down. The recent completion of Route 13 had not brought about the expected increase in motor traffic; most people still preferred to fly ('security'!) and commercial vehicles feared hijackers. The traffic was mainly two- or three-wheeled or four-legged. But despite the numbers of casually wandering dogs and cats, I saw no corpses. A cynical expat, to whom I remarked on this, suggested it may be because victims are at once retrieved to go into the soup. Which is a possibility . . .

I soon realized that one needs a fortnight in Luang Prabang; its dozens of wats demand and deserve considerable concentration. Very often, the beauty is in the detail – quite minute details, easily overlooked and not fully appreciated unless one reads up, on the spot, an explanation of their significance. Also, several wats beckon one back; as with a piece of unfamiliar but appealing music, it seems necessary to repeat the experience.

My aim each morning was to get to the day's first wat target before the *falang* hordes arrived. (But I mustn't exaggerate; even at the height of the holiday season the daily tourist intake was to be measured in scores rather than hundreds.) Always, before sunrise, excited groups gathered to photograph the monks as they processed soundlessly in single file through the dim misty streets, their orange robes seeming to glow. Most *falangs* positioned themselves intrusively, to get close-up shots of both monks and donors. How would Westerners feel if Japanese tourists behaved thus while Christians were going through the 'picturesque' ceremony of receiving Holy Communion? Oddly, there was less ritual than in Vientiane: no chanting of grateful prayers, no obeisances from donors. But there were many more devout young, both sexes wearing ceremonial scarves diagonally across their chests. Back in the wat compounds, the monks breakfasted – rows of novices squatting on *koti* verandas, their elders inside. Those novices were high-spirited schoolboys, much given to happy horseplay, chaffing and laughter. In few wats was there any sense of a rigid monastic discipline; some monks and novices openly smoked cigarettes and within certain compounds the occasional Beerlao bottle might be glimpsed.

The confluence of the Mekong and the Nam Khan, at the end of the main street, has been a sacred place from time immemorial. Here was one of my favourite wats: the small *sim* of Pak Khan is exquisite, standing alone in a peaceful garden compound and cared for by the only surviving monk. His pale green coffin case, most beautifully decorated with mythological figures, awaited him on a pedestal near the Lord Buddha. By now he may have occupied it on the way to the cremation ground; he looked very, very old.

The peninsula's highest point is Phousi Hill, midway between the rivers – conical, conspicuous from afar, the gleaming golden spire of That Chomsi just visible above trees. Phousi is dominant not only topographically but mythologically, spiritually and historically. Long before Buddhism arrived, Thong Kuang, an all-powerful *naga* (cobra deity), dwelt on this hilltop and the building of That Chomsi in no way diminished his importance. He ruled fifteen other *nagas* who inhabited grottoes along the riverbanks, controlling the flow of water on which the rice crop depended. As guardians of the kingdom, those *nagas* were propitiated annually by the King until the 1920s. And, in a special ceremony at the mouth of the Nam Khan, red flowers and a variety of foods were offered to Thong Kuang. Even today, a few survive who know the site of each grotto and the name of its resident *naga*.

As I ascended Phousi's 339 steep steps, Luang Prabang lay hidden beneath a grey cloud-ocean and only the muffled crowing of cocks broke the silence. (In midwinter a dense mist resists sun-power until ten-ish – or later – and the locals find the morning air cold.) Seen close up, That Chomsi is in itself disappointing: too obviously recently restored. But the resonances on that spot are unforgettable. Luang Prabang's rivers and wats and sacred sites, and its patina of myths innumerable, are intimately interconnected in mysterious ways that elude Western comprehension. Yet occasionally, in special places at special times, even a Westerner can fleetingly contact the essence of what has formed the Laotian way of being. Phousi Hill, at sunrise, is one such place.

The *nagas* represented around every corner in Luang Prabang resemble dragons rather than cobras. They support *sim* roofs as brackets, decorate the upturned corners of tiered roofs, and are carved and stencilled on interior walls. Five- or seven-headed *nagas* guard *sim* entrances. One-headed *nagas*, fifteen yards long, form the balustrades of flights of stone steps leading to the bigger wats. In Wat Xieng Tong, a barn-like chapel shelters the royal funeral chariot, elaborately carved and gilded, with a prow of five long-necked *naga* heads. Beneath the fifteen-foot-high canopy lie two royal funeral urns: dodecagonal for the King, octagonal for the Queen. These served as sarcophagi, concealing inner urns which held the bodies before cremation and could be carried like coffins to the pyre. The chariot was last used in 1960 for the state funeral of King Sisavangvong.

Regularly I breakfasted in an eat-drink shop on a corner opposite the Central Market. Mrs Vo, the Lao widow of a Chinese Buddhist, owned this thriving establishment where two ornate shrines, lit from within by tiny electric bulbs, hung high on the back wall and received daily offerings of fruits and flowers. (In the 1930s, when Mrs Vo's father-in-law migrated, a network of some 4,000 Chinese controlled most of Laos's commerce.) As the monks appeared, Mrs Vo and her daughter, Mayvong, donned scarves and went forth to donate steaming rice from large silver repoussé bowls – the sort that take a silversmith hundreds of hours to make. Mrs Vo's only son, a twelve-year-old doing six months at a wat school, then deserted his procession momentarily to collect a thermos of chicken soup, four bread rolls and a basket of sticky rice – all in a plastic bag, placed ready for him on a pavement table. Several other little boys also slipped out of line and made quick purchases: long loaves of hot French bread which they tucked under their robes before hurrying to catch up with their seniors. In theory, monks and novices are solely dependent on alms.

Mayvong spoke some English and I asked if people resented camera flashes going off up and down the streets during their morning ritual. 'We don't mind,' she replied, 'if it makes them happy to have pictures.' Perhaps it was obtuse of me to transfer my own sense of disgust to the laid-back Lao – but then, they find it almost impossible to criticize visitors.

The Central Market – square, tin-roofed, concrete, unbeautiful: built in 1991 – is a smaller though still enormous version of Vientiane's Morning Market. Stalls facing the street sell Thai junk-snacks popular with the friendly toddlers who attend a nearby play-school and whose fond dads cause dental havoc by indulging them every morning. Most mothers are already at work by 8 a.m. and most Lao fathers are what we would call New Men – experts at cleaning infants' bottoms, feeding them with banana or sticky rice, rocking them to sleep in cradle-hammocks woven of palm or bamboo, bathing, dressing and conversing with toddlers, searching for head lice and entertaining older children. Such details are observable because family life happens al fresco during the dry season.

My favourite meander was along the Mekong's high, busy embankment. Here, on the steep slope, pairs of young women saw firewood; their husbands (or maybe brothers) then split the four-foot lengths with great difficulty, using mallets and axes. The length and width of each piece is standard; everywhere in Laos a supply is neatly stacked under the home in preparation for the rainy season. Those smallish hardwood tree trunks come across the Mekong from the wooded opposite shore in long home-made cargo boats with flat tin roofs – the roofs also loaded, rather precariously. An important local trade is the gathering and packing in big bales of the bark of a fast-growing tree, exported in vast quantities to Thai paper mills. It was an LPRP ambition to set up paper mills in Laos but the Thai quashed that.

During King Samsenthai's reign Luang Prabang became a major trading centre – and remained so for centuries. Sitting on the embankment, one can picture the merchants arriving from Tonkin and Dali, from Burma with ceramic and metal wares, from Tibet and China with carpets and textiles. Most transport was by boat, up and down the Mekong and its three nearby navigable tributaries, the Nam Khan, the Nam Ou and the Nam Seuang – which last gave access to the north-east of Vietnam. Around the rivers' confluences the flat lands yielded a surplus of rice for export and the forests produced an abundance of valuable benzoin – a resin used in perfumes and medicines – and stick-lac, an insect deposit found on flame-of-the-forest trees and much in demand for making dyes and varnishes. Where the terrain allowed, bullock carts were used; during the dry season elephants could be ridden across the Mekong at a few fording points, *en route* to what is now the Khorat plateau of north-eastern Thailand. (This remained part of the Lao kingdom until 1893 when France and Britain adjusted the border to suit themselves.) When the capital was moved to Vientiane in 1563 Luang Prabang gradually lost its favourable trading position and generations of rivalry led to the territories of Luang Prabang and Vientiane becoming separate kingdoms in 1707.

The embankment's trees shade many traders' stalls, a few hut-bars and several open-air eat-drink shops. One kindly woman, concerned about my bandaged foot, always beckoned me to have a glass of herbal tea. During one such respite, two emaciated German males stopped for an afternoon coffee and insisted on eating their own bread – apparently distrusting my friend's offered selection of grilled banana strips, intestine kebabs and huge fish heads baked in mud. (These, fresh from the river, are delicious; when the mud is removed the scales come with it and the bony bits are so big one has no trouble discarding them.) The older man had a stringy grey pony-tail, his companion was thirtyish with a crew-cut; both were ragged and dirty, suffered from open sores on their faces and looked quite spaced-out. Then, while sitting only ten yards away from me by the edge of the embankment, they began blatantly to fondle each other's genitals. When my friend turned towards them she almost dropped the coffee glasses. The Lao tolerance of homosexuality had been overstretched; in Laos it is considered ill-bred for even heterosexual couples to so much as hold hands in public, a fact too often forgotten by backpackers.

Those travelling in search of cheap drugs usually look unhealthy and are often morose and short-tempered with each other – not, one feels, people who are much enjoying their 'exotic experience'. During my stay in Vientiane two *falangs* were found dead in their beds, having – presumably accidentally – taken heroin overdoses. In both cases their companions had disappeared before the bodies were discovered. Lao heroin tends to be much purer – more lethal – than the mixtures to which junkies may be accustomed at home.

Luang Prabang is quite often appalled by outcasts from the backpacker fraternity. I noticed passers-by looking away from two American girls wearing pelvic-short shorts, strapless bikini tops and copper rings through their noses and navels. Anywhere they would have seemed off-putting; the Lao must have considered them sub-human. It gave me some satisfaction to observe this pair being refused admission to Wat Ho Xiang.

Two English females, with partners who looked like professional hooligans, arrived at the guesthouse while Mr Somphavan and I were sharing a Beerlao. The young women had large erect penises tattooed on their forearms. Mr Somphavan, seeming as though about to vomit, rose and in his dignified way ushered them off the premises. Such specimens, he commented, seemed to justify the government's previous tourist-exclusion policy. A few hours later he was again upset by three young women – two Israelis and a Swiss – who paid for one night, then went to the spotless, odourless bathrooms and at once reappeared, truculently demanding their money back. They couldn't stay in a place with squat-overs needing to be flushed from an adjacent tank. Silently Mr Somphavan returned their kip.

The Foot continued to protest if I walked a mere mile, yet it had no objection to pedalling up to forty miles a day. One mini-excursion took me east across an unstable wooden bridge spanning a tributary of the Nam Khan and overlooked by a ridge where the leafless branches of tall magnolia trees bore many cream and yellow blossoms. Below the bridge new vegetable gardens were being created by two cheerful young women and three singing men. The women had hauled sacks of rich, dark soil from somewhere and were spreading it along neat stone terraces – being reinforced by the men, using huge bushes felled nearby and dragged downhill. Beyond the river lay miles and miles of flat land, not very exciting but extremely significant: its fertility made possible the founding and flourishing of the Kingdom of Lan Xang. A badly eroded track led to a friendly little *ban* where several satellite dishes sprouted amidst simple dwellings. Villagers acquire TV sets on the never-never, Mr Somphavan had told me, paying 70 per cent more than the marked price; to keep up their payments, many suffer deprivations unknown when they lived outside the cash economy. Quite often sets are repossessed after a few months – then resold as new . . . This *ban*'s concrete, tin-roofed, undecorated wat supported only three monks.

I could hear the Nam Khan before seeing it. Over this wide stretch it is an impressive torrent, even in the dry season, foaming past protruding boulders; the whirlpools in midstream made me feel quite giddy when I viewed them through my binoculars. On the embankment stood two rickety shacks but there was nobody in sight. I sat for a time by a primitive wooden quay, relishing the solitude and half mesmerized by the racing water. From here countless trees are shipped to Thailand. Some lay beside me, clearly lettered and numbered in white paint, victims of the conservationists' failure to alter corporate mindsets and proof of the insincerity of the Lao government's 'dedication to protecting our environment'.

My brooding on the vileness of logging companies and their accomplices was cut short by a spider emerging from between the tree trunks. Terrorized, I fled.

This region's spiders are of mythic proportions – black, hairy, long-legged, bloated – undoubtedly sent by the gods to punish erring humans. At sunrise, fields seem to be copiously strewn with pale grey plastic bags: heavy dew on massive webs. When hanging between electricity cables the biggest webs – some three yards long by one yard wide – look like finely spun bundles of silk containing dead leaves and a multitude of insects. Happily these divine punishments are outdoor types and in my mosquito-proofed room I didn't have to fear any arachnidan invasion. But one evening a monster raced across the guesthouse balcony floor, reducing me to gibbering idiocy; it had to be killed by a gallant young Irishman, in defiance of protests from a young Englishman with Buddhist scruples.

On 8 January Mr Somphavan suggested my cycling south on Route 13 to the site of a jolly Hmong New Year (*Khin Tieng*) party. By then I had become thoroughly addled by the variety of New Years celebrated in Laos: Buddhist, Lao Lum, animist, Chinese, Western, Hmong. *Khin Tieng* happens in late December or early January, on the day following the thirtieth day of the Hmong twelfth month.

Previously referred to as the Meo (a Chinese insult meaning 'barbarian'), the Hmong have become Laos's best-known minority for an unflattering reason: many served the US as mercenaries during the Second Indochina War (the so-called Vietnam War). About 300,000 Hmong lived in Laos before that conflict. During it at least 30,000 were killed; after it 130,000 fled to the USA and Thailand – where even now some remain in refugee camps. Without Hmong recruits the US, prevented by the 1954 Geneva Conference from openly sending American troops to Laos, could not have fought their Secret War – which caused the Hmong villagers to suffer no less than the Pathet Lao and their supporters.

Archaeologists have established that the Hmong lived beside the Yellow River more than 3,000 years ago and occupied western China before the Han arrived. From their sophisticated legal system anthropologists deduce that in the distant past they belonged to a settled, organized kingdom though for millennia they have been semi-nomadic mountain folk, famous as cultivators of the opium poppy. Throughout much of the nineteenth century they were at war with China's imperial forces who at intervals slaughtered whole settlements, sparing not even the children. Large groups then migrated south, into Indochina, where they introduced poppy cultivation and have been practising it ever since. They first appeared around Luang Prabang in the 1850s.

A few Hmong have recently become Christians but most remain staunch animists; they also celebrate many of China's major religious festivals. Their tonal language has eight variations (Lao has six) and each of the three main groups – *khao, lai* and *dam* – has its own dialect. An independent, tightly knit community (though geographically dispersed, especially since the war) they are proud of their culture, cherish their own customs and laws and have always been unwilling to integrate into Lao society. They maintain a rigid patrilinear system; the head of the household, who may be responsible for thirty or forty adults, must always be obeyed. No allowances are made for individual considerations which might compromise the well-being of the group. Invariably the householder is the family's eldest male and property, owned jointly by the extended family, is administered by him. A village's eldest householder automatically becomes the chief. This hierarchical tradition, and the Hmongs' courage and enjoyment of a battle, made it easy for the CIA to transform them into a secret army. Their lack of any national identity – in our sense of the word – was also convenient: they could fight as mercenaries without feeling disloyal to what had become (as the Pathet Lao perceived it) the Hmong homeland. Among their fellow-citizens they had never been popular; post-war they are even less so.

At 11 a.m. the *Khin Tieng* roadside party was in its early stages and as yet rather subdued, apart from the dazzling brilliance of the women's costumes and head-dresses. This is the matchmaking season and nubile girls spend several months creating their festive attire, vying with one another to produce the year's most spectacular ensemble. The skirts – no two alike – are dark blue, batik-dyed, with appliquéd multicoloured stripes and cross-stitch designs embroidered on either side of long pleated aprons. From the back of their wide sashes depend panels of splendidly embroidered silk, adorned with clinking coins; overhanging these are smaller panels, gold-fringed. Everyone wears an elaborate collar-piece and exquisitely patterned blouses and jackets. Old French coins, with holes in the middle, are sewn to many of the head-dresses – some stovepipe, with gay woollen bobbles swinging at every turn of the wearer, others vaguely like Viking helmets decorated with rows of silver pendants. I wondered why one girl was wearing a Lao *sin* – a particularly rich one, but seeming incongruously austere and elegant amidst all that flamboyant finery. The

Hmong have always been implacably against mixed marriages; but perhaps that – like so much else in their lives – is changing.

Having locked the bicycle to a fence, I sat with a few elders under a thatch-awning beside a trestle table displaying fizzy drinks and home-made snacks. I sensed no resentment of the *falang* but the distinctive Lao smiles were absent.

On a level, dusty space in front of us, surrounded by forest trees, twenty or so girls and youths stood in two lines, facing each other, some four yards apart. They were silently throwing tennis-sized balls of cotton to the partner opposite – the girls looking aloof, the youths (wearing dreary European garb) looking slightly sheepish. Anyone who drops the ball must pay a forfeit: nowadays a kiss (or more) when couples wander off into the forest after sunset. This ritual game was less restrained fifty years ago; then the forfeit, for both sexes, was to discard a garment on the spot. Some of the older men, watching from the background, wore a modified version of Hmong male attire: baggy black trousers with crimson and gold sashes and black shirts under Western anoraks.

In features, these handsome Hmong differed little – to the *falang* observer – from the Lao Lum, though some did have a more 'Han' look about the nose and eyes (if I may say so without seeming to echo the Duke of Edinburgh's notorious *faux pas*). Later, in remote areas, I was to meet other Hmong clans who rather resembled the Khambas of eastern Tibet. This didn't surprise me. Hmong folklore (passed on orally: the Hmong had no script) recalls a time when the ancestors lived in a land of snow and ice.

More and more young people were arriving, on foot or by Honda. At noon a tuk-tuk delivered a load of beer crates, and seeing me opening a Beerlao the nearby elders began to thaw. I then took out my packet of baby photographs (that indispensable travelling accessory for all grandmothers) and within minutes a dozen smiling women were crowding around to admire the small *falangs*. As the sun reached its zenith raised umbrellas added to the riot of colour: pink, lime green, blue and white checked, orange and red striped. It was time for the party to descend a steep slope to a cool grove in the forest – followed by the vendors of grilled snacks, steamed rice, noodle soup, bamboo shoots, coconuts, 7-Up and Beerlao. Meanwhile one of my fellow-grannies had been finding me an interpreter – her son, who spoke the sort of English I had by then come to associate with teachers of English. And that indeed was his profession. As we descended the slope he requested, 'You please call me Mr Joe.' (He pronounced it 'Jaw'.) 'I like to have an English name.'

We sat under a very tall tree, its pale grey bark skin-smooth. Soon an elderly man brought a mini-stool for the *falang* and asked if I would drink *lau-lao*? Unwise, I thought, after a Beerlao – with a bicycle ride ahead. Still, it was *Khin Tieng* – so why not. . .?

Now there were at least a hundred couples playing ball and a few hundred of their seniors and juniors relaxing or gambolling in the shade. As the forfeits mounted up, some men shouted what were obviously *risqué* comments and their womenfolk giggled. Groups of children began spontaneously to dance and sing and picnics were laid out on banana fronds. Then my heart sank; two youths were approaching, carrying a music system complete with car battery. Mr Joe beamed. 'We gets listening for music!'

'Hmong music?' I asked, faintly hoping.

Mr Joe wrinkled his nose. 'Is gooder have new music, with Spice Girls! You meet those girls? They come from your place, I think?'

Firmly I repudiated this slur on Ireland.

What little I had heard of traditional Lao music in Luang Prabang enchanted me – an elderly six-man orchestra. Music, song and dance have always meant a lot to the Lao and in times past every *ban* had its orchestra. But in 1975 these were outlawed by a government which unreasonably associated music-making with the bad old days, with royalty and privilege and frivolity. However, the Hmong characteristically preserved their own musical tradition as best they could in their fractured post-war world.

The music system had not been squawking for long when it was silenced by the elders: a four-man band had arrived. Mr Joe noted the names of its instruments in my journal; but he wrote in Lao and I forgot to seek a translation. One was lyre-shaped and played like a Jew's harp; the sounding box of the two-stringed violin was an old oilcan; the bamboo flute was small and keyless; the fourth instrument can best be described as a huge wooden saxophone. These musicians were accompanied by a score of elders blowing large leaves held between the palms of their hands. The result, though undeniably jolly and a vast improvement on, American-Thai pop, was far removed from the complex poignant beauty of Luang Prabang's orchestra.

'We have two thinks,' said Mr Joe. 'Old people wants old music, young people wants new music. When old peole go dead, no more old music!' His tone was disconcertingly gleeful. Old people were in the way, holding all the power, blocking 'progress'.

I asked, 'Is your father here?'

Mr Joe looked towards a group under a nearby tree. 'See my father there, he is not old, he is getting not to say anything. His father is saying what is everyone to do. I want another think. I want to do things for me.'

Here was the contemporary dilemma of Laos (and many other countries): young people scenting the West's individualism and yearning for that freedom. But we achieved it gradually, over several generations. Mr Joe wanted something he did not fully understand and was not culturally programmed to handle – an assessment which may be condemned as patronizing. Yet such condemnations are themselves, in a convoluted way, racist; they ignore the value of other cultures and assume that everyone is capable of successfully participating – suddenly, without preparation – in our sort of society. Or, if they are not, they should be actively encouraged to make the required adjustments.

Time was passing swiftly. Rings of courting couples were dancing around a tree selected by the shaman (its girth prodigious) to ensure fecundity during the year ahead – a good rice crop, many healthy offspring of all species. At intervals giant jars of rice-beer had been carried from group to group and of course I couldn't give offence by declining to imbibe when a jar came our way. Benign elders insisted on refilling my tiny *lau-lao* glass, their pouring increasingly inaccurate. Had it not been empty they couldn't have refilled it – but after all this was a special occasion, for me a unique event, never to be repeated.

As the light waned I stood up and wobbled and realized that cycling was out. Mr Joe stood up and also wobbled but gallantly insisted on escorting me back to the road. We tottered up the slope, stumbling over tree roots – the wobbling leading the wobbling – and my companion diagnosed, 'We are drinked.' I couldn't disagree.

Unlocking the bicycle was not easy. 'It is too much darkness!' exclaimed Mr Joe tactfully. Then he asked, 'Why you make it tied to fence?' The Lao were bewildered to see me attaching my bicycle to something; if they bother to lock their own they leave them free-standing. It shocked people to hear about the level of bicycle theft in Europe; this ill-accorded with their vision of the West as 'more civilized'. Corruption is not unknown among Laotian government officials and the new entrepreneurial breed but everywhere I encountered honesty. Whenever I overpaid (new 1,000 kip notes often stuck together) someone pursued me down the street – once even to my guesthouse – to return the surplus.

During that seven-mile walk to Luang Prabang the Foot – anaesthetized by alcohol – did not complain. Next morning, however, it was swollen and inflamed and very sore. My head felt much the same. Mr Somphavan observed, 'I think yesterday you were silly.' He directed one of his daughters to prepare a healing concoction of herbal essences and porcine gall-bladder juice. This foul-tasting mix healed the head, astonishingly quickly, but did nothing for the Foot. It was not a morning to go watting; those spots in front of my eyes would have blurred the fine details – my liver needed a thorough shake-up on a rough road. The painful pressure as I mounted and dismounted felt like the wages of sin; but pedalling remained – almost – pain-free.

On the Pak Mong road I passed two construction sites within six miles of the town centre. Giant bulldozers were levelling the ground for multi-storey hotels; as Luang Prabang is now a UNESCO-protected World Heritage Site, buildings above three storeys are forbidden. The first site was opposite an attractive roadside *ban*, its house walls of bamboo strips, gold and brown cleverly inter-woven. The residents squatted on an embankment, watching this novel monster changing their environment for ever – changing it radically, within a few hours. Some adults looked bemused, others frightened. Small children whimpered and clung to parents. Their older siblings were excited, awestruck – to them such inex-plicably omnipotent machines must have seemed like something out of a myth. Later, a private enterprise tour operator told me those villagers would have to be 'relocated' because 'our visitors don't like to have dirty villages so close'. The second site had been partially landscaped before construction began; flowering shrubs and sapling trees flourished around a sunken garden with sun-dials and an ornamental fountain in embryo.

Booking space on a downriver boat had proved mysteriously diffi-cult. At the bleak, shabby colonial Navigation Office – the only large building on the Mekong embankment – my request was frowned on by a tight-lipped official in a frayed uniform. I would have to fly or take a bus; tourists could not leave Luang Prabang by boat. That greatly puzzled me; boating on the Mekong is one of the backpackers' delights.

Two days later a badly shaken German youth arrived at the guesthouse. The boat taking him downriver from Pak Beng, and unevenly loaded with cement, had capsized while the captain was struggling to take her through white water. Both his companions – wearing small but heavy knapsacks holding camera equipment and books – were drowned. The captain, the Lao passengers and he himself reached the bank, with difficulty – but all his posses-sions, apart from a waist-pouch, had been lost. This tragedy had evoked a diktat from Vientiane, forbidding tourists to use boats, and I resigned myself to another Route 13 journey. But then came glad tidings on the grapevine: all was well, tourists could now book their places on a boat scheduled to leave at 8 a.m. on 12 January.

The Lao media never reported that boating accident – or the murders of two Dutch hitch-hikers who camped between Kasi and Luang Prabang, within sight of Route 13, soon afterwards.

6

Slowly down the Mekong

———————

The Mekong (2,200 miles from source to delta) can count itself lucky, so far, being the only great river to have escaped major exploitation by Technological Man. It drains an area larger than France and its annual contribution to the South China Sea is 475 billion cubic metres of water. That last statistic – meaningless to me – greatly excites the profit-hungry. In 1957 the Mekong Committee for Co-ordination of Investigations of the Lower Mekong Basin was set up under UN auspices and given a nickname: the Mekong Secretariat. (That was before acronyms took over the world.) The Secretariat's manic planning included a chain of seven mega-dams which would store 142 billion cubic metres of water, generate 24,200 megawatts of power and irrigate 4.3 million hectares of rice fields. The Second Indochina War thwarted those plans and only one dam was built – on the Nam Ngum, a tributary of the Mekong. But now the Secretariat has been reborn and renamed the Mekong River Commission. Its members are Cambodia, Laos, Thailand and Vietnam; since mid-1993 representatives of China and Myanmar (formerly known as Burma) have been allowed to join in the Commission's deliberations. Its plans, though modified by the disrepute into which mega-dams have fallen, are alarming enough – many dams, agribusiness irrigation, foreign-owned industries and mass tourism.

At 7 a.m. on 12 January a long, dove-grey cloud half hid the far bank. Gazing at the greenish-brown Mekong, I wished I could go upstream – up and up, all the way to Tibet . . .

'Why,' wondered Shane, 'did they tell us to be here at seven?'

Apart from Shane and me the Navigation Office balcony was deserted – all doors locked, no official in sight. But Shane, a New Zealander, wasn't complaining. While sharing a breakfast of bananas, we agreed that the Lao are singularly endearing and civilized.

Sean, from New York, arrived soon after and at once I knew he suspected my identity; people looked startled, then incredulous, when they think they recognize someone from photographs.

Next came a middle-aged English couple, Bertie and Bessie, and inwardly I groaned. The evening before, in my favourite draught beer bar, Bertie could be heard loudly explaining that a publisher had commissioned him to find hill tribes as yet unknown to tourists who could be photographically processed for an 'original' coffee-table book. Meanwhile Bessie had been photographing tribal children's skin diseases on behalf of a new NGO in search of an 'original' fund-raising gimmick. ('An easy one to fiddle!' thought I cynically.) The pair were just back from Yunnan and their German companions yawned more than once during Bertie's bite-by-bite account of Chinese meals. When Bessie heard my brogue she screeched, 'I adore the Irish, my favourite people!' Then she sat on my lap and tried to hug and kiss me – whereupon Bertie shouted, 'Come on, my girl! Time for bed, we've an early start!' As Bessie hiccuped and reached for the nearest jug of beer (mine) her husband dragged her off my lap and steered her towards the door. These were not the sort of companions one would hand-pick for a long journey in a confined space.

Soon after eight o'clock the officials arrived, one by one, nobody hurrying. For the next hour we queued. Firstly, to register our exit from the province with an affable young policeman who carefully transcribed passport details into an exercise book, then gave us slips of red-stamped paper (no charge). Secondly, to buy our tickets (approximately US$10) which had to be signed by both seller and buyer and then counter-signed (the third queue) by a stern Navigation Office clerk. Of the assembled backpackers, seventeen were my fellow-passengers; the rest had their sights fixed on the Golden Triangle, a day upstream across the Thai border.

Below the embankment, dozens of river craft were moored in shallow water off the sandy shore. These seventy-foot wooden boats – deckless, capacity about twenty tons – are the commonest craft on all Lao rivers. The six-foot-wide hold is enclosed by side panels, some hinged to serve as doors-cum-windows. The wheel-house in the bows is just big enough to accommodate the helms-man and the inboard engine allows a top speed (not often attained) of 14 m.p.h. Aft is the long-drop, jutting over the water, and a minute galley. Into the seatless hold go passengers, cargo, animals; a few passengers are permitted to sit on the flat roof and some boats also load the roof but our captain forbade that. Boats are numbered, not named: ours was 127.

The duration of these voyages is unpredictable. Much depends on cargo complications, passengers' complications and the vagar-ies of the morning mist. For *falangs*, the language barrier com-pounds this uncertainty. Nothing can be explained; only as events unfold does one grasp their significance.

The Foot had not yet recovered from my 'silliness' and I slith-ered nervously and painfully down a precipitous, pathless slope of loose sand. Then Shane, seeing me in distress, took my rucksack and Sean helped me across a long, dreadfully flexible gangplank – nine inches wide – and through the hold's starboard opening, a method of entry akin to climbing through a window. As the Foot would prevent my reaching the roof, I at once monopolized the best vantage point, by the port opening – about five feet by four feet, giving a fine view of the riverscape.

Everyone else then went shopping; one is advised to be self-suf-ficient in food and water. As I settled down on my rolled-up flea-bag a cock crowed beside me, protesting against being tethered to a flip-flop sandal. A most striking bird he was, one of those tall, trousered gentlemen with body feathers golden and black and a sweeping blue-green tail. The captain's nine-year-old son lovingly fed him maize but I suspected that soon he would be sacrificed to the river spirits. And so it was. While our mooring rope was being hauled aboard, the captain smashed him against the boat's side and gave his beautiful body to the *nagas*. At such moments, one is very aware of Laos's being on the cusp. The captain wore blue jeans, a baseball cap inscribed 'I'm Happy – Are YOU Happy?' and a Nestlé T-shirt – free in the Morning Market if you buy three big tins of infant formula.

As the engine began to growl and throb, the captain's wife noticed that Bessie and Bertie were missing. Seeing no bunks in

No. 127, they had dashed off to buy blankets. Ten minutes later they breathlessly climbed aboard and at 10.55 we pulled out from the shore and slowly drifted past the ancient stone steps leading up to the Royal Palace.

Downstream, the river soon curves and forested mountains close in; here little has changed since de Lagree and Garnier led their celebrated expedition towards China in the 1860s – the first European voyage up the Mekong. Untouched mountains, their karst peaks craggy, rise sheer from rough rocky shores. Lines of flame-of-the-forest blazed near the water's edge. Other trees, even taller, were autumn-tinted or winter-bare but for swags of moss ten feet long. The wild banana groves reached improbable heights and a glorious dark pink flowery creeper flowed over acres of giant bamboo. Everything in sight seemed outsized. Occasionally perpendicular rocks – layered, multicoloured – stood in mid-stream like ruined cathedrals. These create erratic, powerful eddies; as the captain steered a zigzag course, keeling this way and that, excited shouts came from the roof and I was splashed.

The captain's wife was our boss, a tough unsmiling Hmong lady who wore slacks and an anorak. When too many sat on the roof, threatening balance, she summoned three down and delivered a lecture which in its general drift was perfectly comprehensible: her expression interpreted. Half the passengers seemed bored by 'the Mekong experience'. All day they lay on the floor, chatting, snoozing, reading, playing cards. One misfortunate Australian lass was ill; for a week Marilyn had had severe diarrhoea and I became increasingly worried about her.

At one point, on the left bank, the mountains receded slightly to leave space for a series of sand dunes between river and forest. No *ban* was visible, nor any sign of cultivation, yet here we swung around to moor at the base of a dune on which squatted several children, awaiting our arrival. It was only 12.30 and this unexpected stop provoked mixed reactions. I had already identified a minority who were temperamentally unsuited to life aboard No. 127. They had grumbled about our late departure, demanded some covering for the plank floor before they spread their sleeping-bags and sulked when ordered off the roof. Now they scowled and grumbled some more – what the hell was this delay all about? Happily, most of us were disposed to enjoy the diversion.

Soon we heard distant, baffling sounds: hollow metallic bang-ings, much shouting, chanting and laughter. Then the first empty oil drum, battered and rusty, came over the dune top. Three tri-umphantly grinning children pushed it into waist-deep water where Kwang, the captain's eldest son, stood ready. With difficulty he heaved it up to the starboard opening – opposite mine – and his two younger brothers dragged it into the hold. More drums came: ten, fifteen, twenty – after that I lost count. It seems this is a port of some consequence; the nearest *ban* must be the kerosene depot for quite a large area. I moved to where I could watch through my binoculars as three or four children rolled each drum from within the forest, the 'teams' racing each other down the dunes. No adult appeared, this was a job for juveniles and also a game – though pushing large barrels up slopes of loose sand is not easy. Bertie, a self-styled man of action, was now thoroughly enjoy-ing himself – and, to give him his due, being constructive. He organized a *falang* team to take over from the little boys who then worked with their dad, helping him to stack the barrels, on their sides, aft of the passengers' space. They filled half the hold and to reach the long-drop one had to crawl on hands and knees through a low, narrow tunnel between drums and roof. The more daring went outside and crab-walked aft, clinging to the roof, along a six-inch-wide ledge.

By 2.15 we were again on our way and soon the river widened and became less rocky – or rather, less visibly rocky. Bertie had already claimed to be a navigation expert, a yacht-owner familiar with the Mediterranean. Noting signs of submerged rocks, he deplored some of our captain's moves and I reflected that lan-guage barriers have their uses. Given a common language, Bertie would have been trying to take command of No. 127.

Two centuries ago, the Lao divided their stretch of the Mekong into named segments, the length of a segment being measured by the time it took a candle to burn down in the bows. (But what size candle? History doesn't record.) One century ago the French placed navigation markers along the trickiest stretches and some have survived, as have a few little red-tipped concrete posts – high-water marks. But now the navigation markers are of limited value; annually the Mekong manifests its power by changing the position of its 'trickiest stretches'. It rises fifty feet or more when the

112

Tibetan snows melt and the local rains come; abnormally heavy rains flood both Vientiane and Phnom Penh.

We passed only one *ban*, on a high, vine-veiled cliff, its large shabby wat half hidden by teak and frangipani trees. From a narrow sandy spit small boys flew kites so high they were invisible. Swidden patches scarred the least steep of the nearby mountains; behind those, an apparent infinity of rock summits jaggedly crowded the sky.

Then came sandbanks, numerous and treacherous, reducing us to walking speed as Kwang squeezed into the wheelhouse to take soundings. Beyond that hazard, in a narrow gorge, the Mekong foamed between low islets of jumbled, grey rocks, scattered with herbs and a heathery plant. As we approached our sleeping stop, a herd of some twenty buffaloes – fat, as is usual in Laos – came ambling down a cliff path for their nightcap. Never elsewhere have I seen such pale-skinned buffaloes: almost white.

We moored in a right-bank cove where tangled vegetation semi-encircled a sandy space at the foot of partially cultivated mountains. On the far side much higher mountains rose directly from the water. Trees concealed a nearby *ban* where the others sought food and lodgings; no one seemed keen to sleep on board or to camp. I had decided to pander to the Foot by resting it completely for these few days and here I was quite glad not to be among those invading an isolated *ban* in search of sustenance and shelter. Is this travel snobbery? Not really – the arrival of a lone trekker or cyclist sets up a different sort of chemistry. Sean and Shane soon returned; they thought it unfair to expect a meal in that twenty-house Hmong *ban* where only three had been able to find lodgings – three Australian girls.

In 1987–8 there was serious fighting not far from here, near the headwaters of the Nam Heung, where the border with Thailand remains ill defined. The original cause of the conflict, though never admitted by either government, is not a mystery. Most of the few locals were – and still are – Hmong members of the outlawed Communist Party of Thailand, dependent on opium trading for their cash incomes. At that time Lao soldiers regularly received protection money from Thai logging companies who, year after year, stole Lao teak. Then these loggers began to employ instead, as 'security guards', either Thai soldiers or the local Hmong (well armed to defend their opium caravans) and a border dispute was the result.

During a shoot-out in May '87 Lao soldiers captured five Thai loggers, destroyed expensive machinery, occupied Ban Rom Klao and demanded Thai acknowledgement that this village is in Laos. When the loggers continued to claim it the conflict – sometimes verbal, sometimes physical – had to be dealt with by Vientiane and Bangkok. In early November Thai troops attempted to retake strategically important hills, held by Lao soldiers since May. Having failed, they bombed the Lao positions and by January '88 uncounted Lao and some seventy Thai soldiers had been killed. Ferocious artillery duels followed – and many more Thai air strikes. But the Lao continued literally to hold their ground while casualties rose rapidly – to the angry embarrass-ment of the Thai commanders who, in November, had boasted that they could 'get rid of the Lao in only a few days'. Thai alle-gations that Vietnamese troops were involved could not be proved. Finally the Lao Prime Minister, Kaysone Phomvihane, appealed directly to the Thai General Prem, suggesting a pow-wow between the rival military commanders – in lieu of the sterile diplomatic exchanges that had been dragging on for eight months. Sure enough, a ceasefire and a mutual withdrawal from the disputed territory came into effect on 19 February 1988. But, as Shane gloomily observed, 'No one can ever bring law and order to the Golden Triangle. Opium traders and illegal loggers are unbeatable.'

When the rest returned, some had tales to tell of 'instant meals': imported packets of processed noodles which spring to life – of a sort – when boiling water is added. Others remained unfed and the captain's wife (her bark was worse than her bite) gave them a big basket of sticky rice and mugs of chicken soup.

The 'pot lot' then lit a fire on shore and sat around it rolling their joints by the light of a full moon. They were all, according to themselves, loaded with hash – 'cheaper here than anywhere!' The official Laotian attitude to hash seems to be ambiguous; if not actually legal, its use is certainly tolerated. When those eight even-tually stumbled back into the hold – high as kites, speech slurred – they made dull company, giggling like thirteen-year-olds at limp jokes. Yet from the non-participants' point of view people happily high on hash are vastly more agreeable than the average 'drinked' group.

The morning mist was dense – visibility twenty yards – and it lingered. Soon after eight, our theoretical departure time, the three lodgers came aboard looking pleased with themselves. They had slept well, wrapped in cosy quilts – no charge.

'Whose quilts?' I asked.

They stared at me, puzzled. Then one said, 'I suppose the family's quilts.'

'And what did the family use?'

All three shrugged and another said, 'I suppose they huddled up together somewhere.'

Five minutes later a young woman hastened up the gangplank: one of the lodgers had forgotten her pencil torch.

To while away the misty time four of the pot lot shared joints and I wondered about the risk of psychological addiction. (Obviously hash is not physically addictive.) Also, was it mere coincidence that those eight seemed less 'together' than the rest of us? The quartet smoking beside me were all American men in their thirties who marvelled at southern Thailand's 'good value' scuba diving (only US$50 a day!) and belonged to our impatient faction. The captain's refusal to sail blind down the Mekong irritated them – 'That guy has no balls!' Two decided to hire a speedboat, due to arrive from Vientiane at noonish. I then persuaded Marilyn, the diarrhoea victim, to accompany them; six times during the night she had had to crawl through that tunnel to the long-drop. Her companion would escort her to the Australian Embassy clinic – my own destination. Later, I heard that she had been advised to go to the Nong Khai hospital without delay. This reduction in numbers was fortunate; seven Lao passengers came aboard as the mist lifted. Its dispersal was quite dramatic, the still mass of greyness becoming an agitation of shifting, curling vapours – separating into silver cloudlets – then vanishing. At 10.15 we sailed.

Dry season traffic on the Mekong is light: some slender canoes painted bright blue with outboard engines, a few craft like our own, a few snarling speedboats. These can take five passengers from Luang Prabang to Vientiane in six hours and reputedly are as dangerous as they are expensive and noisy. Most Lao passengers wear trendy plastic helmets, made in China and no protection when skulls hit rocks.

I also saw several minuscule canoes, hardly four feet long, being paddled by little boys who had collected baskets of fish from lift nets. Unattended lift nets, popular from south China to Indonesia, are attached to many midstream rocks, their bamboo poles wedged in crevices. The fine nets (usually nylon nowadays) hang from the four corners of large frames which rest on tripod pivots when the net is being used ashore. The blue canoes held cast-net fishermen, sometimes working in pairs with an extra-big net. These nets, made from hibiscus bark fibre, are up to ten yards in diameter, weighted around the edges and generally used by men, who cast from a boat or the shore. Throughout Laos, fish is the main source of protein – if possible eaten three times a day. Although women never hunt in the forest, fishing is among their most important jobs; everywhere one sees them using conical scoop nets on triangular bamboo frames. In 1994 the government revealed a plan to build twenty-nine dams on the Mekong tributaries by the year 2010. If this ambition is even partially realized, the nutritional, social and environmental consequences will be catastrophic. But the declining health of South-east Asia's 'tiger economies' may serve to protect the diet of millions of fish-dependent peasants.

The impatient faction protested inanely when we stopped – at eleven – to take on four more passengers and scores of bales of a red tree bark used to dye weaving thread. A few Hmong houses (unstilted) stood on a sandy bluff just above the high-water mark; in August and September the residents must be able to fish from their windows. My binoculars revealed a toddler leaning on a bench outside a shack-store, nonchalantly smoking a cigarette. Shane was buying Pepsi – not because he's that sort but because there was no alternative. It cost four times the Vientiane price; presumably such goodies are stocked for passing tourists. By then the long-drop had become insalubrious and most passengers disembarked to relieve themselves along the edge of the forest. Here I noticed the book Sean had left on his sleeping-bag: a paperback edition of *Eight Feet in the Andes* containing a recent photograph of the author.

Continuing soon after noon, our zigzaggings became quite

frantic. Between 'cathedral' rocks – themselves a permanent hazard – volatile sandbanks had created an ever-changing pattern of swirling cross-currents and undercurrents. The captain's wife enforced strict controls: no one on the roof and both passengers and rucksacks had to be evenly disposed within the hold. Half-way through a stretch of seething white water we hit a submerged rock, gently but perceptibly. Bertie swore and shouted. 'Hey! See how's it! I told you, this clown, he's no notion how to handle a boat – are we insured?'

Meeting the next cross-current we keeled to port and I noticed that our clearance was three inches. Prudently I removed my binoculars and camera pouch; if it came to swimming ashore, one would do better unhampered. Amidst all this excitement we glimpsed two elephants dragging tree trunks to a wooden jetty. Working (or any) elephants are now rare. In the pre-motor age they were indispensable to loggers and their wild relatives roamed all over Laos.

Two hours of daylight remained when we moored at Pak Lay, the only town (very small) *en route*. At first we assumed this stop to be a mere comma; only gradually did we realize it was a full stop. The impatient faction were furious: when they turned on the captain's wife she withdrew into the wheelhouse and firmly shut the door. A few of the others, including Bessie, appreciated an opportunity to swim; we were moored out of the current, in quite a spacious cove, though for me our position was frustrating. An identical craft (No. 68) was moored between No. 127 and the bank, completely blocking my view. Everyone had to go ashore via this obstacle.

Bessie, Bertie and the pot lot decided to sleep on board, the rest hastened away to book into Pak Lay's only guesthouse. When Bertie had followed them, to scrounge a shower, Bessie borrowed kip from me 'for a few beers', then set off 'to explore the town'. By sunset I was savouring my solitude – but too soon the pot lot returned, scornful of Pak Lay's cuisine. Disarmingly, they asked if I had any objection to their smoking. 'Smoke away,' said I, lighting a health-damaging mini-cigar. A leggy Canadian adolescent then showed me her large carrier-bag of hash. 'All this for less then ten bucks!' she marvelled. 'In the States I could get thousands for it!' No wonder so many youngsters are tempted to pay for their 'travel year' by hash-trading. They often argue (probably correctly) that hash is less harmful than alcohol or nicotine; some potheads eschew alcohol in a pointed sort of way.

As the hold became distinctively aromatic, music was yearned for and to my dismay someone had the necessary technology. Dissonance reverberated around the hold – then faded, as batteries slowly died. An agreeable singsong followed and I noted the universal camaraderie of the hash scene – social, national, educational and temperamental differences not counting as everyone sat cross-legged around a little hillock of 'grass', rolling their joints by candlelight.

I retired early, lying on the floor under 'my' opening through which all traffic had to pass. At once I slept, perhaps doped by the fumes – until Bertie's return. He loomed over me, drunkenly demanding information about his wife's whereabouts. I pretended to be asleep, someone said she'd been away all evening, Bertie swore and turned to go in search of her. Then we heard a commotion in No. 68. Quickly I got up to see Bessie being carried towards us, with much laughter, by four Lao men almost as drunk as she was: a fifth man shone a wavering torch. The two craft were almost touching and they tumbled Bessie on to my bedding where she lay giggling for a moment.

Bertie bent down and said *sotto voce* but with venom, 'You dirty c***! You filthy f****** bitch! Drunken slut!'

Bessie rolled around wildly, trying to get up – then grabbed me, pulled herself to her feet, leaned against an oil drum and shouted, 'I swam in the Mekong, you didn't! You're too scared to swim – shit scared! All day you're the important person, I'm nothing, I'm ordinary, you're important – all day giving orders, smartarse Bertie knows all about currents but too scared to get in! What the f*** d'you know about the Mekong? F*** you!'

The pot lot had tactfully retreated into their sleeping-bags – an option not open to me, my bed space being the battlefield. Fearing physical violence, I had moved instinctively to stand near the misfortunate Bessie. Now Bertie thrust me aside and flung her on to their bedding, beside mine. He was tall and powerfully built, she was small and skinny. In a loud whisper he threatened, 'Shut up or I'll break your f****** bones! You selfish drunken bastard, shut your mouth!'

Bessie's boon companions were peering through No. 68's opening, mesmerized by this sample of *falang* family life. But they were no longer laughing. Coming from a culture that deplores displays of anger, the humiliation of others, physical violence – any loss of control – they must have been shocked back to sobriety.

As I wriggled into my flea-bag Bessie tried to stand up but was roughly pushed under the blanket. 'Lie down and keep your f****** mouth shut!'

A brief silence followed – then came a shrill scream, curiously triumphant. Startled, I looked up. Bessie was standing, stark naked, with one foot on Bertie's face. Her white skin gleamed in the light of two guttering candles at the far end of the hold. The spectators laughed again – though rather uneasily. While scrambling to his feet Bertie struck out at his wife who took refuge between me and the oil drums.

'You don't give me orders!' shrieked Bessie. 'I'll not shut my mouth! I'm not scared – I swam in the Mekong, you were scared – scaredy, scaredy! F****** coward, Mr Know All Smart Arse giving shit to the captain!'

Bertie stood for a moment, swaying, before seizing a blanket. He reached across me to cover his wife, then threw her on to their bedding, even more violently than before. 'We're in Asia,' he muttered, 'they can't take it!' An incongruously thoughtful remark, in the middle of all the rest, and backed up by the disappearance, at this point, of the onlookers. He then said aloud, for the benefit of his reluctant audience, 'I've never been so embarrassed in my life!'

The candles burnt out as Bessie began to scream again – high-pitched, frightened screams, interspersed with pitiful cries. 'Help me! He's trying to break my arm! F****** bastard, he doesn't love me! Love died a long way back – he's important, I'm ordinary!'

Repeatedly I was kicked as Bessie struggled on the floor beside me and Bertie abused her in terms for which there are no asterisks. I began to think I'd died and gone to hell. Given Bertie's disposition, I learned that his wife's repeated taunts (I've omitted the sexual ones) might provoke him to a momentary but lethal loss of control. One hears of such tragedies. When Bessie shouted, 'He's trying to strangle me!' there followed a gurgling, wheezing sound that brought me to my feet. I struck Bertie's head with my torch, then shone it on his face and was about to ask for the pot lot's assistance when abruptly the struggling and screaming ceased. This time I lay on top of my flea-bag, under the space blanket, ready for instant action. Vituperative exchanges continued, being viciously hissed, but soon these were blotted out by the transfer of empty oil drums to No. 68.

I looked at my watch: it was 12.29 a.m. Why rearrange oil drums at midnight? In my already shaken state this prolonged clattering, rumbling, booming and banging seemed a form of torture. Two enraged Australians stood up, yelling futile protests – then sat down and rolled a joint. When half the drums had been transferred the remainder were stacked higher beside me and kerosene dregs began to drip to the floor inches from my nose. To move was not possible; we were packed like slaves on an Atlantic crossing. Then hammering started below the galley and all became clear: that submerged rock had done some damage, now being repaired. But why *now*, when we had moored at 4.20? For more than two hours mighty hammer blows caused the boards on which we lay to vibrate and sometimes sawing accompanied the hammering – patching planks being cut to size.

Despite the noise, it seemed my neighbours had fallen into a drunken stupor. But suddenly Bessie stood up, wearing a long, loose dressing-gown, and made for the opening, tripping over me and mumbling oaths. By then the moon was high in a clear sky and I watched, apprehensively, as she climbed on to No. 68's roof. A moment later she vanished, having stepped on to our roof, from which a lot of liquid could be heard cascading into the Mekong. Bertie raised his head, registered his wife's absence, lowered his head. Doubtless he was feeling battle-weary. For the next ten minutes Bessie paced the roof, excitedly talking to herself – so loudly that her voice though not her words could be heard between hammer blows. On the way back she faltered and for a moment was hanging between the two craft, a hand clinging to each roof, her feet seeking a hold on No. 127. As I moved to help she made it, unaided, and half fell on to my bedding – still talking to herself. Or rather, I now realized, still talking to Bertie . . .

Meanwhile the harsh kerosene fumes were stinging my nose and throat and inducing a faint feeling of nausea. I wished I had something frivolous to read; it wasn't the moment for Eric

Hobsbawm. The pot lot rolled more joints and casually threw their stubs towards the opening. I sternly requested them to desist, pointing out that the nearby floor was oil-soaked. When the hammering and sawing stopped at about 3.30 it seemed we might be able to sleep but that was an illusion. No. 127 had taken on a perilous amount of water and for two hours the baling-out process continued with much clattering and splashing. Simultaneously a very jolly party (to celebrate the mending of the leak?) was happening in the galley. Then all the drums had to be replaced in their original positions, during which operation the morning mist gathered.

At sunrise, to my astonishment, Bessie and Bertie surfaced cheerfully – like teetotallers who have enjoyed an unbroken night's sleep. I was awed; it takes me at least twelve unhappy hours to recover from a drunken orgy. Even more astonishing, they resumed, apparently effortlessly, their roles as united husband and wife contentedly sharing an interesting journey. Bertie pontificated about the leak, the incompetent baling technique, the defective design of these river craft – and Bessie listened passively. Perhaps *in vino veritas* therapy holds this marriage together.

As the mist immobilized us until 9.20 the captain and his family had some sleep. (The parents slept in the wheelhouse, the three boys in the galley.) We then left the high mountains behind and were sailing between lowish hills, some swidden-marked. Here the Mekong is gloriously moody, with many dramatic bends. In places it narrows and is shadowed by sheer cliffs; from their bases grow tall, leafless trees whose flood-exposed, crazily contorted root systems extend far along the sand, mingling with each other. Elsewhere it is 500 yards wide, sometimes smooth-flowing and inno-cent-looking – then suddenly turning treacherous, requiring more zigzagging. A few long high islands stand in midstream, lush vege-tation crowning their crests, fisher folk busy along their shores.

In mid-afternoon the Mekong received the Nam Loei's contri-bution – hardly noticeable, during winter. From this confluence to Paxse, near the Cambodian border, the Mekong forms the Lao–Thai border and immediately it becomes evident that here the right bank is in Thailand. Between the Nam Loei and Chiang Khan, a small Thai town, the riverside vegetable plots were fenced with green nylon netting instead of woven bamboo, and three men – unprotected – could be seen using a pesticide spray. At one point we were close enough for me to read a label – FOLIDOL–E605 M50. This extremely toxic organophosphate methyl parathion is now banned in Laos, having caused many deaths and much chronic illness. Yet I saw it being sold openly in Vientiane. The multinational company's Thai salesmen find it easy to persuade Mekong valley farmers that they really do need this novelty. It will take them some time to realise how seriously folidol depletes fish stocks. Moreover, in southern Laos it is sometimes used deliberately to poison fish, then eaten by the family or sold in the market. Lao rice farmers have also been persuaded to use large quantities of DDT, banned in the Rich World a generation ago. Inevitably these chemicals spread to wetlands and forests until recently pollution-free and conservationists plead in vain for the preservation of Laos's 'biodiversity values'.

Even from a distance, Chiang Khan administered quite a culture shock. Here were the first motor vehicles seen (and smelt) since Luang Prabang. An enormous new tourist hotel overlooked the Mekong. Along the embankment, concrete tables and stools were shaded by Marlboro beach umbrellas. Behind those, garish signs drew attention to twee little cafés and souvenir shops. The embankment slope was in the process of being made 'nice' for tourists. Someone had decided to replace its abundant vegetation and graceful trees with smooth slabs of concrete and long flights of steps leading down to the water's edge. So much for the benefits accruing to a country from a fast-expanding tourist industry.

Opposite Chiang Khan stands Sanakham, a *ban* to which there is no access by road. Not long before, Thailand had kindly provided it with electricity so a few TV aerials rose above the surrounding trees. Its young female population has been much reduced, I was later informed, by Chiang Khan's proliferating 'discos'.

Downstream, the contrasting banks presented a devastating indictment of the logging industry: to the left hills clothed in dense verdant forest, to the right identical hills naked and brown and arid – good for nothing.

Where the Mekong again became frisky the captain did not reduce speed as much as usual and everyone was ordered down from the roof. I noticed a turbulent current racing close to the left bank, foaming between many low rocks. We no longer had a choice of banks, Thailand being out of bounds, and less than an hour of daylight remained. So we couldn't afford to slow down, I deduced, if we were to reach a safe mooring place before dark. Bertie had a lot to say about the captain's recklessness.

At 6.10 we reached our haven, below a high bluff of crumbly red earth. Here the river was a mile wide and a permanent island, partially cultivated with a few houses on its upper slopes, hid the Thai bank. (All the Mekong islands belong to Laos.) Nearby rose a colossal rock – curiously shaped, like a two-humped camel – from which boys were joyously jumping or diving into a river turned to gold by the sunset. Even with two feet I would have shirked going ashore here; the gangplank was precariously propped on a loose stone and all the time wobbling in response to the boat's restlessness. This mooring place was exposed to unpredictable eddies.

In the *ban* on the bluff – invisible to me – few meals and no lodgings were available. Again the captain's wife provided sticky rice, boiled greens, grilled fish. The Lao passengers lit a bonfire ashore and sat around it all night to leave more room for the *falangs*, though by their standards January nights are very cold. Had we all 'huddled up together' there would have been room for them – or the *falangs* with warm bedding could have slept out. But when I tried to get this argument across to the captain's wife she either didn't understand my sign language or didn't approve of my mindset.

We had lost so much altitude since leaving Pak Lay that the next morning was mist-free and memorable for its sunrise – long slim clouds flaming above that gigantic 'camel' rock and the Mekong rippling red. By seven o'clock we were on our way – cautiously at first, weaving between smooth elephant-grey boulders. Gradually the landscape became flatter and on the Lao side many sleek buffaloes grazed along the edge of the forest. On the Thai side a motor road accompanied the river for miles, its speeding traffic an affirmation of that 'prosperity' made possible by loyalty to the United States.

Vientiane's port had not yet adapted to tourism and our disembarking at 10.30 involved another gangplank horror. Sean and Shane carried my gear, then helped me up the steep slope of friable earth to the tuk-tuk stand. I remember my No. 127 friends with affection, especially those two young men and two immensely kind Canadian women who treated me like a granny in distress (which indeed I was) and plied me with arnica pills. From each stopping place they brought me little gifts – improbable luxuries like a packet of four cream crackers made in Bangkok and a miniature (airline) bottle of whiskey distilled in India. Perhaps one day they will visit Ireland and give me an opportunity to show my gratitude in practical ways.

7

Swiftly to Xam Nua

That complete rest aboard No. 127 had done nothing for the Foot. By 2.45 p.m. I was in the Australian Embassy clinic, Vientiane's only source of reliable medical advice. (*Falangs* needing hospital care go to Thailand.) An amiable and confidence-inspiring doctor diagnosed torn ligaments and prescribed a ten-day course of anti-inflammatory pills (cost US$55: no kip accepted). The bad news was that torn ligaments take a few months to heal. The good news was that they don't need cosseting. Said the doctor, 'How much you use it depends on how much pain you can handle. But don't try to walk normally. Limp along, putting most pressure on the heel.'

Next stop, a bicycle shop. I desired a clone of the Luang Prabang Chinese model but only Thai models were available: either a mountain bike (twelve gears, $55) or an old-fashioned roadster (no gears, $40). I chose the latter, having learned in South Africa that a cheap mountain bike brings with it a bundle of troubles. Not much, I reckoned, could go wrong with a basic roadster. (Silly me – the Hare model is designed for use in and around the towns of the level Mekong valley. It is not designed to operate in mountainous areas where roads are indistinguishable from dried-up riverbeds.) I liked the trademark, a beaming hare depicted on the capacious plastic front basket and behind the strong carrier. Adjustable foot-rests were provided for the passenger. A metal stand added considerably to the weight but couldn't be removed. Nor could an ominously soft saddle be changed; just looking at it made my bottom feel sore – and it was covered with a lamentable flowery pattern. (This was my first ever female bicycle, destined to be presented to a Lao woman friend.) The handlebar grips, of hard plastic and roughly grooved, generated spectacularly calloused palms. On all but the smoothest roads the chain-guard rattled loudly. No repair kit or tools were available; it seems cyclists are expected to be always within reach of a mechanic. My request for a preliminary oiling caused consternation. The Lao love to please and two young men turned that shop inside out: but oil there was none. Then the dealer himself arrived, considered the problem and hurried away to borrow an empty motor-oil container from a tuk-tuk driver. Picking a frangipani leaf from the gutter, he used it as a funnel, drained the container – and so Hare had her baptism of oil. Next day, visiting the Morning Market to buy warm trousers and a jacket (Houaphanh Province is high and cold) I found that 3-in-One is among the few commodities not imported.

Within twenty-four hours, yet another of my plans had been vetoed. It would not be possible to cycle north from Pak Xan; that dirt road leads through a Special Zone, controlled by the army since 1994 and closed to foreigners, apart from NGO staff working in the area. Tourists have to fly to Xam Nua. Happily, Lao Air regards bicycles as normal items of luggage.

In the Lao Air city-centre office uncertainty prevailed. Yes, I could book a seat for 19 January – US$70, again no kip accepted. However, winter flights to Xam Nua depend on the cloud cover. If today's service can't operate, tomorrow's passengers must wait until the day after tomorrow – did I understand? I did. All the squiggles on my ticket were of course indecipherable but the woman clerk showed me a timetable: check in at 10.00 for an 11.10 departure.

For some reason that information felt unreliable, despite the timetable – I don't know why. As strong hunches are best acted upon I decided to be at the airport by seven o'clock.

The lack of panniers (unknown in Vientiane) meant travelling even lighter than usual. A little knapsack on the carrier held fleabag, space blanket, books, torch, a few spare garments. The front basket – flexible and quite frail – held water bottle, maps, minitowel, sponge bag and nuts. Everything else was left behind.

On the level tarred road to Wattay International Airport Hare moved fast and smoothly and I foresaw a good relationship. The runway was being extended and a few cranes stood around: the biggest models, far taller than any building in Vientiane. They had been standing around for months, awaiting the arrival of whatever they were supposed to be lifting. The small airport buildings, drably utilitarian, seemed much preferable to the Rich World's equivalents. But rumour had it that Singaporean 'aid' was soon to be invested in Wattay's 'development'. Why? An airport waiting area only needs check-in desks, chairs and lavatories. Wattay also had a grubby little restaurant serving breakfast (noodle soup) at dawn.

When I asked where Hare should check in, an elderly uniformed man viewed her with alarm. He led me to the passengers' exit and pointed to an antique Antonov fifteen-seater with one tiny door – Hare wouldn't fit.

The next hour was fraught. Numerous officials became involved. No one spoke English or French. Everyone wanted to help. We all became eloquent sign-linguists. Would Hare, if taken to bits, fit? That depended on how much luggage the others had. Already, at 8.15, the others were gathering, checking in; my hunch had been correct. All were Lao and, incredibly, two women spoke fluent English. These AusAID-sponsored teacher-trainers – about to run a five-day workshop for thirty of Houaphanh's English teachers – had very little luggage. Hare, dismantled, would fit! Men appeared out of nowhere to do the job – one active, seven advising. Who, I wondered fleetingly, would remantle poor Hare? But that problem lay two hours ahead.

My new friends – Anna and Lulu – were chatty and informative. There must be some little emergency: usually a Chinese Y-12 rather than an Antonov served Xam Nua. Our Antonov was now semi-retired; in times past the Soviets had sold it to the Vietnamese who eventually sold it to Laos, cut price, as part of a 'Helping Little Brother' scheme. As we crossed the tarmac I blenched. The area around the propellers looked as though it had recently caught fire; in Xam Nua I discovered that it had indeed done so. The tyres were almost flat. One teacher cheerfully surmised that our pilot looked so young because he was 'gaining experience', collecting flying hours on domestic routes to qualify for his international licence. Her friend disputed this; domestic routes being radarless, he would be gaining the wrong sort of experience – how to navigate visually.

At 9.20 we took off and almost immediately the young woman beside me vomited on to my knapsack, then was overcome by embarrassment. The cramped seating might have been designed for primary school children. Peering through my minuscule window I glimpsed profound forested valleys but within moments all was hidden – or almost all. Sharp peaks rising above the shifting vapour recalled the Mekong's rocky islets. In December 1993 a Y-12 collided with a cloud-wrapped summit and there were no survivors.

That seemed a long hour and a quarter. With only five minutes to go the cloud cover was left behind – its edges like roughly torn cotton wool – and then we were over a narrow valley. Beside the new (1996) concrete landing strip grazed four ponies and many buffaloes. A small group awaited us outside a two-roomed building flying the hammer-and-sickle and still smelling of fresh paint. Immediately my friends' host, a young man from the Education Department, loaded Hare into a pick-up and volunteered to remantle her with his Honda tools.

During that ten-minute drive Anna and Lulu worried about suitable accommodation for the *falang*. 'This is a primitive place,' said Anna. 'It is our poorest province, tourists don't come, there is no nice hotel.'

'I know,' I said. 'That's why I'm here.'

'But you must take care,' warned Lulu. 'These can be strange people, they are not like us. Don't be curious. When men stop you going in certain directions, don't ask why.'

I remarked regretfully that non-Lao-speakers can't be curious.

The Education Department was a rickety two-storey wooden building near the base of a deforested mountain overlooking the Nam Xam and the town centre. At some little distance sat a score of English teachers (all men) none of whom could speak any English. At 11 a.m. they were a merry lot, their trestle table crowded with Beerlao bottles and shaded by a USAF parachute – that durable and popular awning. Anxiously I watched while Hare was being put together again. Then at 11.15 I bounced and rattled over a rough track towards an ugly new bridge spanning the Nam Xam.

Lulu was right – 'They are not like us.' In the 'capital' of Houaphanh one is at once aware of being in a region temperamentally quite separate from the Vientiane and Luang Prabang provinces. And the town of Luang Prabang, only a thirty-minute flight away, might be in another country.

Vietnam encloses Houaphanh to the north, east and south-east; Xam Nua is much closer, in every sense, to Hanoi than to Vientiane. Twenty-two ethnic groups contribute to the province's population of about 250,000 (in 1995) and 50,000 or so live in Xam Nua. This figure surprised me; the place feels like a large village rather than a small city.

The details of Houaphanh's history are sparse; warfare has destroyed what few documents there were. But we do know that during the past 500 years this region's status changed repeatedly. After the disintegration of the Lan Xang kingdom in the fifteenth century it came under Luang Prabang's suzerainty for only two years (1891–3). Sometimes it was an independent Thai Neua kingdom, sometimes it formed part of Ai Lao, an Annamese tributary state. In the 1880s it was known as Chao Thai Neua and briefly 'protected' by Siam (Thailand). Even in colonial times the Thai Neua *muang* chiefs retained considerable autonomy and by the end of the First Indochina War (France versus the Vietminh) few traces remained of the colonizers.

In April 1953 General Giap's Vietminh forces invaded the provinces of Houaphanh and Phongsali (to the north of Houaphanh) and Prince Souphanouvong (the 'Red Prince', later President of Laos) formally established his 'Resistance Government' in Xam Nua. The Vietminh forces soon withdrew leaving Laos divided, both politically and administratively, into two 'states'. The 'liberated zone', covering much of the north-east, was governed *de facto* by the Pathet Lao with Vietnamese support. The rest of the country remained under the control, ostensibly, of the Royal Lao Government – already an American puppet. Houaphanh was then known as 'the Revolutionary Province' and something of that flavour lingers.

The Secret War in Laos, covertly organized by the CIA and fought on the ground by their Hmong and Thai pawns, was essential – argued the US – to 'protect democracy'. Yet the Americans freaked out in May 1958 when a genuinely democratic election encompassing the whole of the country (the first in post-colonial Laos) sent thirteen pro-Pathet Lao deputies to the fifty-nine-seat

Assembly. On 30 June they stopped all economic aid to Laos and by October they had demolished the all-party coalition government and replaced it with a regime of their own choosing.

For Laos, that marked the beginning of the Second Indochina War. The Pathet Lao, finding themselves excluded from a fair share of political power – a share honestly won through a democratic poll – again picked up their guns and spent the next fifteen years fighting their 'war of liberation' (now inextricably interwoven with the Vietcong's struggle) against what Marxists rightly described as 'American imperialism'. Meanwhile, most Americans were kept in ignorance of this war. It had to be secret for several reasons; one was the likely reaction of American taxpayers/voters had they discovered that it was costing them about $2 million per day (the Pentagon's calculation) to achieve the saturation bombing of a small, wanting-to-be-neutral country called Laos. Professor Timothy Castle, of the USAF Academy, comments:

> A purely Lao solution to the kingdom's political problems would have been achieved with ample compromise and minimal bloodshed. The carnage visited upon Laos was the result of Ho Chi Minh's military and political struggle to reunite Vietnam and the United States' concomitant effort to halt the spread of Communism in Southeast Asia.

The US officials' infinite capacity for self-deception and hypocrisy is only equalled by their naïvety. Why, they wondered, was the Royal Lao Army so ineffective, despite the billions of dollars lavished on it over the years? The Pentagon's Programs Evaluation Office noted: 'Leadership and morale in the Royal Lao Army is extremely poor.' A National Security Council official reported: 'We discovered the Laotians were not Turks, they would not stand up and fight.' In 1970 William H. Sullivan, the US Ambassador who for the previous five years had been running the Secret War from the American Embassy in Vientiane, confirmed that 'The Lao are not fighters.' Another US Ambassador, Leonard Unger, described the Royal Lao Army as 'inept and uninspired'. But why should the ordinary conscript have felt inspired to play the Americans' game by shooting and bombing his compatriots? As for the senior Royal Lao Army officers, they were amazed and delighted by the ease with which they could get their hands on millions of us dollars – simply by making loud anti-Communist noises. Indignantly Professor Castle comments: 'The Lao military had been content to sit out the war and allow the Americans to pay the Hmong and Thais to defend the kingdom.'

During the Second Indochina War Xam Nua – twenty miles as the B-52 flies from Vietnam – was obliterated by American bombs. Now it is a formless, unlovely town rebuilt in a rough and ready way by the Vietnamese. Between 1976 and 1985 Vietnam gave Laos us$146.7 million for the reconstruction of towns, the repair of 200 miles of roads, the funding of 900 'specialists' and the expenses of half the 10,000 Lao who annually went abroad to study. Less than 50 per cent of this aid had to be repaid; the rest was interest-free.

Xam Nua's one street runs level for half a mile along the narrow valley of the Nam Xam. It consists of a tarred strip down the middle, with wide dusty laneways on either side, and is used chiefly by cyclists, pedestrians, wandering buffaloes, playing children and pecking poultry; these rarely have occasion to make way for a vehicle. The town's ramshackle dreariness is more than compensated for by this lack of traffic and by its setting; on every side rise superb mountains, variously shaped.

Seeing no guesthouse, I approached the two-storey hotel, so jerry-built it looked older than its twenty-three years. Formerly government owned, now 'privatized', its courtyard was strewn with empty beer crates. In the forecourt a high, clumsily built stupa seemed out of place. There was no one around. Noticing a broken window in a separate, one-storey restaurant-cum-dance-hall I peered in and saw sheets of the hardboard ceiling hanging loose. At that stage a young woman appeared, stared at me incredulously, then ran away giggling. As I returned to the street a young man arrived. He conveyed that the hotel was booked out (all those teachers?), then pointed me towards an unmarked guesthouse not far from the bridge.

There I was welcomed, with some astonishment, by the owners, a middle-aged Vietnamese couple. Their establishment was shop-house-style, the two ground-floor rooms entered directly from the street; both ceilings were supported by concrete pillars, both bumpy concrete floors were permanently dusty though frequently swept with a grass broom. In the restaurant five metal camp tables were surrounded by plastic garden chairs; a garish Chinese curtain – puce cabbage roses with lime green leaves on a canary yellow background – could be used to partition this space. A few shelves at the back displayed Beerlao, Sprite, Coca-Cola, Lao whisky, mini-cartons of ersatz fruit juices, packets of too-sweet fairy cakes, tinned fish, Nestlé condensed milk, toothbrushes and toilet soap. The adjacent communal sitting-room was furnished with a TV set, a low table, a few chairs and a seven-foot-tall stuffed Asiatic black bear, standing in one corner. Mr Nguyen's father had shot him a long time ago. Here Hare was stabled at the foot of the concrete stairs leading to the bedrooms. My windowless room was filled by an unclean but mosquito-netted double bed. Behind the restaurant were two filthy squat-over loos.

In the kitchen area at the back – twelve feet square, bamboo-roofed, without walls, the floor of packed earth – meals were cooked on a charcoal grill and an open wood fire. *Lau-lao* was served free to residents, a hospitable gesture which must have considerably reduced Beerlao sales.

During my six days in and around Xam Nua I saw no other *falang*, apart from the German leader of a bomb-disposal team and a Filipino road engineer – a fellow guest.

In winter a strong cool wind tempers the noon sun and a two-hour limp revealed that there is much more to Xam Nua than its main street. Between the street and the Nam Xam lies a bustling area of laneways lined with traders' stalls. Downstream is a pleasant semi-rural residential area of small two-storey Western-style homes interspersed with the traditional dwellings of tribal groups – unstilted. There are no opulent villas or mansions such as one sees around Vientiane and Luang Prabang; Houaphanh is far from the source of NEM-generated wealth. As usual the riverbank was the scene of much activity; people bathing and hair-washing women, washing clothes, dishes and vegetables, boys fishing, little girls swimming or just happily splashing around.

Xam Nua is an important military base and in one day I saw more soldiers – unarmed, often riding rusty bicycles – than in all the rest of my time in Laos. An enormous new army barracks stands on a high hill far from the centre, beyond an expanse of paddy-fields. No civilians were allowed near it; a bamboo pole, painted red and blue, blocked a raw red track, bulldozed out of the slope.

Despite forewarnings about Houaphanh's reputation – 'Laos's most beautiful but least friendly province' – I was slightly taken aback, on that first day, by some of the locals' reactions. Often my greetings evoked only hard, suspicious stares – or were ignored. A minority showed the friendliness I had come to regard as 'normal' in Laos but overall the atmosphere could not be described as welcoming. During the Secret War the Houaphanh people endured privations and bereavements beyond reckoning and were conditioned by the Pathet Lao to believe their sacrifices would be rewarded when a socialist government came to power. Do they now feel betrayed by that government's surrender to international capitalism – of which rich tourists are representatives? (In Lao terms, any tourist has to be rich.) The yellow hammer and sickle on a red background, the flag of international Communism, was flying high from the police station, the provincial government offices, the new telecommunications centre, the grotty hotel. And daily at sunrise a rasping, hectoring loudspeaker voice delivered to the town the sort of Party exhortations rarely heard elsewhere.

My limp-about ended in a friendly little restaurant near the bridge where a Beerlao cost double Vientiane's price, for the obvious reason. Here a ground-shaking explosion, close enough to be deafening, interrupted my diary-writing. I looked around in wild surmise. No one else seemed to have noticed the noise, which made me wonder if I had suddenly become prey to hallucinations. But when two more explosions followed, at ten-minute intervals, realization dawned: a bomb-disposal team was at work.

That evening, an English-speaker explained. New water pipes were being laid just beyond the bridge, beside the periphery wall of Xam Nua's high school, and a bomb had been uncovered. When the German-led team were summoned they found the playground stuffed with unexploded ordnance (UXO), not far below the surface – to Xam Nua residents, a commonplace event. Some of the replacement houses hurriedly built by the Vietnamese have UXO beneath them and anyone who chances to use a hammer in the vicinity of a bomb is doomed. For many Lao, the Secret War is not yet over.

My English-speaking informant was a fellow-guest, a senior government minister whose duties required him occasionally to spend a week in Xam Nua. His fluent English and evasiveness about his past piqued my curiosity but I curbed it and we became good friends. Mr Pheuiphanh was the very antithesis of the Poor World government minister stereotype: one couldn't imagine him lusting for the Mercedes, the mansion, the corporate kick-backs. A serene gentleman, he was perfectly happy in our no-star (even minus-star) accommodation.

Juan, the Filipino road engineer, was on recce in the area, a five-day assignment. Although he had then been living in Laos for two years he 'didn't trust the food' and always brought his own with him – and his own water, in two gigantic bucket-thermoses. This I took as proof of the deleterious influence of America in the Philippines.

The guesthouse provided no breakfast, only a thermos of boiling water. While brewing my mug of tea next morning I watched Juan unpacking his hamper. Out came a sliced white pan loaf, wafers of shiny, orange-coloured processed cheese, a jar of Nescafé, a box of Nestlé Coffeemate sachets, a tub of Singaporean jam, a carton of butter substitute allegedly good for the health but certainly containing some menacing mixture of chemicals to create that buttery illusion. I commented on the food industry's over-packaging – another billion-dollar scam. Each of the ten cheese wafers was separately sealed in a triple plastic envelope and contained in a transparent box almost needing a hacksaw to break it open. Juan saw such precautions as 'absolutely essential for hygiene in this dusty country'. I retorted that all market foods are exposed to maximum amounts of dust – especially in windy places like Xam Nua – yet everybody survives. 'They don't,' Juan asserted grimly. 'Gastric infections kill millions.'

Then Mrs Nguyen entered from the street carrying greens and bananas in one hand and in the other a fat, dark grey, coarse-coated animal about eighteen inches long hanging from a vine snare around the neck. Desperately it struggled, its four paws with strong claws kicking the air. It had a blunt nose, small ears, a shortish tail, rodent teeth. 'Jesus!' exclaimed Juan. 'It's the biggest rat ever!'

'Its nose is the wrong shape,' said I. 'It's more like a giant guinea-pig.'

134

As we debated the anatomical structures of rats and guinea-pigs our hostess stood there smiling down at the wretched creature. Finally I said, 'Well, whatever its identity we certainly know its destiny – it's our supper.'

Juan, despite his long residence in Laos, looked disbelieving – then appalled. Pushing aside his breakfast he pointed and asked, 'Food? *Taeng kin?*' (To cook.)

Mrs Nguyen beamed and nodded proudly. Mr Pheuiphanh and his two junior colleagues had invited me to dine with them that evening so Mrs Nguyen went early to the market and made a big effort to secure something special. The creature was in fact a bamboo rat, a choice delicacy. Evidently the rat-as-food concept made Juan extra squeamish; that morning he couldn't face the loo and borrowed a Honda to visit a field. Later I looked into the kitchen and saw our supper crouching in a corner, tied to a table leg. When approached he made a pathetic frantic defensive sound – a hissing snarl – and showed all his teeth.

After breakfast Mr Thongsa failed to meet me at the guest-house. An unusually tall and unusually dim-witted young man, he had introduced himself the day before as Houaphanh's assistant tourist officer. I needed a permit from his boss; he had promised to lead me to the office next morning.

At 8.30 I walked to the enormous, oblong provincial administration building opposite the bridge. On the steps Mr Thongsa appeared and conducted me to a small bare room lacking all the usual posters, brochures, postcards, wall maps. The boss spoke neither English nor French and was not very interested in Xam Nua's sole tourist. He greeted me with a vague smile, shook hands, signed and stamped a sheet of paper (my permit), locked the 1,000 kip fee in a little tin money-box and took himself off to a meeting. ('What about?' I wondered.) Mr Thongsa then filled in the long document which allowed me to spend a week in Houaphanh. Next, he said, I must register with the police and show them my permit. I protested that I had already registered with the police at the airport and produced a chit to prove it. But Mr Thongsa insisted that they must register my permit – a chit giving no details of the tourist officer's permit was not a good chit . . .

Off I went, around the nearest corner and up a slight slope. The dilapidated three-storey police barracks was on an expanse of stony wasteland where numerous policemen stood around laughing and chatting. One strolled away to seek the relevant officer and came back ten minutes later with a smiling young colleague who led me through four long, high, dingy corridors to a cubicle-sized office. There a huge ledger was taken from the top of a tall cupboard, thoroughly dusted, then solemnly opened – as though it were some sacred religious text. But this squat, broad-faced youth was not at all sure what my passport signified and what he was supposed to be doing with it. He studied, intently, the numerous chits I had by then collected and seemed puzzled by the tourist officer's permit. I looked on sympathetically. Why was he expected to cope with a passport in an unknown script? But perhaps he wasn't, perhaps this nonsense was all the fault of the dim-witted Mr Thongsa. When he suggested my filling in the ledger I reflected that few bureaucratic rituals are connected to the real world and amused myself by inserting fantasy details in each column. The young man then asked for a touchingly modest 100 kip tip – a few cents. I gave him 1,000 kip but afterwards felt guilty; the government had recently launched a campaign against the custom of police demanding 'fees' from tourists. In certain remote areas, where *falangs* felt vulnerable, some senior officers extorted considerable sums.

That morning the high school playground was being marked off in squares with white tape. Then three Lao men began to wield their long bomb-detectors; they wore helmets and face shields like riot police but were otherwise unprotected. If UXO goes off by accident it rips through any protective gear so far invented. Bomb disposal is slow work and there was talk of the children's midwinter holiday having to be prolonged.

A mile or so downstream from the motor bridge the Nam Xam narrows to flow through a mini-gorge formed by sheer cliffs bearing an astonishing variety of grasses, bushes, small trees. From here the bulky mountain on the far bank – a Hmong 'suburb' – is reached via a long chain and plank suspension footbridge swaying high above the winter-shallow river. A steep path leads up to a level track, linking several newish settlements. All seem quite impoverished, the shacks crudely built of various combinations of wood, stone, mud, brick, concrete blocks, iron sheeting. Here I felt like an intruder on some private estate. A few women and children smiled tentatively; most of the younger men stared sullenly; their elders – who wore Hmong garb – were polite in a distant way. However, I intuited that had I been able to explain myself, to sit and talk and relax with these people, all would have made me welcome. The Hmong have reason enough to distrust inexplicable *falangs*.

Several small, sturdy ponies were tethered beside houses or grazing on nearby slopes. Always ponies have been indispensable to the Hmong: without them their opium harvests could not be transported to faraway collection points. How much opium do they still grow? This is a question one does not ask in Laos. In theory the opium poppy, traditionally the Hmongs' only cash crop, is outlawed. But how can they be persuaded that poppy growing is now – suddenly – bad/wrong/illegal when for generations the French colonial authorities, and then the CIA, encouraged them to produce more and more opium? Soon after the French grabbed Indochina, the opium tax became their main source of revenue. At the beginning of the Second World War they launched a major campaign to boost Hmong opium production. The annual poll tax was raised from three to eight silver piastres, a sum most Hmong could not possibly save in a year – so they were given the alternative of paying three kilos of raw opium. By 1944 Laos's harvest had risen to about forty tons a year and the administration's opium revenue had increased by 70 per cent since 1939. Subsequently, international pressure forced the French to abandon this source of revenue. However, during the first Indochina War France's approximate equivalent to the CIA (the Service de Documentation Extérieure et du Contre-Espionage – SDECE) ran an underground opium monopoly known as Operation X. This involved close co-operation between the French military and the Binh Xuyen, an infamous Saigon criminal organization – that name rings discordant bells for anyone old enough to remember the Second Indochina War. When opium and heroin trading came to play a crucial part in the CIA's Secret War they learned eagerly from their detested rivals, the SDECE. By then the grievously exploited Hmong had been changed from subsistence rice farmers, who as a sideline had produced an annual kilo of opium per family, to cash-crop opium farmers. Now their way of life was linked to Saigon's opium dens – and, as the Second Indochina War dragged on, to the GIS' increasing demand for heroin. General Ouane Rattikone, former C.-in-C. of the RLA (an army entirely financed by the US government), owned a large heroin laboratory near Ban Houei Sai and another near Vientiane. At the CIA's Long Tien headquarters General Vang Pao, commander of the Secret Army, had his own lab. At Nam Keung, Major Chao La, commander of the CIA's Yao mercenaries, 'protected' another lab. And so on . . . Soon the Hmong, living on high mountain tops, dependent on swidden cultivation, could no longer grow enough rice to feed themselves. Too many men had been recruited, of whom at least 30,000 never came home, and boys of thirteen and fourteen were also sent into action to replace their dead or maimed seniors. At that stage the CIA, as part payment to the mercenary leaders, used their own airline – Air America – to fly free rice to the villages and take raw opium to the heroin labs. Certain districts in Houaphanh province, being both fertile and cool, were among the most productive.

On my way back to the town, I could faintly hear a man with a megaphone warning people to move 200 metres away from the playground, far below me. Then the explosions began and a dark cloud rose high. There were eleven in all, between 3.10 and 4.50; that was the day's harvest. During pauses, traffic was allowed to pass the school – perhaps three mopeds and an army jeep going one way, four cyclists and three buffaloes going the other way. Xam Nua is not prone to traffic chaos. By 4.30 I was on the scene, standing near the playground gate with a group of fascinated small boys. Under the German's supervision, the last two bombs were being prepared for detonation. Then the megaphone man sent us scuttling away. The barrier at the far side of the bridge was a length of pink nylon string tied to a pink bicycle (the colour scheme presumably coincidental) parked at one side of the road: at the other side stood a young man with a foot on his end of the string. What you might call a symbolic barrier . . . The black smoke ascending into a very blue sky smelt acrid. Then the casings and fragments were carried away by the team, presumably to be sold as scrap metal or otherwise put to good use. One wonders what lies under the school building.

At 6.30 the guesthouse generator was switched on and the

bamboo rat served up – stewed and so strongly spiced that I cannot pronounce on its flavour. The texture recalled guinea-pig meat – an Andean delicacy – and those big bush rats so much relished in parts of Africa. Accompanying it were sticky rice, parboiled forest leaves still chewy and slightly sour, delicious beans from a forest tree – small, crisply fried, almond-flavoured – and a sauce based on deer's blood. Next came fish and lemongrass soup, the chunks of white flesh tasty but treacherously bony. To aid digestion, Mr Pheuiphanh produced a throat-searing liqueur distilled from a forest fruit known as 'monkeys' potatoes'. The best liqueur, he explained, is made from bile, preferably a bear's. But that is now very rare and extremely expensive; in Hong Kong, a few years ago, a Chinese merchant paid US$50,000 for the liver and gall bladder of an Asiatic black bear. 'Now we are protecting many species,' Mr Pheuiphanh added reassuringly. 'Though in this province, where people are so poor, we can't be too strict. And there's another problem: most of us prefer the taste of hunted animals. I would always choose wild pig, wild dog, deer, jungle fowl, instead of farmers' animals and birds.'

Next morning, as I arrived early in the market to breakfast at a noodle stall, a hunter was selling his quarry, – a small dainty deer with a richly chestnut coat, all glossy. It was quickly dismembered and soon every bit had been bought; the pretty little hooves were sold in pairs. Then a youth appeared with four squirrels – fawn backs, white bellies, russet tails. One had to walk carefully between the long rows of butchers' stalls where the ground was slippy with blood and guts, and the air rent with the shrieks and squawks of dying pigs and poultry. I paused to watch one elderly woman preparing her stock of a special Lao delicacy: buffalo hide with the hairs still attached, sold in thin eighteen-inch strips. She was using a pointed stick to hold the hide in place and chopping with a heavy sharp knife; buffaloes are thick-skinned creatures and having completed her task she looked exhausted. As usual, the traders were women, many wearing tribal costumes – Hmong, Phu Noi, Thai Khao, Thai Daeng, Thai Neua. Perhaps their presence accounted for the market atmosphere's being so friendly.

Afterwards I cycled to Wat Phonxay ('Victory') at the eastern edge of the town. Its site is very beautiful, on a high bluff overlooking a wide tributary that joins the Nam Xam where it leaves its mini-gorge. To one side stands a grove of giant bamboo and beyond is a *ban* of stilted houses – yet another of Xam Nua's suburbs.

Before the bombings there were three other wats in Xam Nua, of which only fragments remain. Wat Phonxay, begun in 1958 and completed in 1968, was completely destroyed in 1969. Within weeks of the ceasefire in 1973 the local people resolved to rebuild it but by then their resources were drastically depleted and it remained unfinished until 1987. Near the entrance hangs a picture of its predecessor as a foundation, Wat Inpheng, a *sim* in the distinctive Xieng Khouang style, built in 1770 and twice the size of Wat Phonxay with magnificently carved doors and windows. Its famous gigantic statue of the Buddha was bombed to fragments.

This new wat looks neglected and supports only seven monks and novices. An ancient (1565) bronze statue of the Buddha stands under a scarlet silk canopy not enhanced by Christmas decoration baubles depending from the fringe. The unimpressive murals illustrate an uneasy phase in the Buddhist/Pathet Lao relationship. It tantalized me to be unable to read the script on each panel and the long (re-education?) lectures below two large murals flanking the main door. Some panels depict horrific scenes from the eight Buddhist hells: naked men and women being hanged, throttled, drowned, disembowelled, sawn in two, torn asunder by packs of giant hounds, flung into vast cauldrons surrounded by flames or thrown off cliff-tops to feed waiting tigers, having molten metal poured down their throats through funnels, having their eyes and brains pecked at by man-sized vultures and their abdomens torn apart and intestines dragged out . . . Many Westerners, coming East to seek the calming influence of the Lord Buddha, must get quite a jolt when they first encounter those hells. Also, in a wat for supposedly celibate monks it was odd to find naked women obviously modelled on Thailand's almost-naked calendar women. During the 1860s Garnier noted that monastic incelibacy, which carried the death penalty in Cambodia, was tolerated in Laos. Maybe it still is.

Throughout the Secret War the Pathet Lao were greatly strengthened by the Sangha's (Buddhist 'Establishment's') support. Religious leaders saw the American presence in Laos as spiritually corrupting and culturally destructive and all attempts to coax the monks into an anti-Communist alliance were spurned. Much more to their taste was the Pathet Lao's austere Marxism – which they didn't really understand but it seemed preferable to the Americanization of Laos and many young monks left their wats to fight.

Alas! when the LPRP came to power in 1975 the Sangha's support was ill-rewarded. Then the Buddhist and Marxist ideologies were perceived as incompatible and the Sangha was replaced by the Lao United Buddhist Association, its members handpicked by the Party. The enormous ceremonial fans used for centuries by the senior clergy were smashed in public, people were forbidden to gain merit by giving alms and maintaining the wats, the monks were ordered to grow food and breed animals – activities that broke their monastic vows – and the teaching of Buddhism in primary schools was outlawed. Only those who studied Marxist-Leninist philosophy and agreed to interweave it with Buddhist doctrines were allowed to continue teaching. When these compromises had been accepted, Buddhism was officially recognized – as in Tibet in the 1980s. (The worship of *phi* and other manifestations of animism were banned, in theory, but no one made much effort to enforce that ban.) Many monks either migrated to Thailand or returned to secular life; their numbers fell from about 20,000 in 1975 to fewer than 1,700 in 1979. However, the government had reckoned without the inimitable Laotian talent for passive resistance. In their quiet way the people made it plain that they would not co-operate in this downgrading and dilution of Buddhism, just as they would not co-operate to make collective farming possible. And on both these fundamental issues, affecting the spiritual and physical welfare of the ordinary Lao, the government speedily climbed down – thus proving its members to be true disciples of Ho Chi Minh. By the end of 1976 everyone was free again to give alms and the government had decided to present the Sangha with a daily rice ration. There are now some 17,000 monks and Party officials and their wives are often seen at Buddhist ceremonies, seeming as devout as anyone else.

From Wat Phonxay I rattled downhill through the stilted *ban* (its stilts all concrete), forded the shallow tributary and cycled for two hours along a dirt track running north-east across paddy-fields. On both sides, a few tiny *bans* lay at the base of low, rounded mountains – the foot-hills of a distant jagged range. The cold morning mist had dispersed, the sun shone pleasantly hot, the tributary by the track gleamed golden brown, matching the stubble on which buffaloes grazed – rather bony buffaloes as at the end of January not much stubble remained. The traffic was all two-wheeled, cyclists bringing loads of forest produce – including several pheasants and squirrels – to the market. One young woman had to wheel her bicycle; a large pig, its throat neatly slit, was tied to the carrier. Everyone looked more dark skinned, blunt featured and stockier than the Lao Lum. And everyone seemed taken aback by the *falang* cyclist, probably an unprecedented phenomenon on that track.

In the first wayside *ban*, some fifteen miles from Xam Nua, I was advised (not ordered) to turn back. Here the unstilted houses were built of wood – including shingled roofs – and the women wore spectacular piled-up turbans and loose trousers. The courteous elder who stopped me was clad in patched jeans, a frayed combat jacket and a long woollen scarf wrapped around his head. He seemed to be a man of the world, able to take *falangs* in his stride – very likely a Secret War veteran. He made a drinking gesture and invited me into his three-roomed dwelling, the living-room neat and clean, its furniture minimalist, its only decoration a large faded poster showing Ho Chi Minh and Prince Souphanouvong shaking hands. The liquid refreshment came from a bulbous earthenware jar and was indefinable: bland and slightly sweet and certainly not alcoholic so I gratefully accepted three cupfuls. Then, on the way back, I felt odd and wobbly and suddenly life seemed hilariously funny and I was giggling because I was wobbling. In due course Mr Pheuiphanh explained: that jar had contained marijuana 'tea', locally regarded as 'energizing'. He agreed with me that in fact it diminishes energy, both physical and mental.

We had chanced to meet, when I got back to Xam Nua, in the little eat-drink shop near the bridge. It was then 3.15 and Mr Pheuiphanh was relaxing with his two junior colleagues after the day's work – which had entailed an official luncheon party, starting at noon, in his department's local office. I liked the Lao attitude to work; government employees of all ranks eschew stress. Mr Pheuiphanh disapproved of my plan to cycle to Vieng Xai next day; he had come to suspect me of a tendency to stray from the beaten track. Uneasily he said, 'You can't feel free in Houaphanh – too much UXO.' He paused, then added, 'Be careful with those binoculars, don't be seen looking at fields. People might think you were interested in other things, not birds. And don't bother taking pictures of landscapes. People might think you had on of those special cameras.'

Houaphanh's main 'tourist attraction' is Vieng Xai, twenty miles north-east of Xam Nua – a place of pilgrimage for those who admire the Pathet Lao's courage, ingenuity, endurance and determination during the Secret War. There they set up their headquarters in an extraordinary complex of bomb-proof caves in the karst mountains surrounding the little town. Without that natural resource, they could not possibly have withstood so many years of saturation bombing. The USAF put everything they had into pinpointing the Pathet Lao positions, deployed all their most sophisticated equipment, used their most skilled and bravest airmen. Those were volunteers disguised as civilians because of this being a covert operation: in CIA-speak a 'non-attributable war'. One volunteer – Timothy Castle, quoted above – recently recalled: 'Around the airfield at Nakhon Phanom [in Thailand] we were concerned with safe and successful flying, not foreign policy issues. As a twenty-year-old airman I neither knew nor cared about the geostrategic dynamics that had pulled Laos into such a cataclysmic war.'

I left for Vieng Xai soon after sunrise (which was meteorologically silly of me), planning to spend a few days in that area before returning to Xam Nua on my way north. Opposite the guesthouse, on an open space, the day's transport was being organized: a few taxi pick-ups and several Soviet trucks – looking way past their stop-drive-by date – with luggage piled on the roof and passengers packed inside, standing. No buses make it to Xam Nua, not even the sort that damaged the Foot.

That morning was exceptionally cold and misty and soon I passed two old Hmong women crouching on the verge, thawing their hands over a fire; on the ground beside them four bamboo rats, tied together, were struggling to be free. Then three small boys came cycling towards me, each with a kicking bamboo rat hanging from his handlebars – the Lao equivalent of our trucking live animals across Europe.

This tarred road is surprisingly good; the large broken patches might irritate a motorist but rarely slow a cyclist. During the first hour five passenger trucks overtook me, travelling towards Vietnam in convoy with daring young men clinging to their roofs. Questions were shouted at me in a tone not friendly. After that I met only a few Hondas.

Leaving the valley of the Nam Xam, the road climbs gradually through uncultivated mountains – sometimes briefly descending into grassy clefts, then up again, the mist all the time getting thicker. A very steep gradient – Hare had to be pushed – took me on to a long plateau where suddenly the wildness of uninhabited mountains was exchanged for an orderly landscape of hedged fields. Here cattle in poorish condition grazed on coarse grass and I counted four herds of eight or ten ponies, a few with white saddle-sore scars but all plump – they must get supplementary feeding. Near the Hmong village of Naliou I met three little boys wheeling two bicycles; all four tyres were flat. They stopped me with a polite greeting, then shyly pointed to Hare's pump and looked hopeful. Watching them use it, I thought – not for the first time – that on the technological level the average Laotian IQ is even less impressive than my own.

Naliou's one-storey thatched dwellings line the road on both sides. Its school's concrete walls were falling to bits and there was no shop, not even the tiniest store selling shampoo and Sprite. The visible residents were far outnumbered by noisy pigs and bonhams.

Here fog reduced visibility to about fifty yards and a dramatic pass took me by surprise; someone – presumably the French – had blasted a gap in a mountain wall to allow the road through. Then came a descent of four or five miles on the worst stretch of road – flood-torn. Having already made the disquieting discovery that Hare's brakes were unreliable in wet weather, it seemed prudent to walk most of the way down.

Emerging from the cloud, I saw before me a wide, flat, winter-brown valley containing the big rebuilt Hmong village of Hua Khang – by Houaphanh standards almost a town. Here a conspicuous wayside board bears an unusual bilingual legend. The English version says: NOTICE. THE HOUAPHANH GOVERNMENT. THE GOVERNMENT BOARDING SCHOOL FOR THE HOUAPHANH ETHNIC

MINORITY. Several long, narrow, bamboo-walled, tin-roofed huts constitute the school buildings. This institution, so utterly un-Lao, worried me. It recalled Australia's forced integration programmes for the Aboriginals – children ruthlessly taken from their parents to be re-conditioned and 'civilized' by the state. The present Lao government is not, I am assured, attempting anything so drastic. However, it is intent on changing the mountain tribes' distinctive semi-autonomous way of life, allegedly to save the forests from swidden cultivators while creating a united 'modern' nation.

Beyond Hua Khang the road switchbacked to a junction with a small faded signpost in Lao; evidently no efforts were being made to put Houaphanh on the tourist map by 'selling' Vieng Xai. When I turned right the surface at once deteriorated without becoming bad enough to slow a weaving cyclist. Hereabouts were serious-looking little boys carrying slings and bows and arrows: not toys but hunting weapons. It was ironic to see Vieng Xai children wearing Thai-made anoraks with 'USA Army' emblazoned on the back. But of course no local has the least idea what these hiero-glyphs mean.

Now the road was winding between sheer limestone mountains, most free-standing, with yawning cave entrances – some at ground level, others high up, half hidden by bushy vegetation. During the 'non-attributable war' all these caves were occupied by local peas-ants who had to cultivate under cover of darkness; they described this as 'living like an owl during the day and a fox during the night'. Every year airpower – T-28 fighters from Long Tieng, F-4s and 105s from Udorn, B-52 bombers from Uttaphao– destroyed much of that hard-won rice harvest. And these unfortified caves provided limited protection; the Americans soon perfected the art of killing cave dwellers with phosphorus rockets and napalm. The casualties went uncounted. This was what Timothy Castle would then have thought of as 'successful flying'.

Pedalling slowly through two roadside hamlets, I noticed many ordnance leftovers made into fences, incorporated into dwellings, used as flowerbeds and herb-beds and pig troughs. I wanted to find the famous 'garage-cave' which had ample space for the parking of 120 military trucks. But despite Mr Pheuiphanh's coaching my pronunciation baffled the locals and without guid-ance it would have been unwise to leave the road. In another famous nearby cave, at Hanglong, were stored as many of the Lord Buddha's statues as could be rescued – including Wat Phonxay's bronze Buddha of Pra Ong Tu. Ninety-five caves 'of historical significance' have been listed, including a cave school for the children of government officials and a hospital complex some ten miles from Vieng Xai.

Approaching from Xam Nua, a ridge conceals the town and at first I mistook a long roadside *ban* for the Pathet Lao 'capital'. Then a weatherbeaten triumphal arch, decorated with hammers and sickles, came into view at a junction. Passing under it, I followed a rutted road to the ridgetop and was overlooking Vieng Xai, set amidst level paddyfields from which, in Tom Butcher's words, 'startling conical limestone outcrops erupt out of the ground like pieces on a chessboard'. This must be Laos's oddest settlement, neither a town nor a village but with vestiges of urban pretensions. When at last the bombing stopped, in 1973, the Pathet Lao hastily built it – with Vietnamese help – as the capital of the liberated zone. Three years later all zones had been liberated and the Lao People's Revolutionary Party was governing the whole country from Vientiane. Vieng Xai – no bigger than Hua Khang – then assumed village status. Gradually its imposing public buildings mouldered away, its tarred streets (all three of them) crumbled and its power lines ceased to convey electricity. By now the overall effect is visually dismal but Vieng Xai's human content – cheerful, friendly, helpful – more than makes up for that.

The public are admitted to the five main caves, the residences and offices of the Pathet Lao leadership from 1963. These are named after the original Politburo: Souphanouvong, Kaysone, Phonsavan, Phomvihane and Phoumi. During the two years of hard work that went into preparing this spelean accommodation several wooden coffins – elaborate, massive, ancient – were incidentally excavated and dumped with the rest of the rubble. No one had time to take a scholarly interest in mysterious relics and local folklore yields no clue to the identity of these VIPs.

In front of Prince Souphanouvong's cave an ugly damp-blackened wall of concrete trelliswork surrounds a garden planted all over with a low shrub, its leaves wine red. Here stands the two-storey wooden house built by the Prince in 1973 and now apparently abandoned. A nearby shack is the caretaker's office where a generator belches choking fumes and shakes so violently that the whole little building vibrates. Beside the long flight of steps leading up to the cave entrance a fading pink stupa marks the grave of the Prince's son; he was aged twenty-eight when Hmong infiltrators captured him a few miles away and beat him to death.

As I arrived an official Vietnamese delegation (all wearing name badges) was leaving and the pleasant young caretaker hesistated, looking worried – to whom should he now give preference? When the friendly Vietnamese had urged him to attend to the *falang* he again switched on the generator, then pointed out a huge bomb crater and the casing of the 500-pound bomb involved. There were many loose chunks of mountain lying around the entrances to all the caves – not normal rock-falls but gigantic masses of limestone detached from the slope above as time and again the B-52s attacked.

Truly these caves are astounding – and very moving. (In David and Goliath situations, most of us have a built-in prejudice.) They are astounding both geologically and, as it were, architecturally. I marvelled at the enormous grottoes partitioned and ceilinged with planks. Baths and stoves were hewn out of the rock; garages for the Politburo's vehicles were contrived at the base of the karst; a vast cavern was converted to a theatre – its stage a smooth slab of limestone where audiences of 400 and 500 regularly gathered. Also there were hospital units, assembly halls for political education and adult literacy classes, recreation rooms. My guide was particularly proud of the emergency rooms, completely sealed concrete bunkers able to shelter twenty people in the event of a gas attack and equipped with Soviet-donated hand-cranked oxygen pumps. (The young man's expression revealed his pride: he spoke no English.)

Outside one cave, within a few yards of the entrance, are three enormous craters, their rims almost touching. A concrete wall, some fourteen feet by six, shields this entrance. All these caves were heavily fortified with Vietnamese technical assistance. The Pathet Lao's skills did not match their courage: most of the rank and file were peasants unacquainted with modern construction methods.

The weather seemed apt: all day a low, dove-grey sky – no wind – the air absolutely still, the silence unbroken. At the end of our tour, when the young man had gone home, I remained amidst the caves for a couple of hours, taking care not to step off the pathways. The strangeness of Vieng Xai's atmosphere is, I felt, only partly owing to this region's pivotal significance during the Secret War. Those bizarre karst formations rearing up close on every side contribute to it and one is aware of the caves having much older layers of significance – as indeed is proved by the finding of so many mighty coffins.

Back in the village, it felt like Beerlao time. When I sat at a trestle table in a bamboo shack a beautiful young woman welcomed me warmly. Her one-year-old son had a broken arm but was being stoical about it – if not about the arrival of the *falang*. However, he soon relaxed and when shown a photograph of my granddaughters kissed it passionately. Then Granny appeared, conveyed that Vieng Xai's Government No. 1 Hotel was closed and suggested I lodge with the Germans. The bomb-disposal team had its Houaphanh headquarters on the ridgetop dominating the valley. As I departed the little fellow blew me a shower of kisses.

The headquarters used to be Government No. 2 Hotel, a French colonial edifice, its yellow paint flaking. It had a wide veranda and handsome wrought-iron balconies outside the long rows of first-floor windows. Fifty yards away stood a colossal disused hangar-like shed; its doors were half off their hinges and lakelets of rainwater on the floor deterred me from camping there. Two German flags on high poles flanked the gateway; the Laotian flag flew in the background on a much lower pole. The open halldoor led into a vast foyer, empty but for a statistics blackboard: 3,000-plus bombs had so far been dealt with in the Vieng Xai district. To the right, in an unfurnished high-ceilinged room, many of these were on display. When loud rappings on other doors brought no reply I ventured up the grandly sweeping stone staircase to a wide corridor. Through an open doorway a middle-aged German, obese and rubicund, could be seen filling in forms at a rickety desk. Scowling at me, he shouted for an English-speaking colleague, who emerged from another big bare room. This was the supervisor I had seen at work in Xam Nua: tall, lean, narrow faced, with a thin downturned mouth and close-set pale blue eyes. (He reminded me of a certain sort – not the nicest sort – of Afrikaner.) When I sought permission to sleep on the veranda, explaining that I had my own bedding and food, he asked why I had not gone to the Government No. 1 Hotel. 'It's not very good,' he added almost sadistically, 'but you can sleep there if you're willing to pay.' The implication that I might be trying to cadge free lodgings made me wince; always I am reluctant to impose on unknown expats and this experience reinforced my inhibition.

Speeding downhill through the fading light, I wondered if No. 1 really was open. Then I realized that I had already passed it and assumed it to be another derelict residence; nothing indicated its function. In spacious grounds, encircled by towering Norfolk Island pines and bluegums, it was the Houaphanh Hilton during Vieng Xai's brief years of glory when foreign dignitaries and other distinguished visitors came to confer with the Pathet Lao. Since then, the veranda's concrete pillars have half collapsed in what seemed to me quite a dangerous way. The restaurant with seating for a hundred was locked but through the door's glass panel I could see chairs upside down on tables. No water was available in a large communal bathroom with many hand-basins and squat-overs. I shouted and rattled door handles to no effect. Perhaps Granny was right and the German wrong? I wandered up an outside staircase and along a balcony – the boards rotting. Only when I turned on my torch to descend did someone notice me and shout from a house on stilts behind the trees.

A woman carrying a kerosene lamp, followed by two teenage girls, came to greet me shyly, looking bewildered. They were not sure if I could stay . . . Having disappeared for ten minutes they returned with an elderly man who shook hands and closely con-sidered me before saying, 'OK, OK!' Then everyone disappeared for fifteen minutes, leaving me sitting on the edge of the veranda gazing up at the dimly visible crags above Kamtai's cave, only fifty yards from the hotel.

When the generator began to hum my host led me to a memor-able room of lofty proportions where the three single beds had crimson silk counterpanes; ludicrous pink beribboned satin hearts, stuffed with some aromatic herb, adorned the pillow covers. Most of the plaster had fallen from the hospital-green walls, exposing ill-made concrete blocks, the light fitting hung loose and the door lock was malfunctioning. On a splendidly carved table stood a plastic tray bearing a two-litre thermos of boiling water, a bowl of refreshing herbal tea leaves and three delicate porcelain cups and saucers. When I asked, not very hopefully, about an evening meal my host instantly produced from his jacket pocket two of those little packets of dried noodles which swell in boiling water – 500 kip for both. A soup plate, a spoon and chopsticks were soon after provided. Each packet contained a sachet of some horrible synthetic flavouring but I was hungry enough to enjoy that supper; remarkably, there were no eat-drink shops in Vieng Xai. (However, large bundles of freshly made noodles were on sale at every food stall – so why import instant noodles to the Houaphanh outback?)

Mr Pheuiphanh had told me about the Nam Xam National Biodiversity Conservation Area (NBCA), some 380 square miles of forested hills between Vieng Xai and Xam Tai, so designated in 1993 because of its exceptional population of endangered species: tigers, Malayan sun bears, Asiatic black bears, elephants, gaur, banteng, clouded leopards and a variety of gibbons. From Vieng Xai this area is accessible on a cycleable track – or at least a track along which it is possible to push a bicycle.

I rose at dawn, trying not to feel too excited, reminding myself that another frustration was quite likely. In Vientiane I had heard a rumour that at least one Houaphanh re-education camp remains open somewhere near Xam Tai; if true, that could mean a roadblock.

Only one track goes south-east out of Vieng Xai's valley, climbing gently into conventional mountains, swidden-scarred in small patches near the summits. On this cold misty morning I met no one over the few miles to a *banlet* where, according to the map, my track turned right. It alarmed me to see a huge empty loggers' truck – bigger than any of the dwellings – parked in the middle of the *ban*, with no number plate. When I paused to scrutinize it an old man, very small and wrinkled and worried looking, rushed towards me. His sign-language message was that I should (a) move away from the truck and (b) return to Vieng Xai. Had I not already identified my track I might have taken his advice but that track was irresistible, leading directly into primary forest. I tried, unsuccessfully, to soothe him before continuing. Casual visitors can't realistically expect to see endangered species yet merely to be in an area where such sightings were remotely possible exhilarated me and I was equipped to spend a few days in the forest; even during the dry season these mountains have running streams.

Soon my exhilaration had evaporated; that track was sinister – too wide and well engineered, not a peasants' track. An hour later a sound stopped me, distant but unmistakable – the whining snarl of chain-saws. After that I was not surprised to be challenged, on the next mountain, by a middle-aged Hmong wearing blue dungarees and wielding a sub-machine-gun. His message, that I should return to where I came from, was not disregarded. Mr Pheuiphanh admitted next day that Vietnamese cedar loggers simply ignore the NBCA designation. And recruiting local protectors is easy.

Back in Vieng Xai, I consulted the map and decided to see how far I could get on the road to Nam Maew, the Vietnamese border *ban* only thirty-five miles away.

Beyond the archway junction an earth track, quite well maintained, ran through a narrow valley – paddy on the left, maize on the right – with an enticing mountain wall at the valley's end. Here I saw another UXO disposal team, waving their magic wands over sloping paddyfields where five days previously a 'bombi' had killed two young women and a toddler – none of them born when those cluster-bombs were dropped. The black scar of that tragedy stood out on the golden-brown stubble. Then one of the team noticed the *falang* and shouted and came running towards me. I could not continue: this area was temporarily forbidden to *falangs*. To prove his point he bent down and picked up a fallen wayside sign – trilingual: Lao, German, English. To me it said STOP! DANGER WIT EXPLOZONS!

Every day in Laos, as in many other countries, people are being killed or maimed by the leftovers of wars which had to be fought (we were told) to defend democracy and human rights and protect the world from the horrors of Communist domination. Yet now, when the Soviet threat to US global hegemony is no more, the Americans are ingratiating themselves with the Chinese – still in theory Communist and continuing relentlessly to repress the Tibetans, among others. But with a market like China's opening up none of that matters. Democracy and human rights – forget them!

Houaphanh, it has to be admitted, is an unsoothing province – what with its UXO, opium fields, illegal loggers and re-education camps. Those last may no longer exist: who knows? If they do still exist, it is likely their inhabitants are few. In 1995 Amnesty International drew attention to three Lao 'prisoners of conscience' recently sentenced to fourteen years in a Houaphanh re-education camp for peacefully arguing in favour of a multi-party political system. Unfortunately Amnesty International's investigations are not always thorough so this presentation of the case may or may not be accurate; it sounds like less than the full story.

After the Pathet Lao take-over, 40,000 people – it is said – were sent to re-education camps and 30,000 jailed for 'political offences'. Originally that was reported in the *New York Times* (11 November 1976, 3 May 1977); then those figures became accepted and are now quoted in some guidebooks, including the *Lonely Planet* and *Laos Handbook*. However, the historian Martin Stuart-Fox, a Lao specialist, gives 'less than 1500' as the number held in the five camps in the Vieng Xai area, with a similar number held in southern camps – all these being senior army and police officers. Dr Stuart-Fox estimates that probably ten times that number – lower-ranking officers and civilians – were held for a few years, giving a figure of around 30,000 during 1976 and 1977. The inflated figure must be regarded as part of the Americans' vigorous post-war smear campaign. Their 'yellow rain' smear is still doing damage though the accusation that the LPRP government was using chemical agents against 'dissident' Hmong eventually had to be withdrawn, the State Department admitting it lacked any supporting evidence.

During the early 1980s most internees were released – 'it is said' – but these did not include King Savangvatthana, Queen Khamphuy and Crown Prince Vongsavang, who all died in captivity in Vieng Xai, in what is now the Germans' headquarters. (If suitably furnished, that building could well replace the Luang Prabang palace.)

The royal family were victims, indirectly, of Thailand's 1976 military coup which inspired more manic machinations on the CIA's part. In December 1975 the King had abdicated with great dignity, voluntarily presenting to the state the royal lands and palace at Luang Prabang. Immediately he was appointed 'Counsellor to the President' (Prince Souphanouvong) and Prince Souvanna Phouma was appointed 'Counsellor to the Government' and the Crown Prince Vongsavang was appointed a member of the Supreme People's Assembly. ('No guillotines please, we're Lao!') But then came the military coup in Bangkok, leading to a CIA-backed alliance between the Thai military, the Hmong retired mercenaries and the many rightwing Lao then living in Thailand. Their aim: to restore the Royalist regime. Fearing that the ex-King would be seized and used by the conspirators, the government hastily banished him and all his family to Vieng Xai's 'Seminar' camp. This specialized in brainwashing but applied only a token amount to a royal family who had been co-operating amiably with their new Republican rulers.

There is some confusion about the dates of the royal deaths. According to P. Delorme, writing in *Historia* 497 (May 1988), the King and Crown Prince both died in 1978 and the Queen in December 1981. However, the 1997 edition of the *Laos Handbook* reports: 'In December 1989 Kaysone Phomvihane admitted in Paris, for the first time, that the King had died of malaria in 1984 and that the Queen had also died "Of natural causes" – no mention was made of Vonsavang. The Lao people have still to be officially informed of his demise.'

Not much is known about what went on in Laos between 1975 and 1985. All Western media were excluded and the country was almost completely cut off from the non-Communist world. The US Congress refused aid to the new Republic until 1995 – having between '68 and '73 given an average of US$74.4 million per annum to its prodigiously corrupt Royalist allies. Less lavish Soviet funding then flowed in and for twelve years Russian technical advisers replaced American 'aid' workers. Even now, despite 'liberalization', the government maintains that how it chooses to run its domestic political machine is nobody else's business. This partly explains why I hesitated to talk politics, to ask potentially embarrassing questions. The Lao have their own way of dealing with things, a way so unlike ours one senses their diffidence about attempting to explain themselves to outsiders. Also, I was aware of people not feeling at liberty openly to discuss the Party's policies or methods. There is no free press or freedom of assembly or freedom to advocate an opposition political party. Nor, it should be emphasized, is there any popular longing for those buttresses of democracy – the first of which is now being rapidly demolished throughout the Rich World. The Party may have unjustly mal-treated thousands in re-education camps but it has given the majority what they most longed for: peace and stability.

Towards sunset I returned to the Houaphanh Hilton where two fellow-guests invited me to sup with them; they had ordered what-ever forest-derived meat and two veg might be available. Mr Phanivong, a fifty-ish middle-grade government official, had done three years' 're-education' in a camp nearby and was visiting from Vientiane because he liked to keep in touch with friends made locally. His wife, a returnee from Australia many years his junior, interpreted for us. As usual I asked few questions – and those ten-tative. However, Mr Phanivong was more communicative than most Lao, within the limits imposed by his job. Sometimes I sus-pected that his reflections and opinions were being elaborated on by our independent-minded translator who had left Laos as a small child.

Life had been tough enough in his camp, Mr Phanivong admitted. Some older people succumbed to the poor diet and lack of medical care. But it was a learning camp rather than a punishment camp; in the latter the workload was heavier and the death rate higher. The LPRP shouldn't be criticized for punish-ing those who were not simply puppets but crafty exploiters of the Americans' paranoia, cynically indifferent to the devastation being inflicted on their compatriots in the liberated zones.

Mr Phanivong corrected my impression of a government quickly rounding up 'reactionary elements' who had failed to escape over the Mekong. Most of those implacably opposed to the new regime or who, as major criminals, had every reason to fear retribution, fled *en masse* in 1974–5 and were seen as a good riddance. Others gradually seeped away during the next year or so, finding the government's rigid totalitarianism intolerable and being unable to foresee that it would soon become more flexible – more 'Lao'.

Many ordinary folk, like Mr Phanivong and his family and friends, had belonged to the Royalist faction simply because they were born into it. As a reward for backing the US they had gained only to a limited extent, not being placed to have access to big bucks. Such people – most of the educated middle class – were willing to offer their services to a new government badly in need of trained public servants. The LPRP was rightly seen as much less corrupt than the RLG and more concerned about the peasants' welfare. Countless civil servants and police and army officers showed their willingness to co-operate with it by voluntarily travelling to Xam Nua's political re-education centres – known as *samana* – when ordered to do so in June '75. (Re-education was not considered necessary for women.) The show trial *in absentia* of thirty-one Royalist generals and political leaders had given the false impression that only the top layer would be punished. (Twenty-five were sentenced to long terms of imprisonment, the rest condemned to death.)

The *samana* volunteers assumed these courses would take them away from home and family for a month at most and were shattered when their confinement lasted for at least a year – sometimes a few years. However, the majority – including Mr Phanivong – responded positively to re-education and eventually re-entered government service. It had been necessary, in his view, to learn not only about the LPRP's 'Eighteen Points' programme but about US imperialism, to understand why the Royalists had been so easily bribed into serving a cause that meant nothing to them. Surprisingly, his teachers also obliquely conveyed that the Pathet Lao itself had been coerced by the Vietcong in the '50s, when it became clear that Laos's leaders would never be allowed to arrive at their own sort of reconciliatory compromise.

When I mentioned NEM Mrs Phanivong's face lit up. That was the way forward, Laos had been waiting too long for development! Had there been no NEM, she would have stayed in Australia. The French colonists were only interested in Vietnam, to them Laos was just buffer territory. They didn't bother educating even enough Lao to help them run the place. Vietnamese were brought in, same as the British imported Indians to Burma. Mr Phanivong said nothing about NEM; I intuited his enthusiasm was less than his wife's. She of course had never attended classes on American imperialism and international capitalism.

Supper was one course: stewed squirrel and watercress with our sticky rice.

By noon next day I was back in Xam Nua, seeking a bicycle mechanic to overhaul Hare's increasingly unreliable brakes. The young man who spent half an hour on the job, with excellent results, looked shocked and hurt when kip were offered.

At the guesthouse Mr Pheuiphanh and his colleagues were enjoying their two-hour lunch break. I invited them to be my guests for my last supper in Xam Nua but Mr Pheuiphanh wouldn't hear of this. I must be his guest – he'd already ordered grilled jungle fowl for four. He seemed gratified by my reactions to Vieng Xai but the two younger men, Mr Un and Mr Phraxnyavong, looked puzzled. Although they had grown up on a diet of Party ideology, they had no personal memories of the Secret War. When they were in their teens NEM's influence became apparent and they welcomed it. For them Vieng Xai was not a place of pilgrimage. They didn't want to think about the past, they were focused on an illusory future that had to be good because of foreign investment and aid and all those experts and consultants coming in to help Laos. Irish people know about the awful consequences of concentrating on the past, keeping sores open, nourishing ancestral grievances. But in Laos too many are making the reverse mistake, failing to understand what the Pathet Lao struggle was all about and accepting as inevitable their country's again becoming a pawn in a very nasty game – this one economic.

I needed to buy a camera in Xam Nua, having been stupid enough to jam the mechanism by trying to remove a film before it had rewound itself. Mr Pheuiphanh opined that for this momentous purchase an interpreter was essential: Mr Un should accompany me to the large covered market between guesthouse and riverbank.

This is the only dry goods market within a radius of 100 miles but here are no crowds of eager shoppers, as in Vientiane and Luang Prabang. The traders look pleasantly surprised when a potential purchaser of anything comes on the scene and the local demand for cameras is limited; Mr Un had to employ detective skills to track down two in a drapery stall. Outside it sat a young woman and her small daughter, absorbed in a card game. Both these Japanese cameras (US$100 and US$150 respectively) were thickly covered in fine dust, having been displayed on top of their boxes. When I rejected them for this reason they were thoroughly wiped with a damp rag, then hopefully re-offered. I pointed out that one had been dropped – a corner was severely dented – but this damage was laughingly dismissed as unimportant. Finally Mr Un found an elderly woman trader just back from a trip to Yunnan and offering a $24 dust-free Chinese camera. It proved not quite up to Pentax standards but served its purpose.

During supper I casually asked Mr Pheuiphanh how many pupils study at the Hua Khang ethnic minority boarding school but he didn't want to talk about it. As an English-speaker with connections abroad, he may have been sensitive to outside criticisms of the 'integration' policy. And perhaps those criticisms, in which I join, are essentially unfair. The government's ambition to unite Laos's disparate tribes, eliminate 'primitive superstitions' and bring the benefits of modernization to all simply replicates the attitudes, not so long ago, of missionaries and the more benevolent colonial officials. Even now, in the Rich World, a belief that minorities should be allowed to preserve their own cultures is not general – and is scorned if those cultures get in the way of commercial activities.

In Xam Nua my cycling to and from Vieng Xai (twenty miles each way!) was regarded as a fabulous feat, comparable to the achievements of mythological heroes. Most Laotian roads/tracks discourage the notion of long-distance cycling, despite the bicycle's popularity amongst townspeople. As for cycling 150 miles to Phonsavanh – the next town – everyone flatly asserted that that could not be done. In a sense, they were right.

8

Bicycle as Trolley

Before dawn I pedalled furtively out of Xam Nua, lest some policeman or soldier might intervene. At 6 a.m. the Party's daily exhorta-
tion could be heard tearing the silence of the valley, already far
below. By then I was walking – and two hours later I was still walking.
Although the Annamite Chain is not high (8,000 feet or so), it is
very, very steep. The narrow road was tarred but traffic-free and for
miles there were no signs of habitations – no pigs squealing or cocks
crowing in the distance, no pedestrians or path junctions. All
around me the soundless world was hidden in mist, a dense cold
mist creating a soothing sense of total isolation. For a time I enjoyed
moving through that silvery vapour, able to see only the lush vegetation growing tall on either side. Then, on the steepest stretches, a
familiar sensation in the legs suggested that I was near 6,000 feet.
Not quite enough oxygen was getting through and I found myself
stopping every forty or fifty yards to regain breath. The sibilant drip
of moisture from leaves accentuated the silence and occasionally
small birds twittered. Where humans are scarce, remnants of the
avian population survive.

The fog, ever-thickening as I ascended, became frustrating
when I realized it was no mere morning mist but a permanent
midwinter feature of the Annamite heights. However, it did
provide the spice of surprise. Suddenly I was on level ground, a
long ridgetop – cloud oceans below me to left and right filling
immense valleys. Soon after remounting, my hands went numb.
Here stood a Hmong hamlet, the few houses dimly visible, the
porcine residents grunting in alarm and scampering away, two
astonished young men by the verge responding to my greeting
with half-smiles.

A long chilling descent took me out of the cloud – though all day the sky remained overcast – into a wide valley where the tar vanished and a forceful river had to be forded; its footbridge of three slim bamboo poles seemed unsuitable for a cyclist. At the fording point, some way downstream, three kind young men helped me to drag Hare up a muddy bluff – yet another example of essential assistance being vouchsafed to optimistic travellers in the most unlikely places.

Beyond the river, within an enormous gravel pit, a team of tin-hatted Lao were operating Japanese machines, as raucous as they were smelly. A road-building project had just begun, to link Vietnam and China via Xam Nua and Udom Xai – where this section would join the highway from Yunnan already completed by the Chinese.

At the far side of that valley I passed through the day's only large *ban* and was tempted to seek a Beerlao at 10.15. Then I noticed a pair of soldiers guarding a road-construction depot – much machinery, many tanks of petrol – and thought it more prudent to hasten on my way. Before beginning the next climb, I nut-munched and listened to the happy laughter and singing of children cutting bamboo below the road, by the banks of a swift stream. The rural Lao of all ages sing to themselves like no other people I know – while laundering, cooking, spinning silk, husking rice, sweeping floors, humping firewood, fetching water, weeding vegetable plots or just wandering around with babies on backs. For how much longer will their lilting songs survive TV and pop tapes?

This ascent was less steep than the first but its atrocious surface precluded cycling uphill – and freewheeling could not be much above walking speed.

Here I could appreciate the grandeur of the Annamite Chain – range after range of almost sheer mountains, untouched by man, their tropical montane forest extending into long narrow valleys 1,000 feet below me. For hours the road wound upwards through deciduous monsoon forest – not to be confused with rainforest, unknown in Laos. Here the tallest trees attain 100 feet or more, their bark whitish, their single trunks quite slender. Many other hardwoods form the middle canopy – I could identify only Asian rosewood and teak – and beneath them flourish a wondrous variety of shrubs and multicoloured grasses. During my next descent the slopes were bright with blossoming wild plum trees – the first sign of spring, their delicate luminescence seeming quite magical under that grey sky amidst the sombre evergreens.

Only the road-builders marred this paradise. Occasionally an ex-Soviet truck, loaded with gravel and exhaling asphyxiating fumes, slowly overtook me. Or an empty truck came towards me. On a mile-long stretch, recently widened, earth-movers had savaged the landscape, casting magnificent wayside trees into the abyss below. Indisputably, Route 6 needed attention – but if only it could have been of a more appropriate kind, a skilled modifying of the terrain rather than the brutal use of giant machines.

Passing through this desecrated zone, I brooded resentfully, as is my Luddite way, on the many negative aspects of modern technology. Those incongruously aggressive machines were another example of the Rich World's insistence on exporting to the Poor World its own over-dependence on technology. And that over-dependence is dangerous, a point starkly illustrated by a radio interview I heard in Ireland during an American heatwave. Some public health officer speaking from Florida complained that the temperature had risen to 101 degrees F – so people who couldn't afford air conditioning were dying. The Irish interviewer listened sympathetically, apparently unaware that since time began human beings have been routinely surviving such temperatures – and much higher. At an accelerating rate, technology is depriving us of our survival mechanisms, coercing us into believing that if we can't afford an expensive, unnatural device, comparatively recently invented, we are doomed. Our adaptability – our inherent capacity to deal with extremes of heat or cold by using our intelligence – is being ignored or denied. We have become the planet's dominant creature because we can think creatively, communicate lucididly and take responsibility for our personal wellbeing. If technology reduces most people to a state where such responsible thinking is no longer perceived as necessary – or even possible – what is the prognosis for *Homo sapiens*?

I passed three road-workers' camps, a few small army tents looking like Secret War leftovers with bottled-gas cylinders as their only luxury. Later my way was blocked by the workers in action, drilling a deep channel for drainage pipes – which explained the day's complete absence of traffic. (This road, believe it or not, is the only one linking Vientiane and Xam Nua.) The channel was already some four feet deep and six feet wide and as I lowered Hare into it the Hmong drillers ignored me. Then the Lao Lum foreman (reclining under a tree, wearing a neat suit, not engaged in dirty work) realized that I would find it impossible to drag Hare out and ordered a youth to help. He beckoned me to his side and indicated that construction work was blocking the way ahead for many miles I must turn right at a nearby junction – noticing the maps in Hare's basket, he showed me the alternative route. I needed my spectacles to discern the faint detour squiggle; it was a 'route temporaire' and appeared to end, quite decisively, on a 2,062-metre mountain top. But that problem lay in the future and I rejoiced at the immediate prospect of escaping from the road-makers' ambience.

This encounter took place at the end of a long descent during which Hare's front brake became alarmingly enfeebled. After so many miles of walking up and cautiously freewheeling down, it was relaxing to be able to pedal to the junction over level ground, through a shadowy gorge between bulky mountains with a lively river racing on my right.

Emerging into a bowl-shaped valley – some two miles in diameter, rimmed by magnificent ranges – I found myself beside the junction and was relieved to see a small *ban* lining the road ahead. At 4.15 it was time to seek shelter for the night; already I could feel the temperature dropping. Slowly I pedalled past the thirty or so houses, deducing from their design that this was a Tai Dam (Black Tai) or Tai Deng (Red Tai) village. Most dwellings stood on tall stilts, their high embankment backed by secondary growth merging into thick monsoon forest. These were longer and narrower than Lao Lum houses, all built of wood with vertical rather than horizontal wall planks. The steeply pitched roofs were grass-thatched, the windows small with finely carved shutters, the front balconies spacious and overhung by bulbous thatched eaves. When my arrival was noticed and the residents hurried out to stare I saw that they were Tai Dam, the women wearing black *sins* – the hems exquisitely embroidered – and black scarves with coloured borders over their chignon top-knots. Among Laos's minorities, enforced mass movements during the Secret War undermined many tribal traditions. But this seemed to be a long-established settlement – perhaps so tiny, isolated and enforested that the B-52s never noticed it.

My greetings evoked only a few nervous responses so I dismounted at the end of the *ban* and walked back to give people time to adjust to the *falang* presence. I knew the Tai Dam to be a tribe esteemed throughout Laos for their honesty as traders, their craft skills and their diligence as workers. However, they are also celebrated for the complexity of their ancient non-Buddhist religious beliefs and strangers do not enter Tai Dam villages without an invitation. Instead of a wat, each *ban* maintains a spirit house and domestic spirit altars. A large tree, marking the entrance to the village, represents the community's guardian *phi* – and here that tree was easily recognized by the many little balls of rice stuck to its bark.

Back at the junction, I sat on a rock and waited hopefully for some positive development: the chief or a priest might offer hospitality? Or what about the row of unstilted roadside shacks opposite the embankment and possibly unguarded by the *phi* tree – could those be approached without impropriety? Moments later the door of the nearest shack opened and a young man appeared carrying a Scotch whisky bottle full of kerosene. The *falang* on the rock stopped him in his tracks. Then gingerly he approached – as one might approach UXO, curious but not wanting to get too close. Pausing at a distance of several yards he stood looking from me to Hare in total bewilderment. I asked 'Beerlao?' and made a drinking gesture; by then Beerlao was my prior need, coming even before shelter. Immediately the young man relaxed, grinned and beckoned me to follow him into the shack – also the village shop, though no external sign indicated this.

A middle-aged Tai Dam woman was sitting on a low stool by the one small window spinning silk from her own silkworms (later proudly displayed to the guest). I forgot to note her name so let's call her Mrs A. This one-roomed shack, measuring some twelve feet by twenty, had a small fire burning in the middle of the earthen floor – the window served as chimney – and a high ceiling of smoke-blackened thatch. Opposite the door was a long communal bed of bamboo stakes, raised some four feet from the ground, the many quilts neatly folded. Well-worn garments hung from vines strung between the tree-trunk struts supporting the roof. A small table and bench completed the furnishings. In one corner was the 'shop': three short shelves holding a few bottles of Sprite and a meagre stock of toothpaste, instant noodles and cigarettes – alas! no Beerlao. A barrel of kerosene with a patch of oil on the floor beneath its tap stood close to the fire, from which sparks flew at intervals. On the wall beside the barrel hung an abacus on which Mrs A. did mysterious calculations when kerosene customers arrived.

Having drunk all three bottles of Sprite (a singularly repellent amalgam of chemicals), I hinted at my need for a night's shelter and Mrs A. looked momentarily disconcerted – then pleased. Exchanging laughing comments with the young man, she indicated the communal bed and pointed to the quilt that could be mine. I thanked her profusely before unpacking my own bedding and signing that I would be happy on the floor. Mrs A. fingered my thin flea-bag and mystifying space blanket, then frowned and dismissed them. She was a fluent sign-linguist and her simulation of the cold *falang* shivering throughout the night provoked a gale of giggles from our attentive juvenile audience, gathered inside the doorway. (These were filthy children, some with the concomitant skin diseases, but none looked underfed or had any of the obvious symptoms of vitamin deficiency.) For the self-invited guest this situation is tricky: how to explain that one has no objection to communal bedding but wishes not to deprive any family member of their quilt? But there was no problem here. Two sons were away working on the new road, sleeping in tents. While conveying this information Mrs A. used the space blanket to create a tent shape – more giggles.

That was a happy evening. The headman soon arrived to welcome me, accompanied by an adolescent grandson who had been taught a little English by an American road engineer. A little English can go a long way and here it went far enough for me to gather that Grandad regarded the road as an appropriate post-Secret-War gesture of reconciliation. I didn't try to disillusion him.

The Tai Dam recognize three social classes – nobility, priests and commoners – and Mrs A. (in material terms at the bottom of the commoner pile) deferred humbly to the headman. When he realized that she had no *lau-lao* to offer her guest he assured me that a bottle would be sent from his own supply – and would I also like some special tea? Recalling the 'special tea' served near Xam Nua, I firmly said 'No, thank you.' Then, looking slightly embarrassed, the grandson explained that I was not being invited to the headman's home because his daughter-in-law had recently given birth. After a Tai Dam or Tai Deng birth, neither mother nor baby may leave the home for a month lest they meet a stranger. Should any non-family-member chance to glimpse the infant, elaborate and expensive purification ceremonies are compulsory. Until Tai Dam babies are three months old everyone believes them to be only half in this world – and half in the spirit world. Then an aunt names them while placing a plaited cotton cord around the neck, and they are regarded as fully paid-up humans.

At sunset Mr A. returned from the forest with one squirrel, several small birds and a large leather pouch full of insects – unidentifiable by firelight. Everything went into the soup. The squirrel was skinned but not gutted before immersion, the birds were plucked only when cooked. The insects seemed to be regarded as the choicest morsels; carefully Mrs A. dredged most of them out of the cauldron for the guest. That was OK by me. After a long day in combat with Annamite gradients I would have eaten my grandmother.

The Tai Dam are a patrilineal tribe – and it shows. While Mr A., his widowed brother, two teenage sons and the *falang* were sitting on straw mats around a capacious basket of rice – each with a bowl of soup and plate of watercress – Mrs A. stood in the background, ready to replenish plates and bowls. Only when the replete males had settled down by the fire to play cards (an odd game, like a cross between poker and bridge) did she and her two daughters take their places around the basket. Ample rice, watercress and soup remained, but no protein.

By 8 p.m. I was asleep, cocooned in a cosy quilt stuffed with locally grown cotton.

All my Laotian days were enjoyable, despite 'security' frustrations and the Foot, but I particularly treasure the memory of that detour day. I met no one, the sun never shone, the gradients were severe, the surface forbade freewheeling, the Foot protested against overuse – yet from dawn to dusk I was exultant, awed by the surrounding magnificence, blessed by the silence, feeling privileged to be on a track unsullied by tyre marks. Although no dwelling was ever visible a few footpaths, narrow and overgrown, led from hidden *bans* to the track. The 'route temporaire' on my 1986 seemed unrelated to this route, but the headman's grandson had confirmed that it did eventually rejoin Route 6.

Without a tent one couldn't camp at such an altitude and in mid-afternoon I began to look out for a footpath, planning to park Hare and trek to a *ban*. Then I reached a mountain top – and was startled by a long shiny metal bridge, its floor of planks spanning a wide half-dry riverbed far below. Here was something aesthetically abhorrent, in such a setting, yet at that moment part of me was quite pleased to see it; the 'romance' of fording rivers with a bicycle tends to wane after the fifth immersion of the day. Did the bridge lead back to Route 6? I hoped not. In fact my track went nowhere near and the final steep climb to a biggish *ban* on a ridge-top felt longer than it was; I had been in action for eleven hours.

On this bare windswept ridge, where the atmosphere was welcoming, many large houses had intricately woven bamboo-strip walls and roofs thatched or shingled. In the Central Business District (five stalls selling basic goods) a row of Beerlao bottles cheered me. Human beings really are inconsistent creatures; such items as Coca-Cola or Nestlé tinned milk for sale in rural shops make me foam at the mouth, yet I seem to have no objection to the Beerlao brewery (recently taken over by some reprehensible TNC) penetrating to the remotest areas. Those dusty bottles – costing four times the Vientiane price – were probably stocked for visiting government officials.

My arrival perplexed the friendly stall-owner – she wore an ankle-length Soviet army greatcoat – and wildly excited the enchanting children who rapidly accumulated around me. By 5.30 it was extremely cold and large bonfires blazed on open ground between the houses. Around them sat groups of child-minding fathers and grandfathers, some with babies in slings. One little fellow led the fashion: he wore a shocking pink woolly cap with earmuffs, an orange anorak inscribed 'Tom & Jerry' and nylon trousers striped purple and yellow. Fascinated by the beer-swilling *falang*, he insisted on his father's escorting him to inspect me at close quarters; he must have been disappointed by Dad's failure to comprehend and explain. Again I noticed how good relationships are between different age groups as home-made spinning tops and high-flying kites are shared.

This settlement qualifies as a *muang* (town): it had a one-roomed school, a non-functioning hospital and a new Government Hotel – also one-roomed, its three beds a foot apart. Two had no bedding, the third remained as the last guest had left it. Each was equipped with a mosquito net, not needed hereabouts in winter. A generator powered a 15-watt bulb but there was no light switch.

In a minute eat-drink shop next door two young men and I were served with instant noodles and spring onions, the only dish on the menu. The men had brought raw eggs which they broke over the noodles before adding hot water; then the bowls were covered while the noodles swelled. While our meal was brewing I wrote my journal, inspired by two liqueur glasses of *lau-lao*. The young men, sitting opposite me, leaned forward – almost holding their breath – intently watching the movement of my pen.

And so to bed, where I slept without stirring for ten hours.

Breakfast consisted of more noodles (two packets) and three glasses of Ovaltine – inexplicably popular throughout Laos – made with condensed milk. A full stomach was needed to receive a dose of Ibuprofen. By then the Foot was swollen again; had I been able to cycle downhill it could probably have coped with the uphill miles but being in constant use did not suit it.

At 7.00 I set off, pedalling towards the distant bridge – then my host called me back. He was a poor sign-linguist but eventually I got the message: beyond the bridge Route 6 was blocked, I must continue north. This gratified me; I was in no hurry to re-enter the desecrated zone. The track climbed relentlessly for more than two hours into cloud-wrapped mountains. Although by no means unique in my experience, it did belong to the 'Most Horrendous' category – which includes certain main roads in Persia and Afghanistan (1963), Peru (1978), Madagascar (1983) and Tanzania and Malawi (1992). The fundamental defects of roads, as of human beings, are universal, not varying from continent to continent.

I passed one Hmong *ban* on a summit – half a dozen houses – and met a few groups of barefooted women carrying large loads of thatching 'panels'; nowhere is the Annamite Chain densely populated. Then, on a level saddle where stood another *ban*, the track joined Route 6, recognizable because it was slightly wider and bore truck tyre marks. Here I was able to pedal for a mile or so and at the start of the next descent the Foot prompted me to freewheel, very slowly, as far as the surface would permit. If in full possession of both feet I would have preferred to walk; freewheeling over such a rough surface – eyes fixed on the road, brakes held tightly – is both exhausting and nerve-racking.

Five minutes later both brakes failed completely and I discovered that a runaway bicycle is much more frightening than a runaway horse – an animate creature with its own sense of self-preservation. Obeying a law of nature, the unrestrained Hare soon gained the sort of speed (30 m.p.h.? – maybe more) that is fun on a tarred road but here was potentially lethal. On one side lay a sheer drop of hundreds of feet, on the other rose a rock cliff. The surface presented multiple hazards: large stones, embedded in the earth or loose – mega pot-holes – wide patches of fine dust six inches deep – erosion channels between corrugations. Most terrifying of all was the ghastly possibility that a stream might cross the track in a gully bridged by one wooden pole. These gullies remain invisible until one is almost upon them – and anyway could not now be avoided. To hit one at speed must mean disaster and already I had walked across three. I considered trying to fall off sensibly, injuring my arms rather than my head, though in the circumstances the likelihood of being able to manage things so cleverly was remote indeed. I was aware of operating on two separate levels, being emotionally sickened by fear while remaining mentally in control, totally focused on judging in fractions of seconds how to negotiate the hazards. Sometimes using the gravelly verge above the drop was the only way to avoid erosion channels which would certainly have unseated me. As Hare's speed increased: I would have been shaken off had I not kept my feet forced down on the pedals with all my strength. No doubt a half-century of cycling experience helped; a bicycle – even an out-of-control bicycle – feels like an extension of my body. Apart from possible streams, the three sharp bends – the steepest stretches and the roughest – posed the greatest threat; Route 6 was not well engineered. As we came to the last bend – mercifully not the trickiest – Hare's rattling chain-guard prevented my hearing the approach of a truck. Here the road had been reduced to a single lane by high piles of gravel and the truck had to be on its wrong side – not that the concept of right or wrong sides means anything in outer Houaphanh. Rounding the bend I saw its grey bulk only yards away, apparently blocking the entire track. 'This is it!' flashed through my mind before I saw a narrow space between truck and cliff. Swerving into deep dust, I glimpsed the driver's alarmed face. With only inches to spare on either side, I wobbled wildly – then was beyond that hazard and continuing to hurtle downwards, bounding over ridges and stones. (Not until later did I register a bleeding cut on my left hand where I must have touched the truck.) Now my ordeal's end was visible, the beginning of the next ascent. How long did this ordeal last? The distance covered was about three miles so assuming an average speed of 30 m.p.h. – because in places the gradient eased slightly – it lasted mere minutes. Some minutes!

Our momentum took us a little way uphill. Then I dismounted, sat on a fallen tree trunk and ate a portion of my emergency rations (Kendal Mint Cake) while feeling blank – not relieved, or shaken, or triumphant, or grateful to Fate. The experience that had just ended seemed quite unreal, like something that had happened to somebody else.

Later, in Ireland, a neuropsychologist friend explained that danger triggers a special chemical in the brain, preventing panic by numbing emotion, leaving the mind clear to make whatever judgements are necessary to increase one's chances of survival. Far be it from me to argue with so eminent a specialist, but I do know that the emotion of fear was not numbed on that mountainside. However, this chemistry would explain my 'separate levels' awareness, the feeling compartment not inhibiting the action compartment.

Excluding certain nightmarish episodes when my daughter travelled with me as a small child, this ranks as the most frightening experience of my life – even more so than an encounter with Ethiopian *shifta* thirty years ago when four men were debating whether or not to murder me. Yet at sixty-six one should be more accepting of death than at thirty-six – so does personal responsibility come into the equation here? If *shifta* on the wildest shore of Lake T'ana decide to murder you, there's nothing to be done about it. And while the debate goes on you are in no immediate physical danger but merely standing there awaiting the verdict. Yet in 1967 I also reacted on two levels, as I wrote in my journal at the time: 'Beneath the seething terror was a strange, indifferent acceptance, a feeling that gamblers can't always win and if this was it, it was it . . .'

Towards noon the cloud lifted, without breaking, and I calculated that it was four days since last the sun shone. By then the road-construction zone had been left behind but I continued to enjoy its one benefit: no traffic. At 12.30-ish, while fording a wide shallow river, I paused to refill my water bottle and wash my bloody hand. Climbing slowly from that small circular valley – where grazed many buffaloes and several piebald ponies – I was overlooking a *ban* of dark-roofed houses on tall stilts and could hear vigorous hammering, sawing and chopping: a new home being built. In most *bans* home-building is an ongoing activity; with construction materials growing in abundance all around, there is no housing shortage as the population expands. Soon after came the sound of a colossal explosion, quite close. I hoped it had been deliberately set off though hereabouts that seemed unlikely.

When another *ban* appeared far above me, the Foot suggested stopping there for the night. However, a number of scared glances or suspicious stares made it seem the residents would find it hard to cope with a *falang* guest. Here were many mini-huts – no more than four feet by six – on low stilts and too casually put together to protect from the summer rain or the winter cold. Such temporary dwellings shelter semi-nomadic swidden farmers when an advance party moves to a new area to do the initial slashing and burning. Perhaps this community had only recently been moved from some mountain top where *falangs* are never seen. They looked exceptionally ragged, unwashed and underfed.

The next climb (after another Ibuprofen) was the day's most gruelling. Having scrutinized sections of this track through my binoculars, from the far side of the valley, I knew there would be no reprieve; disdaining graded curves, it went straight over the summit of a majestically magnificent but seriously precipitous mountain.

Half-way up the knocks threatened and I stopped to nut-munch, overlooking a profound green-forested valley many miles long, with range after range of bluish mountains beyond. Now a little breeze was stirring, after a very still forenoon, and I delighted in the graceful response of the bamboo groves, gently bowing and swaying along the edge of the precipice. Then I heard distant singing in the forest – male voices. Moments later two young men jumped on to the track almost beside me, wearing axes and long knives strapped to their backs. Finding themselves eyeball to eyeball with a solitary grey-haired *falang* they looked utterly terrified and fled downhill, throwing apprehensive backward glances until reaching the corner. Interviewers often ask, 'But aren't you frightened to travel alone?' Usually it's the other way around and I do the frightening.

Over the last few miles to the top I nibbled continuously on Mint Cake and often had to pause to regain breath. In this more populated area swidden cultivation scarred many of the higher slopes. However, it affects only a minute fraction of the primary forest that in these provinces covers hundreds of square miles. A logging company does more damage in one month than swidden farmers could inflict in three decades.

On the summit swidden land surrounded a small *ban*. I had by then been pushing my trolley for some nine hours and it felt very like Stopping Time but this securely fenced *ban* had a five-foot-high bamboo gate barring entrance from the track. Moreover, the natives were unmistakably hostile. Not that I blamed them; their mountain provides a classic example of swidden erosion and is cited by conservationists (foreign and foreign-inspired Lao) intent on relocating hill tribes. I too would be hostile to anyone I suspected of trying to uproot me from my home territory.

From that mountain top I was looking down on every other summit in view – and the panorama stretched for at least fifty miles to the east. The descent was complicated by an anti-human gradient and my arms ached from restraining the brakeless Hare on a surface entirely composed of large sheets of loose rock. I passed a few groups of small boys bearing muskets longer than themselves, though shorter than adults' guns. As they fired repeatedly into tangled scrub, or tall trees, or stands of bamboo, it occurred to me that these hunters may present a greater danger than UXO to unnoticed pedestrians.

This descent ended on level ground, in the Annamites a memorable rarity. I pedalled on beneath forest giants that met over-head, wondering where I was going to sleep. Then faint motor engine sounds arose from an invisible valley on my left and soon the track joined an old tarred road. Here were two crowded truck-buses on their way from Phonsavanh to Muang Ngoy; they had paused briefly in the little *ban* Nam Noen to buy firewood. As the tar begins/ends here, and the rest of the long way to Muang Ngoy is akin to the road I had just traversed, I didn't envy them their nocturnal journey. But they were in high spirits – 'spirits' being the operative word as several men greeted me by waving bottles of *lau-lao* and urging me to have a swig. A few women passengers, squatting on the floors of the trucks, were cuddling earthenware jars of rice-beer wrapped in straw to protect them from the bumps.

When the trucks had departed I registered this *ban*'s odd vibes and on the following day learned that it is locally rather notorious. Its people belong to an obscure tribe (the name escapes me) with a reputation for powerful magic of a sort that intimidates their neighbours. However, it was too late to be again deterred by unfriendliness: here I had to find shelter.

The 'commercial centre' consisted of one small store at the junction corner, where the tarred road abruptly dropped out of sight into a hidden valley. A surly young woman refused to serve me a Beerlao until I had handed over the cash; neither bottle-opener nor glass was provided. She lived in a shack adjoining the store and her husband, a shifty-looking character, at first treated me almost with contempt. As I sat on the exposed 'veranda' in a piercingly cold wind a line of silent children assembled nearby; their laughter and play had ceased on my arrival. A score of adults, mostly men, also gathered to stare and exchange muttered remarks. I was relieved when a distracting rat hunt eased the build-up of tension. Suddenly a man raced across the road, pursuing an ordinary brown rat, flinging stones at the fast-moving creature with uncanny accuracy. Twice it was struck before taking refuge among the boulders below the opposite cliff. How badly injured? I wondered – then wished it had been killed. The hunter persisted in poking a stick between the boulders, but unsuccessfully. This seemed like a pursuit inspired by protein deficiency rather than vermin control.

Partially restored by my Beerlao, I cycled the level length of the *ban* in fading light, hoping for a friendly face. Many of the hundred or so houses were quite spacious and on high stilts, built more closely together than is usual because of the nature of the terrain. All livestock were returning to base, not being rounded up but following their own routine: hairy piebald pigs of many sizes but the same shape; spectacularly colourful turkey cocks and hens (a small breed); ducks and drakes, goats and kids, hens and chicks and cocks. Most residents had already retreated indoors from the icy wind. A few elders smiled at me hesitantly but quickly turned away – probably uncomprehending – when I requested sleeping space in sign language.

Back at the shack several men had lit a bonfire below the raised veranda of packed earth and were huddled close to the flames. I envied them as I drank a second Beerlao and decided to ask the unpleasant young man's permission to sleep on the veranda; its tin roof would partially protect me from the mist. Permission was granted, with a mocking laugh, and I was about to unpack my supper when a friendly face at last appeared – the headman, I deduced from the deference shown him. He made no attempt to converse with me but left the young couple looking rather chastened, having indicated that I should sleep inside.

The one large room held an L-shaped bed capable of comfortably accommodating sixteen adults; thick bamboo poles, lashed together with vines, stood on four-foot legs and a mosquito net was provided for each couple or pair of sleepers. (The provision of nets in every Laotian home, however poor, impressed me; evidently someone had done a good health-education job. But in Phonsavanh I met a Vietnamese doctor who drily commented that nets are valued simply as decorative furnishings and rarely used effectively.) In the dining-room corner my host ate alone: steamed rice, fish soup and greens, cooked on an outside fire. His wife stood silently behind him, serving more rice and soup on demand. I had been half-heartedly offered supper but the relief was obvious when I displayed my own food supply – by now dwindled to a fistful of nuts and half a bar of Mint Cake. There were no children or elders in residence but two truck drivers arrived after dark – so this was the *ban*'s guesthouse.

Having spread my bedding on the floor, where I would be least in the way, I put my waist-pouch and new camera in the knapsack, fastening it securely and placing it by my head. During this operation someone briefly switched on a torch to observe the *falang*'s activities. The extreme cold of the bumpy earthen floor dismayed me. Eventually I found a comfortable position (ribs and hip between bumps) but my body took a long time to warm the ground sufficiently for sleep to be possible. This crudely built shack, with four-inch gaps between the wall planks, was that night receiving the full force of an icy gale.

Meanwhile four men, wrapped in quilts, were playing cards above me by the light of a tiny wick-in-tin lamp. Three couples (truck passengers) had also retired, though not to sleep; they were chatting and laughing and arguing (amiably) just as we do in our sitting-rooms at the end of the day. A difference here was the Lao peasants' addiction to expectoration. Being indoors inhibits no one and spits were coming from all directions, landing near my head (well protected by the space blanket). This addiction, almost universal among men, women and children, is sometimes associated with a hacking cough (in winter chest infections are common) but more often is mere spitting for spitting's sake. One sees people working to collect a little saliva, then disposing of it with an evident sense of achievement. This unattractive habit may be linked to betel-chewing, still popular in rural areas, even among the young. Over-indulgence is alleged to cause premature ageing and most chewers do over-indulge – like most cigarette smokers.

Against all the odds, I slept deeply. Yet I awoke feeling rather shaken, as though during sleep I had belatedly reacted to the narrowness of my escape on that hill – literally narrow, when confronted by the truck. This delayed reaction surprised me but was I'm told quite normal.

Then I discovered that I had slept too deeply; my new camera was missing, though the knapsack appeared untouched. I blamed myself for not having used it as a pillow instead of sybaritically choosing to rest my head on my little bundle of spare garments. Self-indulgence rarely pays and in this case was plain stupid, especially after that flash of a torch at a vital moment. My host merely smirked when I protested at the theft; there's nothing a *falang* can do about stolen property in the fastness of the Annamite Chain.

By 6.45 I had begun what proved to be the longest and most precipitous descent of my journey, an hour and fifty minutes of very brisk walking. The heavy unbraked Hare determined my speed and this was what the Australian doctor had advised against: fast walking on a hard surface. After such a windy night the air was clear and from far, far above I could see Ban Phiangdang on its riverbank, where a Soviet-built bridge spans the Nam Neun. Although described as a *ban* on my French map, Phiangdang looked more like a *muang* and a good place to rest the Foot, seek repairs for Hare, recover from my delayed shock, bring my journal up to date and eat (with luck) three or four square meals.

Only in the Andes have I so abruptly trekked from one climatic zone to another. As the road plunged down, the vegetation frequently changed: around Nam Noen, cedars and pines covered many slopes, at river level papayas and bananas flourished, and in between were several layers of unidentifiable trees and shrubs. The prospect of R and R in Phiangdang was pleasing, yet I had mixed feelings as I lost altitude – always a vaguely dispiriting experience. However, I would soon enough be regaining it; immediately beyond the Nam Neun rose a mighty mountain range to match the one just crossed.

The heights on either side make this valley seem cleft-like. To the north the river emerges from tightly packed mountains and after a few miles it disappears into more tightly packed mountains. Phiangdang stands some way off Route 6, downstream from the bridge, and is a two-street *muang* – short streets. Yet it is important as the only market centre between Xam Nua and Muang Kham, a small town far away in Xieng Khouang province. And it has a police station, a shabby two-roomed breeze-block bungalow opened once a month (or so) when a policeman comes from Muang Kham. On my arrival people seemed unsure about how to deal with a *falang* who had not emerged from a four-wheel-drive or a helicopter. But friendliness burgeoned as I wandered around in search of a mechanic, demonstrating Hare's problem. Understandably, cycling is not part of the Phiangdang way of life; there is virtually no level ground, nor are there any gentle slopes, within a radius of fifty miles. However, it was suggested that one young man, a resident government official from Vientiane, might be able to help – but he wouldn't be around until sunset.

The Government Hotel is run by a kindly elderly woman who reacted to my limp (rather pronounced that morning) by producing a basin of some herbal distillation in which the Foot remained immersed for a few hours while I wrote my journal. This liquid, though cold, had a warming, slightly stinging effect and wondrously reduced both the swelling and the pain. My hostess also produced three large meals: sticky rice and omelette, sticky rice and boiled chicken, sticky rice and grilled fish. Since this was the Foot's rest-day my Beerlao intake had to be limited: the communal loo was some 200 yards away, down a pathway running between the neighbours' back gardens. (The key hung on a nail in the restaurant when the last user remembered to put it back there.) Beside a smell-free long-drop stood a bucket of wood ash, to be shovelled over one's deposit, and another bucket received loo paper made in Vietnam. In less sophisticated and more ecologically sound settlements, the rural Lao use large leaves.

Three bedrooms led off the restaurant and my hostess emphasized, in sign language, that at night the windows must never be opened – to exclude mosquitoes, I wrongly assumed. Later I learned that hereabouts daring rats are inclined to gnaw guests' belongings. No doubt when caught they become supper.

By 11.00 the sky was cloudless and soon I had begun to sweat, as I sat writing. The afternoon heat recalled Vientiane – probably at about the same altitude – and I lay reading on my bed (the Foot elevated) until summoned for another herbal immersion.

When the young official from Vientiane returned to the hotel (his base) it transpired that he had spent the day very profitably fishing, an activity unrelated to his job – though a sensible activity in Phiangdang, given government salaries and the local demand for dried fish. He spoke enough English to opine that Hare's disability was merely a result of her having been put on the market wrongly adjusted. He then worked on the brakes for half an hour, by the light of his jeep's headlamps, before going for a reassuring trial run down the steep slope from Route 6. Elated and grateful, I stood him several beers as we supped together. He was not surprised to hear about the camera theft. 'You were lucky,' he said. 'Those people have poisons to kill and then they steal everything.'

Hare's brakes were not tested next day though the Foot was. This stretch of Route 6 sports chipped and faded kilometre stones, enough of them legible for me to calculate that by 5 p.m. I had covered thirty-three kilometres – and all but three were uphill.

Luckily the Foot benefited much more from its Phiangdang immersions than from its daily doses of Ibuprofen.

The first three kilometres took me through a narrow, deforested side valley to the provincial border – a pole across the road and an empty lean-to in which a tattered file and a rubber stamp lay on a metal camp-chair. I walked around the pole and was in Xieng Khouang province, at the start of my nineteen-mile climb. Hereabouts wild banana, low scrub and thick secondary growth covered the slopes and singing groups of women and children were descending to the market, loaded with firewood, forest produce, rice-beer, thatching panels, coiled split bamboo. A steep hour later I was back in Cloudland, meeting no one.

There was an aura of improbability about that exhilarating day as I moved ever upwards, from high mountain to higher mountain, expecting descents which never happened. But here most gradients were reasonable, though never cycleable – at least not by a geriatric without gears. When the sky cleared the sun felt agreeably hot and again the altitude enforced quite frequent pauses – not that that mattered, I was in no hurry to get anywhere in particular. The day's traffic amounted to four vehicles: a taxi-jeep, a truck-bus, an army truck full of soldier-loggers and a Beerlao truck which I longed to hijack.

Not long after midday I came to the only roadside settlement, a nine-house Hmong *ban* where everyone wore traditional attire and my stopping to ask for water greatly alarmed the women and children. Hastily they retreated towards their homes, leaving two young men to deal with the crisis. One scowled at me suspiciously, the other smiled and took my water bottle and beckoned me to follow him. I was led to the headman's house – no different from the rest – and invited to sit by the door on a block of wood. My helper entered the earthen-floored wooden hut and after some moments returned with the headman – ancient and stiff. He greeted me affably and had a great deal to say, seeming not to realize that a language barrier existed. Then he directed the young man to fill my water bottle. An hour later I discovered that it had been filled not with water but with some mysterious red-brown liquid, spicy and mildly alcoholic.

All afternoon I was overlooking Laos's most precious possession: immense expanses of virgin forest, the ranges sometimes divided by ravines 1,000 feet deep, sometimes separated from my vantage mountain by wide valleys containing rounded, free-standing hills. Often I heard monkeys barking and the harsh call of jungle fowl. Otherwise all was silent and still – no running water, no breeze. Viewing this terrain, inviolate since time began, I wondered if the almost vertical slopes and moat-like ravines could for ever protect it from loggers. Later I learned that the technology needed to 'develop this resource' already exists.

By 4.30 the road was climbing towards swidden slopes and a few little *bans* could be seen beyond a deep jungly valley – shelter for the night? But no pathways appeared. Little daylight remained when I heard the chopping of bamboo: a distinctive sound, more hollow than the chopping of wood. Then a hunter came leaping down the nearby slope, weaving between bamboo clumps, dangling four thrush-sized birds on a vine string. This engaging young man – Mr Phyvan – was cheerfully outgoing and a dogged sign-linguist and had soon invited me to sleep in his home, a mile farther up, on a ridge below the summit.

At the communal water source – a cold, clear, delicious waterfall, bamboo-piped from a cliff face – Mr Phyvan went ahead while I drank avidly and washed perfunctorily. Several amazed youngsters, queuing with buckets and yokes, stood aside in deference to the elder. During the final climb I realized how tired I was – the happy sort of tiredness caused by enjoyable exertion. From here countless lower ranges were visible, stretching away to the east and the south. This Khmu *ban*, a score of small houses, occupied a ledge on the very edge of the ridge, overlooking a grassy ravine 500 feet below – the drop sheer. Mr Phyvan came towards me followed by neighbours of all ages – excited, curious, smiling shyly, some barefooted, many raggedly clad. Clearly he was enjoying this moment of glory as host to the *falang*.

On either side of the Phyvan dwelling a four-step ladder led up to a narrow balcony where shoes were left by those who wore them. In one corner of the living-room a straw matting partition formed a small bedroom. Crossed roof beams supported the thick thatch and split bamboo walls were nailed to a wooden framework; on one hung sheaves of tobacco leaves, on another a small *phi* shrine. Between the doors, Mr Phyvan had built a large mud-brick fireplace, a foot high, edged with stones. The smoke escaped through two little windows until at sunset the shutters were closed and it drifted around the room. But everyone took care to feed the flames cleverly, keeping smoke to the minimum. High above the fire hung an enormous shallow wicker basket containing soup bowls, cooking implements, condiments and precious seeds for the next rice planting. Only a few age-polished stools – six inches high, eight inches wide, twelve inches long – furnished the Phyvan home. For me a mat was unrolled in a corner near the fire.

The animist Khmu are one of the thirty-seven (some say forty-five) different ethnic sub-groups who make up the Lao Theung, approximately 25 per cent of Laos's population. Their languages (not all mutually comprehensible, none with a written script) prove their Austro-Asiatic origin. Probably they are Laos's first inhabitants, a people who in prehistoric times moved north up the Mekong valley, then were pushed into the mountains when the Lao Lum arrived. (A rough translation of Lao Theung is 'the Lao up there'.) Ever since, they have been subordinate to the Lao Lum – socially, politically, economically – and in times past were known as *kha* (slave). The Khmu are the most numerous (about 400,000) Lao Theung group and in their *bans* the shaman, rather than the headman, wields the greatest power. (The Numbri, hunter-gatherers who lived on the highest mountains in the densest forest, are the least numerous – now fewer than 100, so many died when forcibly relocated.)

Tentatively, Mr Phyvan offered rice-beer. My appreciation of this, and my skill at imbibing through the bamboo tube, delighted the family – which included Mrs Phyvan's thirteen-year-old sister and Mr Phyvan's mother, her teeth and mouth hideously disfigured and discoloured by decades of betel-chewing. Mrs Phyvan remained slim, supple and serene-looking after bearing five children, aged nine years to six months. Her husband looked eighteen but was thirty-one; he used his fingers to convey people's ages and everyone watched, giggling incredulously, while I similarly conveyed 'sixty-six'. By then the juvenile neighbours had arrived *en masse*; I counted twenty-five adolescents and children, many with babies on backs, as they sat on the floor, wide-eyed, speculating about me in half-whispers. Photographs of my family, including cats, enthralled them. These, accompanied by the oil-wick lamp, were passed from hand to hand almost reverently, the little ones not being allowed to touch them. For some reason my cats – especially in conjunction with my granddaughters – aroused most excitement.

At the conclusion of this soirée Mr Phyvan cooked supper while his wife fed the pigs and the eldest daughter fetched firewood from under the house. First my host concentrated on the soup, already simmering gently over glowing logs. Repeatedly he tasted it while adding bits of this and that – dried leaves, crushed nuts, pinches of powder – from the overhead basket. Here was a serious cook, getting the balance of flavours precisely right. (At this point I longed for my camera, as the toddler solemnly squatted on the stone edge of the fireplace, holding out her tiny hands to the heat in imitation of the grown-up pose.) Next Mr Phyvan plucked the four birds, having singed their feathers, before grilling them on a bamboo spit: one for each child. The seven-year-old girl then grilled five baby bamboo rats; her eldest brother, assisted by the family bitch, had found a rats' nest in the forest. Small fingers dextrously wrapped the tails around a skewer and when half cooked the fur was neatly scraped off with an incongruously enormous knife. These too were for the children; both birds and rats were eaten whole, guts and all – beaks, legs and tails being crunched with relish.

When everyone had gathered around the rice basket – the adults on stools – Mrs Phyvan ladled the tasty soup into our wooden bowls. It contained chopped bamboo shoots and many interesting small corpses; I recognized only the crabs – an unexpected ingredient, presumably from the nearest river. Raw greens were also served: very palatable, with a strong peppery flavour. This plant grows profusely by the wayside and I was pleased to learn that it could supplement my nuts. The two-year-old sat on her father's knee being fed by him; the baby was on the maternal lap eating soupy rice in a desultory way. Here, too, the older children were included in the animated mealtime conversation and everyone fed the dogs. The bitch had three puppies whose tails, unusually, had been docked. Later, after we had all settled down for the night, there came a desperate whimpering and scratching at one door; a precociously rambling pup had been locked out. When admitted by Mrs Phyvan – in her night attire – he joined his family between me and the fire.

After supper the eldest girl took her baby brother outside. I followed in search of the long-drop and could hear the standard suggestive noises. This Laotian equivalent of potty-training greatly impressed me. At dawn and dusk, and after feeds, babies are taken outside and held in the appropriate position while their minders make a 'Ps-s-s-s-s' sound which almost invariably has the desired effect. How the other excretory activity is coped with I know not, but most Laotian babies look and smell clean at all times. The same cannot be said for 'tribal' children in remote regions and some *falang* passers-by, noting their filthy ragged clothes, deduce that these must be unhealthy youngsters. A minority are of course sickly; this is inevitable where no medical service exists. But on seeing such children naked one is reassured by their well-developed and beautifully proportioned bodies. And their strength astounds as they carry heavy loads up precipices at speed – loads I couldn't carry far on level ground.

Back from the long-drop (communal, on the far side of the *ban*), I retired to my flea-bag and found it complemented by a quilt mattress and cover though the fire blazed only two yards away. Before the family retired my host went to the overhead basket and took something – I couldn't see what – to place in the *phi* shrine. The older three children and their young aunt slept on the far side of the fireplace; Granny occupied a hammock in the bedroom. Twice during the night she emerged to feed the fire and I half woke to hear her chiding the puppies for their mistimed playfulness.

Perhaps the Reverend J.H. Freeman, an American missionary, visited many homes like this. In 1910 he wrote about Laos affectionately if somewhat patronizingly and noted:

> Neither the husband nor the wife is expected to enter upon any important business alone. They share the work, the responsibility, the rewards of their labour. The whole atmosphere of a Laos home is on a plane distinctly higher than we find in any other non-Christian land.

When I stood up next morning the Foot protested and I examined it by torchlight – swollen again, in need of another herbal immersion. But it seemed likely that soon I could freewheel; even in the Annamite Chain, ascents can't go on for ever.

As I was packing up Mr Phyvan reached into the overhead

basket, then offered me one rice seed on his outstretched palm. How was I to react to this obviously significant presentation? Should I eat it, or take it home to Ireland and plant it – or what? Laughing, Mr Phyvan led me towards the *phi* shrine, bowed to it, then indicated that the seed should be put in the shrine for a moment before being transferred to my shirt pocket. Presumably this little ritual gave me a blessing from the household *phi* – but it also aggravated my quandary about offering kip. To do so didn't feel right; not to do so felt mean. As I had feared, the offer offended – but then Mr Phyvan asked for something and when I failed to understand took the packet of photographs from Hare's basket. He wanted a group photograph of my family and gladly I gave it – plus a few others, including the portrait of my cats which had particularly appealed to his children.

At 6.20 I limped off into a freezing fog (visibility ten yards) and within minutes my hands were numb. As the ascent continued – not steeply, by local standards, but relentlessly – that seed in my pocket engendered gloomy thoughts. If Monsanto et al. have their way – as there is every indication they will – no twenty-first-century farmer, anywhere in the world, will be allowed to save seeds. Of all the dirty tricks practised by multinationals, the proposed creation of the Terminator seed, genetically engineered to ensure sterile harvest seeds, is surely the most despicable. And the WTO colludes in the campaign to force all farmers to buy new seeds annually, despite this being so blatantly unjust – a direct bullying attack by the richest of the Rich World on the poorest of the Poor World. Why does the 'international community' cravenly condone such immorality? Why is it not being opposed, with maximum publicity, by the UN High Commission for Human Rights? It is hard to think of any human right more basic than the right of a peasant (or any) farmer to save his or her own seeds. In Laos, and many other countries, seeds have been carefully bred over centuries and are precisely suited to the soils, gradients, competing vegetation, insect populations and climatic caprices of specific areas. Political and civil rights are indeed important. But to millions of Poor World peasants, dependent on subsistence agriculture, the right to save their own seeds is incomparably more important than freedom of assembly, freedom of speech, freedom of the press and so on. In

November 1997, soon after her appointment as UN High Commissioner for Human Rights, Mary Robinson affirmed that 'the whole range of human rights issues must be addressed'. Words cost nothing . . .

Within an hour the cloud began to thin (visibility 100 yards) and I stopped to breakfast: bamboo shoots, provided by Mrs Phyvan. As I chewed enthusiastically a middle-aged, barefooted hunter appeared out of the mist and paused to smile at me, not looking surprised; evidently he knew about the *falang* with the bicycle. Then a nearby bird called twice. The hunter moved to spot his prey, crouched down to aim, fired, dropped his musket beside me and swiftly ascended a steep slope. Ten minutes later he returned, beaming and waving his starling-sized bag. Given the mistiness, how had he seen it, targeted it so accurately – then found it in thick undergrowth? He plucked the wing feathers before putting it in his wicker hunter's pouch, slung over a shoulder.

As the road and the invisible sun rose higher the mist re-thickened, again reducing visibility to a disconcerting ten yards. Then came the relief of a steep descent and cautiously I freewheeled, using both brakes – but not cautiously enough to avoid colliding with a buffalo bull who misfortunately stood ruminating in the middle of the road, his dark grey coat exactly matching the mist. For the Foot this was the last straw; on impact I automatically used it as an extra brake and when the buffalo bellowed I almost did likewise. Here blew a strong cold wind, not shifting the cloud but driving it into me as a chilling drizzle. The next shortish climb was steep yet I shivered despite the exertion.

My mind-over-matter technique was failing, *re* the Foot, when a continuous twenty-two-mile descent, round and round mountain after mountain, delivered me from physical pain. But soon came another sort of pain. Before emerging from the cloud I could hear the ugly whine of electric saws, then a devastated area became visible. For miles the mountains had been stripped naked and churned up by massive machines. On one slope I could see them operating – picking up their victims, carrying them to the road, stacking them for collection by army trucks. Countless trees 'of no commercial value' had been felled by hand to make way for those machines. Anger and grief overwhelmed me. This process is grotesquely described by timber companies as 'harvesting the forest'.

'Harvest' is a comforting, positive word; when the harvest is in, people can feel happy and secure and next year there will be another harvest. The felling of primary forest is the very antithesis of a harvest.

Three times I stopped to try to thaw my frozen hands and to rest my wrists – aching from braking. On this side of the range only patches of tar remained and a Vietnamese-assisted government team had recently begun major repairs. My first stop was outside a road-workers' shack where five men were sitting on a bamboo bed drinking Beerlao for breakfast. I hoped they might sell a bottle to the weary traveller – but one was an army officer so I sped away.

The present role of the Lao People's Army is controversial, not least because of the Mountain Area Development Company, run by the Ministry of National Defence. Between 1991 and 1994 army numbers were reduced from 55,000 to 37,000 and since Soviet subsidies ended the LPA has received no outside funding and neither bought nor repaired weapons – a healthy situation, in my view. Less healthy is the new dependence of ill-paid (or unpaid) soldiers on 'private enterprise'. The US State Department alleges that the Lao government and army are into drug trafficking and encourage the Hmong to grow both opium and marijuana. Given the source of this allegation, one's first reaction is scepticism – nor is there any shred of evidence to link the government with such trafficking. However, the army's peculiar circumstances (local commanders unable to pay their men) make it seem likely enough that certain LPA officers, following the French example, are taxing rural opium traders.

In the old Pathet Lao days the military were required to be versatile, not confining their activities to battlefields but involving themselves, throughout the liberated zones, in political education and socio-economic development. The latter included adult literacy classes and initiating subsistence farmers into the mysteries of collectivization, a daft Marxist notion the peasants soon rejected, quietly but firmly. Now this tradition of versatility is, ironically, being commercialized. Since 1985 exporting timber has been the army's most profitable (legal) activity, yet none of the military personnel involved has been given even the most rudimentary training in conservation.

In *The Quest for Balance in a Changing Laos*, published in 1995 by the Nordic Institute of Asian Studies, the authors issue a warning that the Lao government would do well to heed.

> The minorities are becoming increasingly marginalized in the economic field. They live in the areas that are the least affected by foreign aid and investments and new job opportunities. The most important problem is the conflict over the use of forests. Several provinces, and possibly the army as well, depend on income from the export of timber. For environmental reasons, the central government imposed a general ban on logging from 1991 to 1993 and then a system of quotas, but regulations can be circumvented by arguing that trees need to be cut in connection with the construction of roads or dams. Roads must be constructed in connection with the government's policy of resettling people to stop them from practising slash-and-burn agriculture. Thus, trees can be cut in order to stop the minorities from cutting trees. If the minorities are neither left in peace nor allowed to get their share of the benefits gained from economic growth, the result may be the outbreak of local revolts.

During the last few miles of this descent my hands began to tingle and thaw as the temperature rose perceptibly. Below me lay a sunlit, fertile, bomb-cratered valley – the first expanse of level ground since leaving Xam Nua, so it looked enormous though scarcely six miles wide. A sequence of *bans* lined the road to the little trading centre of Muang Kham at the far side of the valley, below another, lower, mountain range.

9

Trapped in Xieng Khouang

The province of Xieng Khouang became part of French Laos under the terms of the 1893 French–Siamese treaty but it cannot be said that colonialism brought strife and misery to this region. Strife and misery pre-dated 1893 by a few centuries.

Being so close to Vietnam, Xieng Khouang was on the route for numerous invasions into the kingdoms of Luang Prabang and Vientiane. The province once formed part of the Kingdom of Lan Xang and in the fifteenth century its rulers were granted the title of Chao ('king' or 'prince') by the King of Luang Prabang. Later, it sometimes paid tribute to the Annamite emperor, sometimes to the King of Vientiane. In the eighteenth century the Burmese several times made trouble. In 1814–15 the young King Noi had some difficulty defeating a major Kha rebellion. Sixteen years later he was executed by the Annamite emperor; unwisely, he had allied himself with the Siamese, then intent on controlling north-eastern Laos. Subsequently Xieng Khouang came completely under the control of Annam and was renamed Tran Ninh ('Maintaining the Peace') and grievously oppressed. The Lao had to pay high taxes to Annam, as well as to Luang Prabang, and were forced to adopt Annamese clothes and hair styles. When they appealed to Siam for help chaos ensued and thousands were displaced from their homes. In the 1870s the infamous Ho bandits invaded Laos from China and Xieng Khouang suffered more than its share of their devastating attacks; the courageous inhabitants of the city of Xieng Khouang withstood a two-year siege before fleeing to the forest.

Then came the French who inflicted on the peasants corvée labour and exorbitant tax demands – hardships unprecedented, even in Xieng Khouang. The Hmong, especially, detested the colonists and from 1900 to 1922 fought a sporadic guerrilla campaign against the occupying army.

In the 1890s, the French administrator Auguste Pavie chose one of King Noi's sons, Kham Ngon, as puppet ruler. His son, King Sainavong, lived to the age of 102, dying in 1952. The last King, Sai Kham – born in 1918 – was deposed when the Pathet Lao liberated Xieng Khouang.

After the Annamites, that road across the valley seemed crowded; I met three Honda riders, four cyclists and dozens of pedestrians.

Muang Kham is another hastily constructed replacement town and its long straggle of shophouses, bungalows, shacks and small stores seems at first glance characterless. The flags flying from every building puzzled me: the hammer-and-sickle, the Chinese and Vietnamese national flags – but not the new Laotian flag.

Freewheeling slowly down the only street, I looked for an eat-drink shop; at 1.15 p.m. my priority was the satisfying of thirst and hunger, in that order. (Genuine thirst: a need for water.) On a patch of dusty ground, outside a machine repair shop, some twenty men were sitting around a long table, loaded with food and bottles. I stopped and asked, '*Mee nam baw?*' (Do you have water?) Everyone looked pixillated but welcoming and an old man handed me a full tumbler. I half emptied it at a gulp, as one does when very thirsty – then gasped and lost my breath as all that neat *lau-lao* hit an empty stomach. Amidst roars of laughter, I was invited to sit down. A man wearing a suit and shirt and tie – evidently the host – offered me his chair. The other men (this was a mixed-age group) wore casual dress – and not what is known in South Africa as 'smart-casual'. Moments later everyone seemed to have two heads and I felt myself swaying slightly . . . The chuckling old man on my right piled a plate with rice, chicken, pork fat, fish, beef, greens and from somewhere in the background a youth appeared with chopsticks. My inability to use these caused a long search for a spoon. Meanwhile I was urged to eat with my fingers and having started on a second helping of everything I began to understand that this was a Chinese New Year party – hence the flags – being given by the local authorities in honour of Muang Kham's sizeable community of Chinese traders. The guests' intake of *lau-lao* awed me but seemingly the vast amount of food being eaten absorbed it; everyone was merry – some more so than others – yet no one became footless. The only English-speaker (Vietnamese) stood up to tell me that all were pleased to have a foreign guest – but where or what was Ireland? My having come from Xam Nua with a bicycle strained credulity until an army officer gave evidence; he had been in that logging truck met *en route*.

The guidebooks briefly mention Muang Kham and are misleading. 'No accommodation,' they say, ignoring the Government Hotel, run by a charming family and serving excellent food in a large eat-drink shophouse. The owner, Mrs Yinglao, is the keystone of a family of thirteen comprising maternal grandparents, husband and wife and nine good-looking children aged from twenty-one (a son) to three (a daughter). The restaurant prospers, Muang Kham being on the road to the important trading post of Nông Hèt, thirty-eight miles away near the Vietnamese border.

Soukue, the eldest daughter, led me up a slight slope behind the main building to the tin-roofed sleeping-hut (two plank beds in one room, four in the other) built on a stone foundation with walls of wood and wicker. I shared the bigger room with three road-workers who had come to town for the New Year revels. (There is something profoundly civilized about a society where the sharing of sleeping accommodation by strangers of both sexes is taken for granted.) The two-bed room was occupied by Mr and Mrs Bounyong, a congenial Lao Lum couple who, to my delight, spoke quite fluent English. Mr Bounyong, a senior road engineer, was spending a fortnight in the Muang Kham area supervising Route 6. His wife had 'come along for my own reasons'. She was, I later discovered, a senior officer of the Lao Women's Union (LWU).

The loo shed, close to the shophouse, provided no washing facilities and was an unfortunate compromise between Ancient and Modern. A porcelain squat-over had recently been installed but there was no plumbing to match; flushing water had to be fetched from the well and Soukue indicated that used loo paper must be deposited in an open bucket in the corner. A long-drop furnished with squares of banana fronds and treated daily with wood ash is far more hygienic. But Mrs Yinglao was looking forward to the tourists who may soon be streaming – or at least steadily trickling – through Muang Kham. Mrs Bounyong described the loo shed as 'interim'.

Cooking and washing-up were outdoor activities. A hired Khmu youth toiled beside a well from which buckets of clear water were hoisted on a long pole. A wood fire heated cauldrons of washing-up water and boiled the kettle from which mega-thermoses in the restaurant were kept topped up. Dishes drained on the stony ground and food was chopped on a section of tree trunk. Muang Kham is fly-plagued and I tried to imagine how the EU's paranoid health inspectors would react to this juxtaposition of used lavatory paper and a kitchen area . . . But such standards breed fewer diseases than our experts would expect. According to Mrs Bounyong, diarrhoea and dysentery are rare in this region though gastro-enteritis kills quite a few babies.

Hanging from a low tree near the well were two cruelly small cages containing a raven and a larger grey and white bird with bright red legs and a long yellow beak. The latter – his owners claimed – spoke Lao with a Vietnamese accent. Both much enjoyed social intercourse; passers-by who ignored them were summoned back by indignant squawks demanding a civil exchange of greetings.

The guesthouse was pivotal to Muang Kham's Chinese New Year celebrations; in the restaurant, throughout the afternoon, ground-shaking rock music was played non-stop by a group of young men, mostly Chinese and Vietnamese. Finding the decibels intolerably stressful, I went walkabout.

On an adjacent expanse of wasteland brown grass grew raggedly around the rims of five colossal bomb craters and the edges of this expanse were marked by faint traces of house foundations. A few buffaloes and calves and many fowl grazed and pecked between the craters. In the middle of this parody of a village green stood a new gold-painted quasi-Buddhist shrine – no bigger than a household's *phi* shrine – awaiting the installation of President Kaysone's bust. Each city and town thus honours the late President, who died in November 1992. However, no personality cult involving a living leader was encouraged by the Party; nobody's photograph is seen in every government office, school, hospital, police station.

The Vietnamese and Chinese dominate Muang Kham's commercial life – such as it is. In a Vietnamese eat-drink shop I asked for Beerlao but was given instead a small glass of warm, murky brown, home-brewed Vietnamese beer – at least, it was thus described though the effect was almost spiritual and the flavour of almond and cinnamon. Then came a tiny glass of *lau-lao*, a large tumbler of coffee and a plate of sweet titbits – for none of which I was allowed to pay.

At 4.00 I visited the enormous police station to register my presence and found off-duty young men all over the place – sitting chatting on the veranda, cross-legged on their beds playing cards, asleep in offices, repairing a Honda, washing clothes on what might in another environment have been the front lawn. When so many police are stationed in such centres, why does one never see them around? A young man lounging on the steps told me to come back next morning at 9.00 – he pointed to that figure on my watch. He was a Hmong, as were most of his colleagues.

Back at the guesthouse, Mrs Yinglao was negotiating with a hunter. Less than a dollar bought a cock pheasant, much bigger than our breed but less colourful – pale brown back, grey-white flecked breast, very long dark brown tail.

I chose my supper of fried rice, omelette and a salad by pointing to those items in the kitchen. When the meal was served an enormous dead green-brown beetle garnished one lettuce leaf – whether by accident or design one wouldn't know, hereabouts. Surreptitiously, lest it might be rated a choice morsel, I flicked it over the balcony.

The revellers had disappeared – to sleep it off, I over-optimistically assumed – and the tape-deck was silent. As the sun set I bought a packet of candles from Mrs Yinglao and was writing my diary when the young men returned, their numbers considerably augmented by Lao lads and lassies. Then a Toyota van arrived, towing a mobile generator, and much electronic music-making equipment was carried in and set up at the back of the restaurant – while three sons cleared the floor of tables and chairs. The revels, I realized, were only beginning . . . For some reason this generator produced no light and a huge petrol lamp gave trouble as three men tried to pump it into action and then regulate its flame before hanging it from the ceiling. Finally it went 'WHOOSH' and all three – and those gathered around them to give advice – lost eyebrows and forelocks and suddenly regained sobriety. The macabre smell of singed hair still lingered when I retired at 7.30.

Pausing near the door, I looked back at the dancers – illuminated by a row of electric torches placed on a high shelf. Two young men were yelling into the microphone while imitating the sort of demented convulsions indulged in by pop singers on TV. Only a few days previously I had been reading Eric Hobsbawm on the global pop culture: 'even the language of the urban lower classes setting the tone for the patrician market'. And here in Muang Kham was a vivid illustration of the conquest of folk culture by the transnational music and fashion industries. I walked up the slope grieving over all that that conquest entails, in terms of the loss of integrity and individual skills.

Half an hour later a Lao youth arrived to present me with my share of party goodies: minced pork and rice steamed in banana leaves, long strips of sweet coconut, wrapped toffees and tiny nuts coated in hard sugar. I was very touched by this gesture.

Until 2.40 a.m. the generator – parked close to the sleeping-hut – tortured me. It made shuddering, grating, screaming noises like several road drills operating simultaneously and discharged foul fumes that seeped through the wickerwork walls and made my eyes water. I would have gone for a long walk towards Vietnam had the Foot not been in rather a bad mood – so bad that I decided to spend a few days in Muang Kham.

When at last silence fell both Mrs Bounyong and myself had ghastly nightmares. We wondered over breakfast – could so many hours of aural torture, and those poisonous fumes, have induced our exceptionally nasty dreams? The climax of mine was a dead body (strangled, the tongue sticking out and eyes popping) being lowered down a glass shaft in a transparent plastic sack, followed by the murderer who had Hitler's face and slowly sank a few yards from my bed. I closed my eyes to deceive him into thinking I hadn't seen the corpse. But I knew he had observed them open and would return to murder me as a witness. I woke then, my heart hammering, and felt that absurd but very real relief that marks one's escape from a nightmare. There was nothing odd about Hitler's featuring: he is depicted on the cover of Hobsbawm's *Age of Extremes*.

Mrs Bounyong's nightmare also had to do with being threatened, by a man who stole her Honda in Vientiane, pushed her into one of the deep new drainage channels, then went to fetch a bulldozer to bury her alive and however hard she tried she couldn't climb up the slippy mud wall – at which point she awoke screaming and clutching her husband. We realized then that we had been nightmaring at precisely the same time – a slightly disconcerting discovery.

Post-party, my room-mates looked frail at 7 a.m. when they were supposed to return to their high mountain camp. As the jeep wouldn't start and no one could fix it they sat silently on a bench outside our room in identical postures – elbows on knees, heads in hands, occasionally belching or groaning – like allegorical figures on some total abstinence society poster.

At 9.00 every police station door was locked and silence prevailed; one could too easily imagine the hangovers within. I wandered off to the nearby covered market where more than half the stalls were unused and the range of goods was extremely limited; Muang Kham's rebuilders had been too sanguine about its future as a trading post. However, the women merchants kept each other's spirits up by a constant exchange of banter and anecdote.

Poor Hare, having forded so many swift, gravelly rivers, was creaking and squeaking with every revolution of the pedals. At the cycle repair shop almost opposite the guesthouse Mrs Bounyong interpreted for me. A young man diagnosed divers diseases and half dismantled Hare in his determination to cure her. The slightly buckled back wheel was straightened, brake pads and ball bearings were replaced, all the spokes were tightened. The high-tech equipment in use amazed me – though it should not have, given the state of the local roads and the numbers of local bicycles. Cycling fatalities caused by brake failures are common, said the young man. (Like myself, Lao cyclists don't wear helmets – though most affluent urban Honda riders do.) I asked why the sturdier Chinese machines are not favoured over these Thai disasters-waiting-to-happen and the reply was: 'Too many kip for the Chinese and the Thai look better.' Which of course they do if you fancy pink bicycles with Laura Ashley patterned saddles.

At noon, on the police veranda, I passed a subdued, unhealthy-looking queue of men, women and children; the local clinic had recently been closed and the police delegated to dispense such pills, lotions and bandages as were available. This horrified Mrs Bounyong but, remembering Luang Prabang's hospital, I doubted if Muang Kham's clinic would contain anything beyond the capacity of the police to administer.

In the relevant office, a young policeman was dozing on his desk – a New Year victim, eyes bloodshot, mouth dry. He transferred me to a young woman who wrote my 'details' in the usual exercise book which was then locked away in her desk drawer and the key hung on a hook behind the door. There is an endearing *Through the Looking-Glass* flavour about Laotian bureaucracy. But it is also alarming, as the free market wolf pack converges to hunt down profits. Laos is pathetically vulnerable to that pack's propaganda and bribery.

My limp worried Mrs Bounyong and she sent forth a bevy of children to search in the surrounding *bans* for a 'special' ointment. Meanwhile, her prolonged and gentle massaging and manipulating eased the Foot wonderfully. 'Now you put it up on that table,' she ordered, 'and be still.' I obeyed and we talked throughout the afternoon.

The people of Nam Noen – the junction *ban* – are much feared, said Mrs Bounyong, not only because of their magic powers (unusually strong) but because their arcane knowledge of forest poisons makes them seem omnipotent: no one has any antidotes. These poisons are created by mixing juices from the barks of certain trees and one drop on an arrowhead or home-made bullet is lethal to a tiger or a bear – and also to a human, if put in food. When a solitary hunter uses a poisoned bullet or arrow on any large animal, his victim's ears, tail and feet must be cut off and taken home; otherwise the corpse will revive and kill all those who come to carry it back to the *ban*. Nam Noen is one of the few *bans* of its size without a Lao Women's Union group.

According to Marie in Vientiane, the LWU was a rubber-stamping offshoot of the Party until 1988 when suddenly it became effective, perhaps because the Party was then loosening its grip and women like Mrs Bounyong could exert influence. As one would expect, given the traditional role of women in Laos, it operates with more vigour and flexibility than the male-dominated bureaucracies. Its relationships with certain government departments – notably Health, and Agriculture and Forestry – are not always tension-free. Each department tries to relegate 'women's issues' to the LWU, as though these were secondary to 'important issues', but Mrs Bounyong said strenuous efforts are being made to counteract this buck-passing. Now the LWU has more trained staff working on 'integrated rural development' than any other official institution and prides itself on forming strong links with remote communities of little interest to anyone else. Mrs Bounyong (in Xieng Khouang to visit such *bans*) invited me to ride on her carrier next day. 'I'm borrowing a Honda to get to a "model village". You must see how with good leadership even our Khmu people can thrive.'

It impressed me that a senior official of a government institution thought in terms of a borrowed Honda rather than a four-wheel-drive – and also that this couple had preferred Muang Kham's Government Hotel to the Big Spring resort ten miles away. President Kaysone's wife established this resort (roomy bungalows surrounding hot mineral springs) to accommodate state guests from Vietnam – and elsewhere, but not many from elsewhere reached Muang Kham.

Mr Bounyong joined us for an early supper; the New Year party was to be continued after sunset. On the way from Xam Nua, Mr Bounyong informed me, I had passed through territory inhabited (far from the road) by wild buffaloes – Laos's most dangerous animal – by wolves which kill goats and calves, by many deer, many gibbons, a few Asiatic bears and even fewer tigers. Deer are fatally attracted to secondary growth (their equivalent of a five-star hotel) and on such comparatively open ground they become easy game. Mr Bounyong agreed with Mr Pheuiphanh that there is little hope for the most endangered species, so valuable are their livers, gall bladders and other body parts. Nowadays professional poachers, killing for the international market, use AK-47s and sub-machine-guns. The peasants' muskets are partly homemade, the barrels usually modified versions of discarded French army weapons. The shot is bought cheaply by the kilo in local markets, made from those countless tons of metal bequeathed by the USAF.

That evening's party ended at 10.30 when Mr Bounyong, whose government department owned the generator, insisted on his workforce going to bed. Such an exercise in authoritarianism, coming from so mild a man, surprised me – until I divined that

Mrs Bounyong was behind it. She couldn't take another prolonged aural torture session.

At elevenish I was awakened by the arrival of three new room-
mates, young Lao men who, noticing an occupied bed, at once
lowered their voices. They played cards by candlelight until long
after midnight, to the accompaniment of tuneful Vietnamese
tapes. Even without understanding the language, one can enjoy
listening to Lao conversations; people never sound argumenta-
tive, complaining, angry, peevish. And, judging by the laughter
content, most Lao believe in looking on the funny side of
life.

Mrs Bounyong had ordered two early breakfasts and as we ate
our noodles I asked if cows are milked anywhere in Laos. My
friend looked bemused and said of course not, people would
laugh at the idea – they don't know milk is nourishing and anyway
couldn't afford such expensive machinery. Having seen cows in
milking parlours on TV she assumed this food to be available only
to Rich World farmers and looked disbelieving when I recalled
that for millennia all farm animals were milked by hand.

Bumping along a dirt track, we passed a few Thai Dam tombs,
big whitewashed stupas with prayer flags fluttering above them
and piles of rice and the deceased's deliberately broken tools laid
at their base. We also passed a few clusters of four or five houses
where poppies were brazenly blazing in front gardens. When I
drew Mrs Bounyong's attention to these she shouted back over her
shoulder, 'I have not seen them – right?'

Parking the Honda at the beginning of a steep footpath, we
walked up towards the as yet invisible *ban* between plantations of
avocado and bluegum saplings. 'Tree growing is part of this programme,' explained Mrs Bounyong. 'Before, that land was wasted,
only weedy bushes. These people moved from near Nam Noen in
'75 – in a bad way after a cholera epidemic. The bombing made
their water dirty. Here they were hungry for years, with little land
and only rain to water the rice. They were borrowing rice at 300
per cent interest, they were exploited with many children dying
and no hope. Then the LWU got them a UNICEF "integrated rural
development programme" and in '92 they were given fifteen tons
of rice. Their LWU leaders set up a rice bank charging low interest
and in two years saved enough rice to sell and get money to build

a reservoir and irrigation canals. Everyone gave free labour, even small children did small jobs! With water this ground is very fertile, now each hectare gives five tons – maybe more – and nobody is hungry and the children grow strong.'

The *ban*'s forty-two houses stood in groups of four or five on a wide ledge, below the sheer upper half of the mountain. We were received with respectful joy; Mrs Bounyong was a regular visitor and, as a UNICEF success, this *ban* is quite used to admiring *falangs*. Unluckily Haki, its LWU leader, had the day before gone to Pak Xan where her mother was dying. Mrs Bounyong gave Haki much of the credit for the *ban*'s prosperity. An educated Lao Lum, she fell in love with a Khmu man when he was wage-earning as a builder in Pak Xan, to help pay his family's debt to the exploiting rice bank. In defiance of her parents, Haki married this thoroughly unsuitable young man and moved to his desolate *ban* where she has been living happily ever since.

'That was lucky indeed!' said Mrs Bounyong. 'Without her leadership, how could they have known where to look for outside help? In Pak Xan Haki joined the LWU so she knew how to make things work and get everyone motivated. And how to run the programme when it started. Our ignorant minorities need educated leaders. They need more people falling in love with the wrong people! If you didn't fall in love, you'd surely never move from a Mekong town to this mountain – right?'

We walked up to the reservoir, well stocked with fish that need no feeding. Their numbers are carefully controlled; over-fishing is forbidden. From that height we had a splendid view of the whole crater-pocked Muang Kham valley, stretching away to the base of the aloof blue-grey Annamites. Directly below us lay the paddy-fields, a total of sixty-eight hectares; the villagers planted seven hectares of cleared land in '93 and another ten the following year. Each family now has some land but for the clearing of this much the LWU had to fight a long war with the Provincial Agriculture and Forestry Service – a much longer war than if they'd been a logging company.

Returning by a different path, we stopped to admire the new rice-mill, generator-driven, and the four fifteen-foot wells, which never run dry. Then Mrs Bounyong photographed the one-roomed school's new roof. This little building serves too as a health education centre, and an Oral Rehydration Scheme has saved many children's lives. A credit system for rearing pigs and poultry has been set up, with training for those who never before could afford to own livestock. The 'development committee' has also bought a bicycle for communal use and everyone was fascinated to hear that the grey-haired *falang* granny was travelling by bicycle. Leaping on to my soap-box, I asked Mrs Bounyong to translate a message from me: 'Stick with your bicycle, or bicycles if possible – then when you're old you will be healthy like the *falang* granny!'

We drank herbal tea with four Lao Lum women who now live here and are teaching their neighbours how to weave – not, traditionally, a Khmu skill, but in Phonsavanh there is an expanding tourist market for weavings. 'This is what our government wants,' said Mrs Bounyong, 'to have people nicely helping one another, not being superior about minorities. Here our programme has gone so well because the LWU has a good policy against people getting greedy and lazy. After all the war traumas, and sitting waiting for rice from Americans, Chinese, Thais, Vietnamese, we want our people to do for themselves again, to be independent like always before. We don't want them to get the habit of looking for more and more help. UNESCO offered more to this programme but we said no. Fifteen tons is enough for a small community, with that they can make things all right – the way they have done.'

When Muang Kham's populous valley was carpet-bombed uncounted thousands died and eventually 365 villagers from Ban Na Meun decided to take refuge in Tam Phiu, a vast limestone cavern similar to the Vieng Xai caves. Within, they built a two-storey bomb shelter, then tried to conceal the entrance with a high stone wall. For almost a year they lived there, emerging at night to cultivate their fields, but reconnaissance planes spotted the entrance in February 1968 and, allegedly, the American military commanders suspected that here was a Pathet Lao hospital. On 8 March, at sunrise, two T-28 fighter-bombers took off from the Udon Thani airbase in Thailand to attack Tam Phiu. The defensive wall was demolished by the first rocket. The second rocket penetrated to the back of the cave before exploding. No one survived.

To find Tam Phiu I retraced my wheelmarks along Route 6 for a few miles, then turned on to a little-used track undulating along the base of the Annamites. Barbed wire fencing, rarely seen in Laos, enclosed a scrubby area where UXO abounds. I pedalled slowly, my eyes nervously fixed on the track, remembering the warnings received about 'bombis' working their way to the surface as time passes – especially on slopes. After a few miles I parked Hare where an expanse of liquid mud, bridged by bamboo poles, blocked the track – which then became a footpath winding through dense bush beside a stream. Quite soon a small concrete irrigation dam appeared – built in 1981 – and directly above it, half-way up the steep side of a low mountain, was Tam Phiu. I decided to stop there; a path exists but was invisible and I didn't feel like searching for it among UXO. Not long before, the UK Mines Advisory Group had defused a mighty bomb found in the stream below the dam.

Coincidentally, this was another still, silent, grey-skied morning – recalling Vieng Xai. All around the cave mouth (some thirty yards wide and fifteen feet high) a tall auburn grass covered the slope. Lower down grew silver-tipped feathery bamboo and golden elephant grass and masses of blue-bush. At the base of a nearby jagged karst hill are buried the 365 men, women and children of Ban Na Meun, slaughtered by youngsters who took their orders from the Pentagon's war criminals. The most infamous of these was the late unlamented General Curtis Le May. His ambition 'to bomb the Communists back into the Stone Age' has often been quoted but repetition does not lessen its chill factor.

I sat on the dam and thought about the fear and suffering and bewilderment of those who sought refuge in Tam Phiu – families such as I had been staying with, knowing nothing of superpower rivalry, no more 'Communist' than I am (maybe less so), only aware that to have any chance of survival they must hide. Which of us can appreciate the terror felt as T-28s swept down that valley day after day, month after month, year after year? It is salutory to focus on specific examples of twentieth-century brutality; deluges of statistics merely numb us, which is dangerous. The next stage may be the sort of callousness that accepts such brutality as 'regrettable but inevitable', to quote President Clinton on Serb civilian casualties during another illegal war.

That evening Mrs Bounyong triumphantly produced the 'special ointment', allegedly a blend of tiger bone marrow, bear fat, the ground horn of a wild sheep (or goat), the essence of a cobra's spine (simmered non-stop for seven days and nights) 'and other things'. She completely trusted the medicine woman who sells these cures but I hoped she had been cheated. Who knows what this precious unguent cost, yet an offer to pay would have grievously insulted my generous friend.

Again we supped together, by the light of a storm lantern which drew an entomologist's cornucopia to our table. Mr Bounyong asked about my future plans, then broke the bad news. His job required him to be aware of the real (not rumoured) local security risks and the roads from Phonsavanh to Pak Xan and to the Route 13 junction had recently been closed to all traffic. 'A temporary measure,' he added, 'but you're trapped in Xieng Khouang! There's no way out on a bicycle.'

Like most Lao, Mr Bounyong was noncommittal about the nature of this recurring security problem. But by then I felt sufficiently at ease with the Bounyongs to speak out; they were already aware of my political position. Boldly I recalled that conversation in Luang Prabang about the heroin component in security 'situations'. Mr Bounyong smiled and said drily, 'Different people have different theories – and they may all be right.'

Mrs Bounyong drank only Pepsi but her husband enjoyed his *lau-lao* of an evening and as time passed he became more expansive. It was well known, he declared, that for many years after '75 remnants of the Hmong army had been encouraged to 'keep up the struggle against the Commies', a way of life not easily abandoned when NEM made that struggle superfluous. Those remnants cherish their own 'ideology of opposition' and have a vested interest in dominating remote districts where flourishes the poppy. More than 10,000 Hmong remain illegally in northern Thailand, hiding in a warren of karst caves and regularly crossing the Mekong with supplies of dollars and weapons for the guerrillas or bandits or drug traders – however one chooses to describe them. It is unlikely that they make their return journeys empty-handed.

The Lao government accuses the Thai-based militia and the wealthy us-based Lao Family Community (LFC) of 'encouraging rebellion'. The LFC, founded by 'General' Vang Pao, commander of the Secret Army, is supported by 100,000 Hmong exiles and their American sympathizers. In November 1997 they organized a rally on Capitol Hill and demanded Washington's help in their campaign to overthrow the Lao government and 'recapture their homeland' – as though the Hmong had once been in control of Laos! The troglodytes in Thailand are lavishly funded by their Californian cousins, all us citizens. Many male exiles of the older generation still express a willingness to 'fight the Commies'.

I said, 'You are the first Lao to tell me plainly how things are. And I get the impression most Lao genuinely don't know – are confused, only hearing rumours. Why the official secrecy?'

'People don't need to know,' replied Mr Bounyong. 'It is unbalancing the country if there is talk about rebels and guerrillas. After so much conflict, our government's priority has to be stability and calm.'

In consultation with the Bounyongs, I then made a new plan: fly to Vientiane after some days in Phonsavanh, take a bus south to Tha Khaek and from there cycle back to Vientiane when the Foot had recovered from its over-exertions *en route* to Muang Kham. Mrs Bounyong would soon be in Phonsavanh and we arranged to meet again.

The road to Phonsavanh – narrow and semi-tarred – passes through several *bans* before leaving the valley. In one I observed a most ingenious example of private-enterprise-cum-intermediate-technology. A roadside stream had been dammed and within it a metal wheel – probably donated by the USAF – was connected to a thin wire, available in any market, which ran up to the top of a high bamboo pole and then across the road to a house on stilts. When I dismounted to view this contraption a smiling young father, his newborn baby in a front sling, proudly switched on the two living-room bulbs that reward his ingenuity. Being technologically uneducated, I would not have known what questions to ask even had I spoken Lao. But I presume this innovation was possible because his home happened to be opposite a fast stream where it could be dammed – and because he had somehow acquired that wheel and the necessary know-how, both foreign imports.

On the first bumpy stretch Hare's basket fell off, to the great amusement of five schoolchildren who stopped to watch me securing it to the handlebars with an elastic web. That seemed a bad omen – and it was . . .

A rattling wooden bridge spanning a lively little river marked the beginning of a gradual climb. This was mostly cycleable, around mountains still forested – unlike the severely swidden-spoiled slopes beyond a deep valley on my right. By 10.15 the road was running level below a long karst wall; here the clouds suddenly dispersed and the colours of the rock peaks glowed: russet, silver, pinkish. Then, without warning, Hare ceased to function; for some esoteric reason the pedals simply wouldn't revolve.

Given my disability, a twenty-mile walk was not to be considered. I sat hopefully by the wayside. Thus far two vehicles had passed me: an antique overcrowded Peugeot saloon and a truck-bus containing as many calves as people. Close to the road, at the base of the karst wall, avocado trees half hid twenty or so stilted wooden houses. Dozens of seven-foot-high tiptanks fenced their large vegetable plot and two half-bombs formed the gate of an approach path. The women's headgear – colourful scarves, worn turbanwise – indicated that here was another Khmu *ban*.

Soon the volume of traffic increased: two jumbo taxis, a petrol tanker coming from Vietnam, two road-workers' trucks loaded with tree trunks, an army jeep, another truck-bus. Nobody could or would rescue the *falang* though most drivers slowed to stare. Meanwhile the villagers had been observing me from a distance and when the bus failed to stop, despite my frantic gesticulations, an elderly woman and a one-armed youth came slowly towards the gate. I stood to greet them and the youth said, 'Madame, you are with a problem?'

As I explained my problem his grandmother looked from me to Hare and back again with a mixture of puzzlement and pity – why was this old *falang* lady so poor, not able to buy even a Honda? Then she invited me to spend the night; next morning, when her nephew passed, driving a truck to Phonsavanh, he would give me a lift.

Mr Bounkhoun, the eighteen-year-old, wheeled Hare up the path and told me how he began to learn English – in Vientiane's hospital after an encounter, while ploughing, with a twenty-pound fragmentation bomb. The Mennonite Mines Advisory Group gave him 'Teach Yourself' tapes and a Walkman but sometimes he couldn't afford new batteries. Having lost his right arm from near the shoulder he was determined to become a tourist guide 'after my English is more improved and I get money for a wood arm and a Honda'. He begged me to correct his mistakes as we talked.

My hostess, Mrs Bounthanh – the headman's wife – looked much older than her sixty-five years. Her husband was the only septuage-narian in this community of 160 or so, the majority aged under twenty. He could just remember the move down from Houaphanh; he was then a small boy. Having cleared some land, these Khmu bred big herds of cattle and buffaloes and 'nobody was hungry'. When the bombing started they couldn't understand it, they had never before seen an aeroplane, they knew nothing about places called the United States and the Soviet Union. For the children they dug shelters at the base of the rock wall – here are no caves – but those pathetic attempts at self-defence were futile. In 1969 a bomb killed Mrs Bounthanh's first three children, aged six, four and two. In June 1970, when everyone was out working in the fields, another bomb killed Mr Bounthanh's three sisters and two of his wife's brothers. Within the next month, all the *ban*'s homes were levelled and all their cattle killed. The survivors fled to an overcrowded displaced persons' camp near Vientiane, where malaria and dysentery killed many more children. In 1975 they returned and for several years lived in rattan shacks on the ground, while collecting the wood for their present homes.

All afternoon we sat on the balcony with Grandad, who moved stiffly and breathed with a whistling wheeze. In 1988 a man working two fields away from him struck a bombi (cluster bomb) with his hoe and died instantly: bombis inflict damage over an area of 5,000 square yards and Mr Bounthanh will never fully recover. He lifted his shirt and pointed to his ribcage; numerous steel pellets were visible under the skin. Others are invisible – the cause of his difficult breathing. In 1996 his niece was killed with her four small children while weeding in her field between Muang Kham and Nông Hèt. In the same field, her husband had been killed five months previously. But this was their only field; if they didn't cultivate it they would have no food. Several years ago, said Mr Bounkhoun, the American Mennonite Peace Church donated 30,000 shovels to replace hoes, which strike the earth like hammers. But shovels, though less likely to detonate UXO, do not suit the Laotian terrain and the loss of efficiency tempted many to revert to their hoes.

This was the poorest *ban* I stayed in – UXO poor. Cultivable land was nearby; I had been overlooking it, far below on the banks of the Nam Ghouan, as I sat by the roadside. But everyone feared its contents. And their poverty was exacerbated by the government's attempts to 'modernize' Laos. Like Mr Tang, Mr Bounkhoun resented official interference with 'the ways we had for living'. He complained, 'Before we go cut firewood, to sell in Phonsavanh, we must to buy permit from the District [Agriculture and Forestry Service] Office. Bombis stop us to use all our land, we have not half a hectare for each family, but everyone must sign a document not to clear land in the mountains. My grandfather must make everyone sign this before he take to District Office. For people who cannot sign, he makes their markings. The same time a big wind [a typhoon, in October 1994] spoiled most of our rice. All here was hungry and hungry next year for we have no enough seeds. And that year they said we must to pay land tax. It is not possible! Many babies are born here but maybe one from three die before talking. They have no strength for living. There is families in this place never have kip, never touch or use it – how can they pay tax?'

Under the house next door I could see five old women making roofing panels, their worn fingers still swift and nimble. Khmu women are famous for this skill. 'They bring important kip to their families,' said Mr Bounkhoun. The gathering of the grass, from far away, takes much time and energy – but that, to the Lao, doesn't seem like a problem. This was the re-roofing season: all over the country thatches were being repaired or replaced. Often I had passed women carrying loads of these beautifully made panels to the nearest market.

The *ban*'s pig population seemed reassuringly high but there was an odd absence of poultry; during the last rainy season all had died, within a week, and people hesitated to invest in replacements. Such epidemics are not uncommon in Laos. At sunset numerous cattle were herded into a communal corral; each family owns three or four, said Mr Bounkhoun, but there are only five buffaloes to do all the ploughing. Then he pointed to two bamboo pipes fixed to a stream racing down the cliff: 'This way we are lucky, good water comes to us every time in the year.' Both men and women were fetching water but only men – accompanied by their older children – were returning from the forest with head-loads of firewood. Khmu women leave this task to their menfolk who now – Mr Bounkhoun said bitterly – need the headman's permission to cut even enough for domestic use. 'So many laws is bad, no one can do what they say to do in the offices but we are made afraid what will happen us if we get seen doing the wrong thing.'

Traditionally the Khmu are patrilocal but the disruptions of the war and post-war years, and contact with Lao Lum families around Vientiane, have brought about adaptations. The headman's household consisted of grandparents, Mr Bounkhoun the young-est grandson, a married granddaughter and her husband and five children. Normally, after the first birth, the young couple would have built their own home. But having to pay for a permit to cut trees made this impossible. The grandson-in-law, a shy man who seemed almost scared of me, came from a highland *ban* and before moving he had to sacrifice a pig to placate his parents' house *phi*. Since the war, many Khmu have given up paying a bride price though the bride's parents still try to endow the young couple with quilts, pillows and some livestock.

Here my presence did not attract the usual juvenile attention; tourists take taxis from Phonsavanh to view nearby 'minority vil-lages'. We dined by oil-wick light, my host and Mr Bounkhoun sitting with me on a mat near the door – all these houses were windowless. The others ate at the shadowy far end of the room, beyond a large *phi* shrine decorated with fresh flowers. This was the only piece of furniture, if it may be so described. Our noodle soup, faintly onion-flavoured, contained none of the interesting ingredients to which I had become accustomed. There was nothing else; Mrs Bounthanh apologized for the lack of rice. The children looked – were – underfed. To the outside world, the Second Indochina War is away in the past – history. To many thousands of Lao, it continues to determine their present and future.

Mrs Bounthanh's nephew stopped his covered lorry by the gate soon after 9.00. It seemed to be a retired military vehicle, much modified – in fact 50 per cent home-made – and the cab's passenger seat was piled high with rusty bomb casings. (In Phonsavanh such scrap metal was then fetching 200 kip for ten kilos.) When Nephew had roped Hare to the plank roof I climbed inside. On three layers of rice sacks sat a Hmong granny, her daughter, two grandsons and a Khmu couple with a year-old baby who was being fed a banana in tiny pieces. The adults welcomed me with shy smiles, the children at first looked uneasy. I settled myself on the end of the load, my legs squeezed between the sacks and a pile of bamboo poles. While cycling, this road surface had seemed tolerable – now it seemed positively dangerous as we hit the tarless hollows. I remembered breaking a rib in similar circumstances in Madagascar and, since this journey had so far been rather jinxed, I clung to a metal strut (ex-USAF) which did not save my head from being banged repeatedly on another strut supporting the roof.

This district is quite densely populated and we stopped in a few biggish Hmong *bans* to deliver rice, take on huge bundles of sugar cane and roofing thatch and exchange some of the bamboo poles for more bomb casings – tightly packed around my legs. During the first stop three pigs (two grown sows and a half-grown male) were dragged screaming from a hut to be loaded on to the tailboard below me. When their feet had been roped together they shrieked with pain and struggled desperately as three men – two operating from within the lorry – lifted them by the ropes and by their long ears. Once in place (on their backs, the ropes tied to a strut) they were silent – apart from piercing squeals when the more sensational bumps hurt them.

Thinking about our ill-treatment of animals in transit, I wondered if such cruelty almost inevitably goes with butchering. Here a certain malformed logic is dimly discernible: if an animal is about to be killed, why treat it kindly? Consideration for individual animals involves forging an emotional link – which contradicts slaughtering them for food or profit.

What baffles me about Western animal rights campaigners is their failure to protest loudly enough against the separation of calves from their mothers, surely an even greater cruelty than that inflicted during comparatively brief journeys to abattoirs. In Laos and elsewhere I have often observed bovine family life and mutual affection is evident, the calves not only suckling but at intervals bounding over to seek a few reassuring licks, then taking off again to do their own thing. Amongst African cattle-owning tribes, where milk is part of the daily diet, it is shared with the calves. But commercial farming eliminates civilized behaviour.

10

In and around Phonsavanh

Phonsavanh, meaning 'Heavenly Ground', is something of an overstatement. This new provincial capital (population about 25,000) was founded in the mid-'70s to replace Xieng Khouang, twenty miles to the south. At that date Laos had none of the resources needed to create a new town/city, yet one can understand why Phonsavanh was improvised. The total destruction of Xieng Khouang will be long remembered as the Secret War's worst act of cultural vandalism. That ancient city was much more than a provincial capital; for 500 years it had been one of Laos's three religious capitals – Luang Prabang and Vientiane the others – and its numerous rich and beautiful wats, some dating from the sixteenth century, were distinctive in design and decoration. Now nothing remains: not a stone is left upon a stone. And Xieng Khouang, spiritually and architecturally so precious and significant, could not be rebuilt. Its reduction to rubble had to be accepted as final. A dismal little town – Muang Khoune – today occupies that site. I funked visiting it.

Phonsavanh's setting on the northern edge of the Plain of Jars, semi-encircled by wooded ridges, is pleasant enough. But the town's shapeless sprawl of concrete slabs and tin sheeting, with a tarred strip running down the centre of two wide main streets, seems closer to hell than to heaven. Other roads overlook the surrounding cratered paddyfields and a few large stagnant ponds. The banks, government offices, police station and post office stand on wasteland. Everything looks unplanned and unfinished, as though this urban project had been abruptly abandoned at an early stage – which may well be the case, given the circumstances of the 1970s. Phonsavanh is also the dustiest town I have ever been in – and before pronouncing this judgement I searched my memory carefully. Motor traffic is minimal but on windy winter days a dust cloud replaces vehicle pollution. And the social atmosphere is uneasy – not tense but curiously restless, as if people feel they don't belong (which in a sense they don't, being recent transplants) and can't take seriously Phonsavanh's status as a provincial capital. Yet individually the inhabitants, representing a bewildering tribal mix, are friendly.

The Plain of Jars is not really a plain but an undulating plateau: altitude a bit above 3,000 feet, area some 650 square miles. As for the jars – who knows? They have been around for at least 2,000 years, man-made and standing all over the plain. Now they attract a steady trickle of tourists; many fly up from Vientiane before noon, 'do' the jars that afternoon and fly away next morning. However, some locals evidently have faith in the future and Phonsavnh is over-supplied with hotels for the rich and guesthouses for the rest. Not that the rich would normally stay in such hotels but everything is relative – and more relative than usual in Laos.

In the Vinhthong guesthouse – a bungalow, with annexes, on the main street – everything was simple but clean. My US$2 room had a squat-over and hand-basin *en suite* and the plumbing worked; electricity was restricted to 6–9 p.m. but candles were provided; through the rattan walls I could hear my neighbours snoring. No food was provided but guests were invited to help themselves to boiling water from the thermoses behind the 'bar' – four empty shelves and a locked tin icebox containing Beerlao and Pepsi. (A Pepsi factory is one of Laos's few industries.) In the bar much ordnance was on display and, illegally, for sale to *falangs* craving bombi souvenirs. The affable middle-aged owners were shrewdly entrepreneurial in a gentle way. ('Gentle' is the word that most often springs to pen when writing about the Laos.) Every forenoon the eldest son, who spoke a little English and more French, drove their smart new minibus to the airstrip to offer rich tourists transport to the jars' sites. His younger brother pursued the more thrifty backpackers, hoping to be hired as a guide when they clubbed together to share a tuk-tuk. The youngest brother, aged ten, was to be seen every morning watering a rockery which their resourceful mother had recently created below the veranda.

In the central market, meagrely stocked and apathetic, I sought a basket for Hare and another camera. At one stall a young Vietnamese merchant, sharp eyed and sour faced, tried to over-charge me 90,000 kip for a Japanese Konica. Ten minutes later an agreeable Lao woman sold me the same model for 50,000 kip (£16). Nowhere could I find a bicycle basket.

Not far from the market was a mechanic's empty shophouse – smelling of incense, as most homes do after the morning offering to their guardian *phi*. I sat on a stool and waited. The young man who appeared twenty minutes later had been taught English by his Hmong grandfather who fled to Thailand in 1975, learned English in a refugee camp and returned home in 1992. When Mr Khamvone condemned poor Hare as 'a very bad bicycle' there was nothing I could truthfully say in her defence. It seemed the Muang Kham mechanic, despite (or because of?) all his high-tech gadgetry, had done more harm than good when replacing ball bearings. Mr Khamvone devoted forty minutes to repairs, then set off on his Honda in search of a basket. Returning half an hour later, he would accept payment only for the basket. He smiled and bowed and said, 'I enjoy helping you.' Too soon he was to have more enjoyment of the same sort.

At sunset I supped in an eat-drink shop tempted by tourism to pretend to be a restaurant. The menu read: 'Offal Salad – Friend EEGS – Cooked LAP – Raw LAPP – OB JAN – Sukiyaki – Bred&Butre.' I chose the salad, ob jan and sukiyaki, being unable to imagine the nature of these dishes. But alas! none was available and I had to settle for mundane EEGS and Bred&Butre – the butter Thai margarine.

Mrs Bounyong's ointment did provide some relief, but not much. At 6.30 next morning I ate stale buns in my room to accommodate the essential painkillers; now, for the first time, the Foot was throbbing when not in use.

An hour later Phonsavanh was beginning to wake up but it does not cater for early breakfasters. In a dimly lit eat-drink shop opposite the guesthouse a charming man had problems preparing my coffee and repeatedly apologized for the delays. As his primus wouldn't light he had to borrow a thermos from a neighbour. Then he could find no milk in his cupboard and my pleas for black coffee went unheeded – or not understood. His expedition to buy a tiny tin of Nestlé's condensed milk took fifteen minutes. A plate of revoltingly sweet biscuits was served with the coffee (no charge) and those I left were presented to me in a plastic bag. Given the cost of the milk and the biscuits, and the few kip I paid for the coffee, there can have been no profit in this transaction.

Hare seemed in good form when we took off; for some twenty miles south of Phonsavanh I could cycle unhindered, Mr Bounyong had assured me. Then comes the military roadblock at Ban Hai.

In midwinter the Plain of Jars does not look at its best. Beyond Phonsavanh rise low hills, meanly wooded or bare and eroded, and the pulverized expanses of grassland are an unpleasant brownish black; few natural colours displease but this was quite depressing. Many bomb craters are thirty yards wide and twenty feet deep; in some trees have taken root, others are now fish ponds.

Most of the Secret War's ferocious ground fighting took place on this plain. Seasonally it changed hands – being held in the dry season by the Pathet Lao and North Vietnamese, in the wet season by the RLA and 'General' Vang Pao's Hmong troops. When the shooting started the RLA Lao Lum usually and very sensibly ran away, leaving the Hmong to do the killing and be killed. Mrs Bounyong had described Xieng Khouang as 'our victim province' and quoted a Lao proverb: 'When the buffalo fight the grass is flattened.' It is hard to believe that this was once a self-sufficient region where large cattle herds thrived and French planners dreamed of colonists happily settling here to grow tea in the cool climate on the fertile soil. I passed a few dejected-looking Hmong resettlement *bans* and a Swedish conifer plantation covering miles of hillside. A notice on the wire fence said: REGENERATION PROJECT, 1992. If only regeneration were so easy!

When the morning mist lifted, high mountains were visible away in the distance, dusky blue against a clear blue sky. Somewhere among them was the hidden city of Long Tien, the US/Hmong army headquarters, founded in 1962 by the CIA and soon the second biggest city in Laos, with 20,000 inhabitants – yet never marked on any map and only referred to by its code name 'Alternate'. Its amenities included all-weather airfields, the most modern communications equipment and a US-style hospital.

Nearby was a resettlement area run by USAID for hill tribes (60 per cent Hmong) who had fled from the bombing. By mid-1971 USAID reckoned they were looking after 150,000 displaced people, incorrectly referred to by them as 'refugees'. These unfortunates were running away from the USAF but American propaganda used their migration south to 'prove' that the Communists were 'hated and feared'. Their concentration in area one also had another use, as Professor Alfred McCoy explains:

> This area served as a buffer zone, blocking any enemy advance on Vientiane. If the Pathet Lao and North Vietnamese chose to move on Vientiane they would have had no choice but to fight their way through the resettlement area. Hmong leaders, well aware of this danger, pleaded with USAID to shift the resettlement out of the probable line of an enemy advance. Knowing that the Hmong fought better when their families were threatened, USAID refused . . . Most of the Hmong had no desire to continue fighting for Vang Pao. They regarded him as a warlord who had grown rich on their suffering. But since USAID decided where the rice was dropped, the Hmong had no choice but to stand and fight.

Those rice drops were important American weapons; the threat to stop them was repeatedly used to force those left in the *bans* to obey CIA orders. Rice could no longer be grown when all the men, and boys as young as ten, had been recruited. Therefore opium production greatly increased. Women had always grown this crop unaided and since the beginning of the twentieth century the Plain of Jars had been north-east Laos's opium trading centre.

In Long Tien, Vang Pao built himself a large heroin laboratory supervised by a Chinese chemist. For a few years raw opium was flown to this 'facility' from all over northern Laos by Air America planes and helicopters. Then, in 1967, the CIA and USAID helped the 'General' – financially and otherwise – to buy two C-47s and form his own private airline, Xieng Khouang Air Transport. On the Long Tien–Vientiane run, opium and heroin were the main cargoes. Air America helicopters, piloted by Americans, dropped Vang Pao's agents – uniformed Secret Army majors and captains – at certain *bans* where they spent a few days collecting the local harvest before radioing for the 'copter to return and take them and their merchandise to the 'General's' laboratory. In 1971 Hmong farmers received US$500 for ten kilos of raw opium. After processing, that became one kilo of No. 4 heroin worth $2,500 in Bangkok and about $23,000 in the US when sold in bulk to a dealer. Adulterated and packaged, the $500 worth of opium bought in a Lao *ban* was worth $225,000 on the streets of New York or San Francisco.

When Ban Hai came into view it was identifiable through binoculars because of the army trucks parked nearby. I turned back then, lest some soldier might think it his duty to drive me to Phonsavanh.

Three hours later, Hare's chain not only fell off but came to pieces. Mercifully I was by then within a mile of Mr Khamvone, who welcomed me back with a bow and a concerned look. On his removing the chain-guard, we saw that not a speck of dust had penetrated it – so after all Hare did have one redeeming feature. We also saw a multitude of tiny bits and Mr Khamvone spent over an hour linking them together. (A new chain was not an option in Phonsavanh.) He then took Hare for a trial run – and, incredibly, the back brake cable snapped. Again my knight rode off on his steed, leaving me in charge of his three-year-old son. As the boy played with a small plastic fork-lift truck, no more than six inches long, his ingenuity and concentration greatly impressed me; clearly this toy was being 'imagined' into various other forms. I remembered the Lao children's concentration span when Joan Clanchy wrote in the *Independent*:

> There are middle-class children whose cupboards of toys are enough to equip a nursery school, but they rarely play with them for long. This is partly because plethora works against play, partly because their pace of life does not encourage any sustained activity. They rush from stimulation to excitement and then flop in front of a video . . .

When Mr Khamvone had fitted the new cable I didn't ask 'How many kip?' but firmly handed him 20,000. Equally firmly, he returned 19,000; the cable, he affirmed, had cost only 1,000.

It was 3.45 – linnertime. In what was to become my favourite eat-drink shop, the Nang Phonkaew on the main street, I shared a table with two young Norwegians who were horrified to see me eating roast pork. They were not vegetarians, they explained, but 'It's so dangerous to eat meat in these countries!' To them, unhygienic slaughtering methods and flies and 'what the pigs eat' spell danger; they looked baffled on hearing that I operate in reverse. To me, pigs who include human faeces in their diet (as pigs will, when such delicacies are available) seem much safer, as well-cooked pork, than pigs stuffed from the moment of birth with antibiotics, steroids and unnatural feeds.

When they heard that I had been trying to trek, Marika and Ton again looked baffled.

'But it's not possible!' exclaimed Marika. 'Our guidebook says in Laos the trekking industry is not yet developed.'

Over the past few decades, the verbs 'to trek' and 'to camp' have changed their meanings. Now most of the young associate those activities with an organized (by someone else) Adventure Holiday. Or, if not travelling in a group, they look for commercial campsites providing hot showers, cooking and laundering facilities, electricity and 'security'. Camping used to mean finding a level spot where you could put up your tent, preferably within reach of firewood and running water. This, I gather, is now known as 'camping wild' and generally regarded as a life-endangering form of eccentricity. Which clearly it isn't or I and thousands like me wouldn't still be around.

As for a 'trekking industry' – apart from making money for those who run it, why should it be considered necessary? Why must market forces intrude into that space where individuals should be at their most liberated – planning holidays or more extended journeys? Much of the happy excitement of travel is in the planning; normally intelligent people are quite capable of organizing their own treks in whatever region most appeals. This commercialization of trekking, camping, swimming, cycling (with a vehicle to carry luggage!) can only breed wimps. But then the consumer society needs wimps. It needs to discourage independent thought and action. While politicians stress the 'rights of the individual', and free marketeers glorify 'freedom of choice', the 'want-makers' are subliminally persuading us that an industry must cater for our travelling impulses.

*

The first vehicle I saw in Phonsavanh was a dusty, well-worn blue Land Rover with a Union Jack sticker on the back – the Mines Advisory Group (MAG) personnel carrier, I rightly assumed.

In Vientiane I had met John Humphreys, MAG's Project Director for Laos. At once we realized that we had met before, in London in 1992 – two years after MAG was founded in Afghanistan by Rae McGrath. Its aim is 'to establish mine survey, mine clearance and mine awareness programmes so that rural communities can live without fear of death and maiming by mines . . . to establish an indigenous capacity to respond to the long-term problem by training selected local people from the affected communities'. By 1998 MAG was working in North Iraq/Kurdistan, Angola, Cambodia – and Laos, where UXO make landmines look like a minor problem.

To try to make comprehensible Laos's record as 'the most-bombed country in the world' it has been estimated, using the Pentagon's figures, that the Secret Air Force flew 1.5 times the number of sorties flown throughout the Vietnamese campaign. Those 580,944 sorties dropped an average of one planeload of bombs every eight minutes, twenty-four hours a day, for nine years, from 1964 to 1973. Approximately 1.9 million metric tons were dropped: ten tons per square kilometre of Laotian territory, or more than half a ton per unit of population.

When 'millions' of anything are mentioned my mind usually goes numb but the wall map in the MAG office got through to me. It shows how contaminated the various provinces are – only three out of eighteen escaped bombing, all in the north-west. Red dots on a white background mark severely contaminated areas and within Xieng Khouang province virtually no white remains visible. The same is true of the southern provinces where ran the Ho Chi Minh Trail. In 1997, twenty-four years after the end of the war, 2,861 *bans* (25 per cent of the total) reported the presence of unexploded bombs within their district and 948 were contaminated in the village centre, where explosions usually claim multiple victims. For 375 *bans*, UXO along local tracks or footpaths limited trade and communications. In 1,156 *bans*, bombs from 100 to 1,000 kilos were present; 782 reported mortar shells, 555 reported projectiles from artillery and armoured vehicles; 'only' 214 had found landmines nearby.

Most UXO consists of anti-personnel cluster-bomblets, found in and around 1,553 *bans* in 1996. These 'bombis', no bigger than a tennis ball, cause the majority of deaths and maimings. The model most often found by MAG is the BLU-26, containing 100 grams of high explosive with 300 ball bearings embedded in a steel casing; each casing held 670 bomblets and more than 90 million were dropped. Between 20 and 30 per cent remain unexploded – most of them lying, as I write, in paddyfields, under bushes and boulders, in the forest, in streams, under houses. Their high failure rate (the expected failure rate was 10 per cent) has a 'logical' explanation. The American manufacturers were using Laos as a testing ground for this new type of ordnance, later dropped lavishly on El Salvador, Afghanistan, Cambodia, Iraq, Serbia – anywhere of interest to the US military. Twelve other types of cluster-bomblets were also tested on Laos but the manufacturers refuse to give any information about these.

Bombis are not like landmines, designed primarily to maim – and thus to demoralize the enemy by overstretching medical, social and economic resources. (Although of course landmines do kill many small children.) Only about 15 per cent of bombi victims survive; these 'tennis balls' can blow children literally to bits and leave adult corpses gruesomely mangled. Usually survivors are so badly injured they cannot be considered 'lucky'.

All the above figures come from a Handicap International report entitled *Living with UXO: National Survey on the Socio-Economic Impact of UXO in Lao PDR 1997*. This survey – the first attempt to assess the extent of the unexploded bomb problem – was commissioned by UXO LAO, a programme established within the Ministry of Labour and Social Welfare in early '96 'to reduce the number of UXO casualties and increase the amount of land available for food production and development activities'. UXO LAO is funded by UNDP, UNICEF, Australia, Belgium, Canada, the Netherlands, Norway, Sweden and the UK. According to a UNESCO bulletin (December 1997), 'NGOs like Handicap International and MAG implement their projects under the auspices of UXO LAO.' This flatters UXO LAO; the British MAG team was working efficiently in Xieng Khouang two years before UXO LAO was invented.

Why did the Lao government ignore UXO for twenty-three

years? Most of the bereaved and injured, and those hungry because they could not cultivate their land, lived in 'minority' regions already utterly devastated by the thirteen-year-long Secret War. (It began on the ground four years before the bombing started.) Would the official attitude have been different had UXO similarly affected the provinces largely populated by Lao Lum? Or is the key to be found in those two words 'development activities'? *Living with UXO* notes that 'UXO contamination is a significant disincentive for economic development and expansion'.

Vientiane prefecture is UXO-free, yet UXO LAO chose to open a national training centre near the capital in mid-1996. Recruits came from contaminated areas to attend courses conducted by US military personnel, under a bilateral agreement with the Lao government. By the end of '96, 147 had completed the course and another 138 completed it in July '97 – but not all were keen to return to their *bans* after several months' exposure to the bright lights of Vientiane. (Many had never before encountered electricity.) The sensible MAG system of training villagers in their home provinces would not work for UXO LAO; US military personnel are allergic to the sort of living conditions on offer in provincial Laos.

MAG's offices in Vientiane and Phonsavanh are small and austere. No superfluous office equipment is imported, no money is wasted on comfort for the expat staff; this is a humanitarian job being managed as such jobs should always be managed – frugally.

In the Phonsvanh office I talked for hours with Paul Stanford, Xieng Khouang's project supervisor and a British army veteran – 'twenty-two years, from Cyprus to the Falklands'. A standard Englishman in the best sense, he understates risks and difficulties and conceals his dedication to his work behind a façade of laconic flippancy. But this façade could not disguise his distress as he recounted the fate of eight children in a hilltop *ban* on 10 January – when I was getting 'drinked' at the Hmong New Year party. The children, aged from three to eleven, were gathering firewood when they found a bombi. Only the three-year-old boy survived; he lost an ear and the shrapnel embedded in his spine caused him excruciating pain as his mother, Mrs Phut, carried him for miles on her back to Route 6, where she hitched a lift to Phonsavanh hospital. Three of those killed were Mrs

Phut's children, the other four were her nephews – now their parents are childless. The three-year-old is unlikely ever to walk again.

Immediately after the war, when thousands of displaced villagers returned home, many dealt with the UXO threat by moving big bombs from their fields and the vicinity of their houses and dumping them in 'safe' places – unused wells, hollow trees, rivers or deep bomb craters. Some were recklessly brave, opening ordnance and extracting the explosive for stunning fish or selling in the market – then using the container for domestic purposes, or selling it to itinerant scrap-metal collectors who encouraged their recklessness. These bomb-openers became important contributors to the national metal trade. Usually they began as the poorest men in their *ban* – then waxed rich, while earning much gratitude by daring to render harmless UXO. Some are still being driven to this rash expedient because their own land is so contaminated they need money to buy food; they reckon it is safer deliberately to dismantle a big bomb than to hit a bombi by mistake when hoeing or ploughing. Twenty-five per cent of all UXO fatalities have been as a result of men opening ordnance. In 1996, when the government suddenly became UXO-conscious, the scrap-metal trade was outlawed; now the army is supposed to bury all UXO remnants. But every day in Phonsavanh I saw huge piles of bomb casings being loaded on to traders' trucks.

MAG began its Xieng Khouang operation in April 1994 and by February 1998 had cleared only 114 hectares in an area nearly the size of Wales, destroying 62,000 pieces of ordnance. Not much out of countless millions, yet Paul and his teams were sustained by the knowledge that they had saved many lives.

Showing me around the headquarters, Paul said, 'We've found more than a hundred different types of ordnance originating in six countries.' (The North Vietnamese and Pathet Lao also contributed UXO, though in a comparatively small way.) When I mentioned Xam Nua's playground bombs, Paul recalled MAG's demolition of a teacher training college in 1997, after metal detectors being moved over the floors went crazy; the foundations yielded up 1,500 bombis. He then showed me, in a corner of the field beside MAG's little bungalow, a display of 450 mortar shells recently dug up in a primary school playground. And outside his office door lay the casing of a 160 kilo phosphorus bomb, found fifty yards from the bungalow, with the potential to destroy a size-able town.

Paul's only expat colleague in Phonsavanh took the 'small world syndrome' to extremes. Edna Dowd is the daughter of a Lismore woman and her grand-uncle was the parish priest of Lismore for many years during my youth. Can the world get any smaller? Laos is globally back-of-beyond, within Laos Phonsavanh is back-of-beyond, Lismore is not exactly a metropolis of renown – yet in Phonsavanh Edna and I meet . . .

In Edna's office hung a poster based on data gathered from 7,675 *bans* by Handicap International and advising Community Awareness teams to concentrate on the ten most dangerous activities, in the following order:

1. Defusing UXO
2. Playing with or throwing UXO
3. Making a fire to destroy rubbish
4. Weeding agricultural land
5. Making a fire to clear a field
6. Walking along paths or roads
7. Making a fire for cooking
8. Fishing with UXO or explosives
9. Ploughing the fields
10. Keeping grazing animals

By this stage I had become accustomed to seeing bits of UXO metal being used for everything from flowerpots and knives to pig troughs, wat bells and roofing weights, from fencing and house stilts to lamps, saucepans and canoes. (Fighter-bomber 'drop' tanks make very fast canoes.) In Xam Nua province, where these grisly souvenirs first came to my notice, they seemed mor-bidly fascinating but one soon adjusts to their local roles This is a major difficulty for MAG's Community Awareness programmes. Children who have grown up so familiar with UXO components in the home, and observed adults removing UXO from fields, are not receptive to warnings about the threat presented by bombis. Boys are most at risk; of all the recorded accident victims between 1973 and 1996, 27 per cent were boys and only 4 per cent girls, though girls spend as much – or more – time in the forest and the fields. (Further proof of the female's greater store of common sense?)

If the statistics on Laos's annual population growth are accurate (3.4 per cent), the unavoidable future use of contaminated land must lead to many more deaths and injuries. Within recent years there has been a considerable increase in child fatalities, as paddy-fields expand to meet the needs of refugees returning from the camps in Thailand (and of relocated 'minorities'). Clearance of *bans* and fields should be given priority but UXO LAO tends to put first the clearance of land for government developments. To speed up the process, it has been suggested that sniffer dogs might be used to detect buried bombs; apparently they have been very successful in Afghanistan.

Edna told me that the commonest maimings are limb losses. Few survivors of a blast have not lost at least one limb – usually an arm – and sustained injuries to the face and torso, often accompanied by widespread burns. All UXO survivors are to some extent handicapped for life – many left permanently blind and/or deaf. Being maimed in Laos has implications unknown in countries where the government pays for your home to be adapted to your new needs. Of the 2,481 amputees recorded by Handicap, only forty-four have been able to obtain an artificial limb. In remote *bans*, some victims receive no medical attention but must recover as best they can. Many are unaware that artificial limbs exist – and anyway how could they afford the fare to a hospital and payment for the limb? None are manufactured in Laos but *Living with UXO* suggests that the existing (very limited) rehabilitation service should produce a simple artificial arm (easily and cheaply done) to enable victims to use hoes and other basic tools. The provision of physiotherapy has also been recommended – but there one's imagination boggles in a big way, given the terrain involved.

There is no hope of accidents decreasing in the foreseeable future unless many more MAG-like enterprises come on the scene and are generously funded. Paul said, 'We have a budget of $1 million annually. And the American bombardment, you'll remember, cost an average of $2 million a day for nine years.'

In MAG's 1997 report, Rae McGrath forcefully argues for the obvious solution to the funding problem:

It is worth restating two facts about landmines which are often overlooked. The military are culpable. Regardless of their reasons for disseminating landmines, there is not a single recorded instance in the past three decades where military forces have successfully cleared minefields following large scale deployment. In fact there are very few cases where such attempts have even been made and little evidence that military commanders have given any thought to the post-conflict impact of landmines . . . The second consideration relates to profit. Who has profited directly from the sale, and therefore the use, of landmines? The arms trade, those companies involved in the manufacture and sale of weapons . . . So from where should the international community source the funds to underwrite the clearance of landmines? These moneys come from budgets designed to assist rehabilitation and development, or from emergency aid or refugee funds, and yet this seems illogical as the presence of landmines already places an extra burden on these budgets. I am suggesting that it would be far more relevant to make mine clearance a charge against military budgets and the profits of arms manufacturers – putting into practice the principle that the polluter pays. It will be argued that this would set a precedent that neither the military nor the manufacturers will find acceptable, that some governments would be reluctant to accept such a principle. But we are approaching the millennium. There is a need to review the norms by which we live, and surely the principle that we place greater value on the saving of human life than on the taking of it is a worthy message to pass on to the children of the twenty-first century.

Hear! Hear!

Handicap International reminds UXO LAO that 'large scale clearance in support of major infrastructure construction projects should remain within the commercial clearance sector. UXO LAO should concentrate its limited resources on its mandate of providing humanitarian assistance.' *Living with UXO* is an impressive report but my toes curled towards the end where 'It is recommended that a follow-on project be established to add to the general survey work already done, to develop technical survey activities and to develop clearance completion survey activities. These measures meet with those specified in the United Nations International Standards for Humanitarian Mine Clearance. In order to better understand the situation it may be necessary to collect additional information on certain issues and continue to develop the national data base on UXO.'

Here we go again! Another outreach of bureaucratic blight, the fatal compulsion to study problems, to write about them, to hold seminars about them, to organize workshops about them – instead of tackling them as, in the UXO case, MAG is doing with few words but much action.

From neolithic times to the beginning of the twentieth century Xieng Khouang's jars remained untouched; a powerful taboo, as mysterious as the jars themselves, protected them from the curious and the greedy. Made of sandstone, or granite, or chalky clay containing lumps of quartz, many hundreds were scattered over the plain – and beyond – with the main concentration (250 or so) at Ban Ang, where almost all were bombed to bits. None of the biggest – between nine and twelve feet high, weighing around fifteen tons – has survived. The smaller jars – three or four feet high – are either cylindrical or shaped like the earthenware pots now used for rice-beer. Collectors have stolen a number of those portable models and two of the biggest survivors have been helicoptered to Vientiane.

When French archaeologists investigated the jars some were found to contain charred human bones, glass beads of different colours, ceramic fragments, bronze jewellery, splinters of metal. Ever since, academics have enjoyed arguing about their function and origin. Although obviously the product of an advanced society, they in no way resemble any other artefacts left behind by the ancient civilizations of Indochina. 'Funeral urns' seems to be the most popular theory, the varying sizes reflecting their inmates' social status.

The few hundred jars left on the plain are dispersed over five sites; only Site 1, eight miles from Phonsavanh, is considered safe, and even there one is advised to stay on footpaths. The road to that site undulates through suburbs of tin-roofed shacks and brick bungalows, between bare hills on which bony cattle graze and past yet another sad-looking Hmong 'resettlement'. Then a pole blocks the track but at 7.45 a.m. there was no one around to take my 1,000 kip entrance fee.

Some visitors come away complaining that the Plain of Jars has been, in the jargon of the tourist trade, oversold. I can sympathize: this is no beauty spot. Beyond the pole two grotty pavilions – a circular rest-room and an oblong restaurant – were constructed a few years ago in a moment of mad extravagance to cater for a visit from the Thai Crown Prince. On what is left of a low hill – some B-52 demolished its southern side – stands the biggest surviving jar and several others. From here one is overlooking level miles of brown, desert-dusty land dominated by an enormous aviation fuel depot, recently built to supply the adjacent airbase and Lao Airforce headquarters. (The airforce consists of nine elderly MiGs; let's hope it never expands.) Also visible is the new airport and a new airforce personnel housing estate. However, this unlovely panorama is hidden by the hill as one wanders around grassy acres strewn with jars of various sizes in various states of repair. A few have lids lying nearby; one is decorated with a crude carving of a dancing figure. There was nobody in sight as I limped between them, pausing often to handle one with the peculiar sort of awe inspired by man-made objects ancient and inexplicable. It pleases me that the experts cannot explain these containers or identify the people who made them. The more scientists inform us about our world and our universe, the more our imaginations need such mysteries to toy with. A local legend insists that the jars belonged to a race of giants – and maybe they did . . .

On my way back I took a path leading past a vast cave, the approach to its mouth made difficult by a series of colossal overlapping craters now half full of scrub and litter. Here the Pathet Lao had one of their bases.

Collecting Hare from beside the rest-room pavilion, I noticed a *Vientiane Times* cutting sellotaped to the inside of a window, commemorating the last time that pavilion was used – on 10 November 1997 when the us Deputy Secretary of State, Strobe Talbott, the most senior us government official to visit Laos since 1975, delivered a speech on the Plain. Even by the standards of travelling statesmen, it was notably fatuous:

Here are three messages to be seen. One is the rich culture of these huge stone jars. Then there are the physical scars on the landscape from the heavy bombing during the war. But there is also evidence of Americans and Lao working together to heal these wounds. I don't think there's any question that we're standing in the midst of evidence that there was a terrible conflict in this area. It is obviously vivid and sobering, but of course what is alive here is the image of Lao civilians and military, and Americans, British and other members of the international community, working side by side in finding these devices and getting them out of the way so they will not harm people. Since 1996, the USA has provided $1.5 million in equipment, as well as training, for the national programme to clear the bombs.

My return route followed a new red earth track through the air-force base, the land all around bulldozer-ravaged, the strong north wind creating a dust storm. It was a cloudy day, the glimmers of sunshine lukewarm; even at noon the Lao were wearing sweaters, anoraks, scarves, balaclavas – sometimes gloves. Then I found myself pedalling along a two-mile stretch of pretend motorway – four-lane, with what somebody hoped would be a central flowerbed, its earth neatly raked between concrete kerbs. This 'development' led from nowhere to nowhere and only one side had been tarred; the other surface was of coarse skiddy gravel so nobody used it.

I thought as I went about Strobe Talbott's speech and wondered how much he, personally, knows about the Secret War. Does he realize that while the Americans were posturing about saving the world from the Evil Empire their own behaviour, in Laos and elsewhere, was consistently evil? Even at night AC-47 gunships patrolled the skies over Laos and when their infra-red sensors reacted to warm flesh the heroes on board fired 6,000 rounds a minute – not knowing whether their targets were Pathet Lao soldiers, buffaloes, North Vietnamese, pigs, nursing mothers, gibbons or children. And B-52 pilots on their way back to base from abortive sorties into Vietnam regularly dropped their unused bombs on Laos, having been ordered not to land with high explosives aboard. The inflicting of so much 'collateral damage' proves that the Americans regarded all Lao within the 'liberated zone' as expendable. Yet if one American pilot had to bale out over 'enemy territory' an elaborate rescue mission was launched within minutes, sometimes involving the napalm bombing of surrounding areas.

To this day the Americans remain obsessed by those who were not rescued – their MIAS. According to *Laos: A Country Study*, produced by the Library of Congress's Federal Research Division in 1994:

> Two key components have dominated the US relationship with Laos: accounting for those Americans classified as prisoners of war or missing in action at the end of the Indochina Wars, and controlling the growth of, and trafficking in, narcotics. As a measure of sincerity for improving relations, the US has sought greater Lao cooperation in providing information on the fate of POW/MIAs and in searching for their remains. As of September 1994, thirty-three joint missions of field searches and excavations of crash sites had been conducted. In August 1994, the two sides agreed to carry out six joint field activities in the future.

How irrational can you get? Why should the Lao government waste its scant resources on searching for American remains? After the unimaginable chaos of the nine bombing years, how many Lao could not locate relatives' remains? Why are American remains so important? The tone of most US official statements on MIAS suggests that the Lao are to blame for the disappearance of those airmen – a perverse carrying through, to the 1990s, of the pretence that the Secret War was justified.

To explain the *unique* bombing of Laos, it has been posited that the Americans behaved thus because they didn't regard the place as a real country/nation/state. At the time, Bernard Fall wrote that Laos was 'neither a geographical nor an ethnic or social entity, but merely a political convenience'. (And maybe the inhabitants of 'political conveniences' are not human beings?) In 1970, during the worst of the bombing, a Rand Corporation report dismissed Laos as 'hardly a country except in the legal sense'. And in words that perhaps hint at the true explanation, Dean Rusk, when

Secretary of State, described Laos as 'a wart on the hog of Vietnam'.

In Phonsavanh, Mrs Bounyong also borrowed a Honda. 'Here we could get a taxi but for visiting very poor people it is nicer to go by Honda.' (Foreign NGOs, please note.) We were on our way by 9 a.m., following the 'forbidden' road for a few miles, then turning off to ascend into a narrow valley between mountains still densely forested. 'Logging companies fear UXO!' chuckled Mrs Bounyong. She had already explained her particular interest in this Hmong *ban*. Its LWU leader, the only literate woman, had sent a note to the Vientiane office asking for help; inevitably, there are many complicated post-war land problems in Xieng Khouang.

A Lao Lum *ban* once stood on the site now occupied by these Hmong; when it was bombed to bits, the survivors took refuge elsewhere. In 1973 the pioneers of the present community (pro-Pathet Lao Hmong) settled on the abandoned land. They cleared the old paddyfields on the valley floor (at the expense of seven lives), dug wells, planted peach and avocado trees, bought a few cattle and buffaloes, established a few opium fields high on the mountains. Soon after their arrival they had felled four rare and precious trees (*mai ketsana*: Mrs Bounyong didn't know the English name) and sold them for one million kip, then a vast sum. That deal enabled them to improve their irrigation and buy more livestock. (Now they would be jailed if they laid an axe on a precious tree; only logging companies are allowed to be environmentally destructive.)

All went well until 1995 when three Lao Lum families moved from Pak Xan to Phonsavanh and claimed this land. A court ruled in their favour – they had ample proof of ownership – but declared that in accordance with present government policy they must share the land fifty/fifty with those who had been cultivating it for over twenty years. The Lao Lum were agreeable to this – so agreeable that they allowed the Hmong two-thirds of the fields, which by our standards is something to marvel at. However, the loss of one-third was serious enough, with an expanding population, and to compensate the villagers surreptitiously cleared a few more plots on the high ground and increased their opium output.

This was a double defiance of the new laws: slashing and burning, then growing opium. Which perhaps explains a catastrophic development in December 1997, when the local administration decreed that they must move to an area recently set aside and irrigated for landless highland folk.

At this point, Mrs Bounyong's help was sought. The villagers argued that they are not landless, having been allocated the usufruct rights to their land in 1973 by the Pathet Lao administration then in control of the Xieng Khouang liberated zone. At that date private land ownership was of course taboo – and anyway it had never seemed very important in Laos where there was more than enough land for everyone.

We walked the last steep mile, out of consideration for the borrowed Honda. From afar we could see the *ban* on the lower slopes of a precipitous mountain at the head of the valley; ledges had been laboriously created by the original Lao Lum settlers, leaving all the valley floor available for rice growing. These seventy-six houses were unstilted, windowless, the walls of bamboo, the thatches – raggedy, not panels – extending over the doorways to form a porch of sorts. All the women wore their traditional floppy black trousers and blue or green turbans piled high; the men, except for a few ancients, were sartorially Westernized. This was not a poor *ban* though there was no school, no health centre, no transport apart from a few bullock-carts and bicycles. The children looked well fed and bouncy, if unwashed; the adults were adequately clothed and generally in good health. The livestock were flourishing and the vegetable plots bountiful – irrigated by streams off the mountain.

While Mrs Bounyong was in earnest discussion with the elders (women as well as men, despite the Hmongs' MCP reputation) I limped around followed by a giggle of half-nervous children. Near some homes the pigsty stood on stilts above a pond and from its slightly sloping floor nourishment slid into the water for the family's supply of carp. Beside one house stood a tall pole from which hung a basket containing a rather smelly pig's head. Later, Mrs Bounyong explained: when the householder recently encountered UXO a pig was sacrificed to Phi Fa, the sky spirit, in the hope that those injuries would not permanently cripple him. The Hmong favour black pigs and everywhere these are made to wear triangular wooden stocks to keep them out of vegetable plots – a precaution also taken with young calves who might squeeze through fences.

We drank herbal tea and nibbled sun-dried raw fish outside the home of the headman, one of five elders who each had two or three wives. Apparently polygamy rarely causes friction in Hmong households; the first wife sometimes contributes to the bride price for the second, by way of halving her own workload. Second and third wives cost much less than the first. From the forest pharmacy Hmong women take their traditional contraceptive – an 'infertility herb', as Mrs Bounyong described it. *Saha* is as final as a hysterectomy and without side-effects. Other Lao women have religious scruples about preventing births – 'the spirits of children want to be born' – but Mrs Bounyong was finding more and more young women, even in remote *bans*, wishing to have 'only four, if possible two of each', instead of ten or twelve with the likelihood of several dying in infancy. However, they are fearful of both the Pill's side-effects and sterilization; the latter is widely believed to reduce women's fitness for physical labour. This anti-contraceptive information came from the Pathet Lao educators.

As the discussion continued, I could sense my friend's concern for the villagers' distress. What to do? As a senior LWU officer and Party member, she could not openly condemn provincial administrative decisions and new central government laws. But no doubt there are Laotian ways of dealing with such conflicts of interest.

Another wee dander took me down to the paddyfields where, it seemed, cattle may safely graze – though I kept cautiously to the bund tops. By then I, too, was worrying about these people's future. How cruel it would be to uproot them again – people who, without any resources beyond their own initiative and energy, had recreated a community in this lovely valley and were making no demands on anybody, only wanting to be left to do their own thing.

As we were leaving, the headman's third wife (younger than his eldest daughter), hurried to present me with a handful of large pink berries. She had noticed my limp; if I boiled the berries with areca nuts and soaked my foot in the liquid all would be well.

That evening Mrs Bounyong and I supped rather gloomily in

the Nang Phonkaew. 'Must swidden farming be outlawed?' I asked. 'Isn't that a debatable point, loggers being so welcome?'

Although Mrs Bounyong's position did not allow her to be blunt she came close to it. More accurate information is needed, she said, before just and practical decisions can be made. Loggers' spokesmen consistently inflate the damage done by farmers and the consultants called in to do reports and surveys and estimates are usually on the side of the people with clout. On my return home I sent her a relevant quotation from Erik Eckholm's *Down to Earth*:

> Traditional systems of shifting cultivation entail lengthy fallow periods during which soil fertility is restored and trees regrow on the cultivated plots. Today [1982] many traditional peoples in the Amazon Basin, Central Africa and Southeast Asia are still practicing shifting cultivation in harmony with nature. It is when such farmers get hemmed in by logging companies, the spread of plantations, or other incursions of modern society that they can become enemies of the forest. In addition, as human numbers in a given region rise and the free forest area about them shrinks, fallow cycles are shortened to the point where trees have no chance to regrow.

We thought next about opium growing – not a debatable issue. Or is it? By now all the world knows (though not all the world will face up to the fact) that 'law enforcement' cannot stop well-organized, large-scale opium growing in Afghanistan, Burma, Laos and elsewhere. It is however relatively easy to detect and punish those who grow just enough for local use, people for whom this is at present their only cash crop of any significance. Those Hmong women, since losing one-third of their paddyfields and being told it is illegal to slash and burn, need opium cash to buy rice. Alternative cash crops (sugar cane and bananas) have been suggested by the authorities but, said Mrs Bounyong, they offer no instruction, no seeds, no marketing advice – and the Hmong come from altitudes at which neither crop is grown. She admitted that opium growing presented her with an ethical problem. For a century the authorities encouraged peasants to depend on poppy growing. When suddenly it is made illegal the little growers ask 'Why?' and are frightened and resentful. They know nothing about heroin – have never seen or used it. In their communities smoking opium is the prerogative of elders who, having worked hard all their lives, are entitled in old age to that luxury.

'If what they call the counter-narcotics programme was working,' said Mrs Bounyong, 'I could tell these poor women "You cannot be the only people breaking the law." But there is a very big new villa in this town – you've seen it – because that programme is not working!'

My friend then gave me a letter of introduction to Mrs S——, the English-speaking LWU leader of a *ban* some twenty miles south of Tha Khaek. 'You'll like this lady,' said Mrs Bounyong, 'and you need English-speakers. You can stay in her home, she's married to a Vietnamese and it's very sad – they have no children. For us, that is the most sad thing. Maybe it's why she works so hard in the LWU. She learned English with a British NGO in one of the Hmong refugee camps in Thailand. Having that job was brave for a Lao Lum, there was too much trouble in those camps . . . She's a good woman.'

On my third visit to the Lao Aviation shed-like office I had at last found someone behind the three-legged desk (a bit of bomb stood in for the fourth leg) and booked my ticket for the following morning: check-in time 9.30, departure time 11.00.

All my Phonsavanh nights were disturbed by a bold rat (standard size and colour) determined to raid the cupboard where my nuts were stored. When I switched on a pencil torch he merely glared at me, sitting on his hunkers with one paw in the crevice between the doors. Although partial to rats, I decline to share my food cupboard with them; the name of the disease carried by their urine escapes me but I know it's a killer. A thrown shoe sent him diving under the cupboard but in darkness he at once re-emerged. Having risen to secure the door, I left him to his hopeless task and slept again; next morning his toothmarks were barely visible on the hardwood. That night he resumed gnawing, with admirable tenacity, and seemed quite an old friend. On the third night, when I put out a handful of nuts to reward his persistence, he ate only a few before briefly disappearing – then returned with a smaller companion, doubtless his mate. By candlelight I watched this loving couple sharing the feast; they devoured the nuts at an apparently reckless speed but I dare say the rat and human digestive systems are quite different.

Given the state of Xieng Khouang's roads, local travellers have to fly almost everywhere (at a government-subsidized rate, I'm happy to say) and the little airport building was thronged at 9.30. Many passengers presented twelve or fifteen large pieces of luggage to be separately weighed – only 200 kip for each ten kilos of excess baggage but the paperwork involved was formidable. One woman – her *sin* and jacket breathtakingly beautiful – put seventeen items on the scales, assisted by two daughters. Some sacks contained rice, others were baffling – strange shapes and colours discernible through nylon mesh – and one was oozing blood from the choicest parts of a buffalo just killed. About this there was a prolonged dispute – amiable, as is the Lao way – and eventually the daughters had to Honda off to fetch plastic bags for a repackaging of the deceased.

At 10.30 a giant helicopter landed and dozens of peasants emerged, dragging sacks and buckets and baskets of forest produce. It took off again at once, without passengers or cargo, and Mrs Bounyong (also flying out) whispered that it was a government 'copter which provides free flights for residents of 'restricted zones'.

At 10.55 scores of cows with tiny calves ambled down the centre of the runway, unattended, their bells faintly tinkling. At 12.20 they ambled back, having presumably dropped in to their local pond for a quick one. Beside me stood a middle-aged American, complete with tropical helmet, telescopic lens camera and well-pressed safari suit; from his belt hung a comical range of gear as though he were about to plunge into pathless jungles. Staring at the cows, he exclaimed: 'Jeez! You get the feelin' this place ain't really knit together!'

By then the tourists were restlessly pacing to and fro, looking at their watches every other minute. Several went to the manager's office to complain loudly and demand an explanation for this wrecking of their schedules. The manager, who spoke only Lao, beamed at them and made sympathetic clucking noises which had the reverse of the intended effect. At noon the adjacent restaurant-hut had closed and the benches were crowded while leaking lavatories sent a flood of reeking water (plus) farther and farther over the concrete floor, lapping around feet and hand luggage – and finally driving all *falangs* on to the veranda where a brisk wind flayed them with fine dust. Meanwhile the waiting Lao, who don't expect anything to be knit together, were happily talking and laughing and playing with their children.

Our Chinese Y-12 turboprop landed at 1.40 and I noticed yet again how often the Lao – laid-back when that is appropriate – prove quietly efficient when action time arrives; within thirty minutes the plane had been unloaded and reloaded.

While observing the day's intake of tourists, I heard a Vietnamese youth, who spoke good English, telling an elderly Australian couple that in Phonsavanh they must have a guide – US$50 a day – because unescorted foreigners may not visit the Plain of Jars. As tourism expands, I fear this young man will have his Lao counterparts.

The flight for which we had waited five hours lasted thirty minutes and was 'tourist friendly' – strong cough lozenges, cold face-wipes, plastic glasses of iced Pepsi. Our hostess wore a very lovely *sin* but was horribly made up, Chinese style: chalk-white face, thin black eyebrows, hair in a chignon with a dispersed fringe.

'Maybe she thinks she must,' said Mrs Bounyong, 'to match the Y-12.'

11

South to Tha Khaek

From Wattay airport it is not far to Marie's home where I heard about the shooting dead of six bus passengers between Kasi and Luang Prabang ten days previously. Some claimed a few Hmong 'brigands' had also been killed by the military escort. On the day following the shooting Marie, travelling by Route 13 for the first time, wondered why there was so little traffic. When she flew back to Vientiane she was unsurprised to discover that no one there had heard about the killings. She only heard, in Luang Prabang, because her taxi driver chanced to be a brother of the bus driver – who had immediately decided to find another job. We marvelled at the government's tight control of information. 'Just imagine,' said Marie, 'such a drama, in Australia would be common knowledge around the world in five minutes. Here, ten days after, no one knows anything about what happened 200 miles away!'

When Marie went out to make coffee I glanced at the *Vientiane Times* and was, for once, riveted. (This has to be the world's dullest newspaper: interesting headlines appear biennially.)

FIVE FOREIGNERS INVOLVED IN ILLEGAL
ACTIVITIES TO BE DEPORTED

Five foreigners who acted in breach of the laws of the Lao PDR at Ban Phonkheng, Saysettha district, Vientiane municipality, last week, will be deported back to their countries. These people include: three Americans, one French woman and a Thai man. Following investigations, the Americans confessed that they were responsible for inviting foreigners and some Lao nationals to hold an unauthorised meeting, violating article 66 of the criminal code of the Lao PDR. They stated that they came to Laos to work for a clean water project. However, they were involved in other activities. The use of an Australian Embassy car with a licence plate 11–21 was not acceptable since they were not granted diplomatic immunity. These foreigners, released from prison on February 4, will leave the country shortly.

'You get it?' asked Marie.

'Fundamentalist missionaries!' said I – then threw human rights to the wind and congratulated the government of the Lao PDR on its decisive action.

Marie agreed. 'Wherever they can find a foothold, those fanatics make trouble. Look at their role in South America, colluding with TNCS. And they're at it here, too, over our dam controversy. They're infiltrating every province, always pretending to be do-gooders. Every week they put ads in Lao language newspapers offering free English classes – our eldest was approached and offered six months' free tuition if he'd attend "unauthorized meetings" every Sunday. They told him if he became a Christian he need only go to church on Sundays, not be worshipping every day of the week. He told them as a Buddhist he need go to the wat only when he feels like it!'

On the 216-mile bus ride to Tha Khaek, I paid little attention to the landscape. Soon I would be seeing it again from (I hoped) the more favourable vantage point of Hare's saddle. And beside me sat a most remarkable young man – we had already been talking for half an hour at the bus station.

A scion of the former royal family (there are many such), Jaques was taken to Paris in 1976, at the age of five, by his fleeing father. In '93 he left the Sorbonne with a philosophy degree and decided it was time to make contact with his own culture. He then spoke no Lao, only French and fluent English, the latter acquired while visiting his mother in California. (His parents divorced in 1977; his father's second wife is French and he has two much younger half-siblings.) Father – a businessman with 'large interests' in Thailand, Singapore and the US – opposed his son's plan, not believing Laos would ever 'reward investment'. But back Jaques came, found his maternal grandmother in Luang Prabang and, through her influence, was accepted into a prestigious wat for three years – or as long as he wanted to sample the monastic life.

It seems contemporary wats in one sense resemble British educational establishments, ranging downwards from the Eton/Oxford equivalent. However, this comparison is limited; Jaques's three-year experience was comparable to life in a medieval Carthusian monastery. His morning begging round provided an adequate but monotonous rice and vegetables diet; meat was not allowed, never mind alcohol and cigarettes, and celibacy was strictly enforced with no homosexual compensations. The days were divided thus: four hours of prayer and meditation beginning at 4 a.m.; eight hours of intellectually demanding study which made his Sorbonne course seem like a doddle; another four hours of prayer and meditation; eight hours' sleep. This, Jaques admitted, was an exceptional wat; few maintain such standards. He could have left after three weeks without losing face but felt a need to 'stick it out' if he wished to describe himself as 'Lao' after growing up in a rich cosmopolitan milieu.

Now Jaques was cautiously running a one-man anti-NEM campaign. Cautiously because what he called his 'alternative attitude' (the opinions he shared with Marie and me on 'development' predators) could get him deported – or worse – if publicly voiced. The Lao, he argued, are not being given a choice between their own way of life and the 'globalized' way; to choose you must be informed and changes advantageous to the Rich World are being relentlessly imposed on uninformed peasants. Through his father's contacts ('My pappa is a very cunning predator!') he hoped to find opportunities to talk with, and possibly influence, some of those threatening the peasants' future. If he and others of like mind could communicate directly with the decision-makers among the developers, some of them – argued Jaques – might think again about what they are doing to an ancient but fragile culture, a rare and precious ecosystem and a self-sufficient (in peacetime) subsistence economy. The damage-doers despise peasants and rarely come face to face with the Jaques-type. In their target countries they meet only those in power, men who relish the glamour of being publicly associated with some marvel of modern dam engineering or some shiny new factory which, when switched on by the relevant minister, will produce chemical 'inputs' never previously needed by Lao farmers. Said Jaques, 'My targets – UNDP king-pins, corporate planners, IMF consultants – they're not bad people, only ignorant. They were born with no opportunity to know another way. They have goodness within, like everyone has, but they need help to find it.'

All that may make Jaques sound like a silly New Age dreamer but to me his thinking and feeling seemed an unusual blend of Buddhist spirituality and occidental liberal aspirations. ('Liberal' in the original sense.) His opposition to Capitalism Unbound was not a source of angry frustration, like mine, but was calm and constructive – at the age of twenty-eight. Perhaps I need three years in a wat.

On the outskirts of Tha Khaek I mentioned Marie, guessing Jaques would know her. His eyes glowed. 'She is my second mother! I love her, she is my anchor and inspiration! You struck lucky, meeting her! She can tell you more about my family than I can, she's somehow related to my Luang Prabang grandmother – a few generations back.'

As I watched Jaques walking towards the tuk-tuk rank outside the bus station – a small, slight, very ordinary-looking Lao – it suddenly seemed fitting that he should be trying to defend his 'kingdom'. Although scions of the royal family are numerous, they are also hallmarked – so Jaques carried immeasurably diluted but authentic Fa Ngum genes.

Tha Khaek is at the other end of the chronological scale from Phonsavanh – probably older than Luang Prabang. A thousand years ago, as Sii Khotabun, it was a remote border post of the Mon-Khmer empire and a Mekong port for Indian and Arab traders. When the French army first appeared, in 1893, the town was named Muang Tha – Port Town. The unsuspecting Lao graciously welcomed the foreigners, referring to them as 'guests', and soon Muang Tha had become known throughout the region as Tha Khaek – Guests' Port. Now, as the capital of Khammuan province, it is an agreeably run-down French colonial outpost dating, architecturally, from 1912 and as yet not much afflicted by 'development'. Pre-1975 the population was 85 per cent Vietnamese. Some had been imported by the French to administer the area (in so far as the colonists bothered to administer any part of Laos), others had fled from northern Vietnam when Ho Chi Minh took over. After 1975 the majority – staunch capitalists – moved on to more lucrative pastures in France or the USA. The present population – mainly Lao Lum – is nearly 70,000 including 'suburban' *bans*. But the town is uncrowded and slow-paced even by Lao standards. Soon I realized that I had left the best wine to the last and was somewhere exceptionally congenial.

The Khack's few VW 'Beetles' and antique jeeps are far outnumbered by Hondas, tuk-tuks and bicycles. The attractively dilapidated colonial dwellings, Vietnamese shophouses, eat-drink shops and noodle stalls are all approached via footbridges of wood or scrap-iron over wide drainage channels. Beyond the compact centre, Tha Khaek becomes a collection of *bans* linked by rough laneways that end where the paddy begins and bells tinkle as buffaloes graze.

On the way to the centre from the far-out bus station I noticed a conspicuously new building: Hotel Phoudoi. Behind it is the Baw Phaw Daw disco, named after a military conglomerate which owns the hotel and controls Khammuan province, politically and economically. In 1997 this conglomerate ran into financial trouble and their second hotel, overlooking the Mekong, was abandoned when half built. A five-storey, crescent-shaped mass of concrete slabs, it now serves as an ugly memorial to greed and bad judgement. Who, I wondered, would have slept in its 200 beds? Tha Khaek attracts few tourists or backpackers and is already over-bedded. Things were different during the American era when the town was a notorious gambling centre, drawing Thai visitors by the boatload at all seasons.

In the Inter Hotel – a flat-roofed, two-storey 1960s construction, its cream façade darkly damp-stained – both the restaurant and the bar had ceased to function. But free *lau-lao* was offered, with roast corn on the cob, by the large jolly family who ran the place and seemed unworried by their lack of guests. I stayed in the one-storey annexe, where my enormous high-ceilinged room (the only dirty room in my Lao experience) lacked a mosquito net, window screen, fan, towel, candles – though the electricity went off at 10 p.m. In the filthy mosquito-infested bathroom a dip-and-pour shower was occasionally possible. The family lived in the other half of the annexe and it worried me to see, near their veranda, two monkeys roped to a huge wooden chest amidst a pile of old tractor tyres. But everybody loved them and they were often released to sit on family laps being fondled and fed leftovers.

The Mekong embankment is, naturally, the focus of Tha Khaek's social life. Here the river is narrower than at Vientiane and on the Thai bank bustling Nakhon Phanom is very visible. Several times a day ferries cross, carrying passengers and goods and the occasional truck, and most locals long for a bridge. They reckon that would transform Tha Khaek into a favourable (cheap labour) site for Thai industries and bring much truck traffic in transit to Vietnam; here Laos is at its slimmest, the Vietnam border only 170 miles away. People looked puzzled when I remarked that cities everywhere are now desperate to reduce their truck traffic – so Tha Khaek should be counting its blessings, like clean air and tranquillity. But already the consumer society is dripping its poison into this region through TV advertisements.

By sunset on that first day I had acquired four charming self-styled 'interpreters', all eager to practise English; when job seeking in Thailand, English-speakers are at an advantage. From all these riverside towns, and from the interior of the southern provinces, thousands migrate to work in Thailand – including children as young as eight, many of whom (both boys and girls) end up in Bangkok's 'specialist' brothels. One youth asked, 'Is Ireland civilized same like Hong Kong?' At this stage the answer, unfortunately, is 'Almost . . .' As we talked by the river – a bicycle or Honda passing now and then – we could see a stream of fast cars flowing along the far embankment and my young friends eyed them enviously. A cool breeze blew, wrinkling the Mekong, and under a nearby tree small boys were using catapults to knock off those furry pods – precious pods, and hard won, yet the smallest boy spontaneously ran over to present me with one. Tha Khaek is like that.

Then a beautiful young woman joined us, looking twenty at most, and surprised me with the information that she had spent three years in Leningrad studying science and Russian.

'I liked it there very much, the big fine city and kind people and work and language interesting. I admired how they looked after old people, and young people if they were ill or disabled. No one was cold in winter or without food – not nice food, like our Lao food, but enough. I am sad Communism has gone for those people. Now we hear no one is looking after them and they have bad crime, no jobs or no wages, no medical care like before.'

Mrs Shayamang was the first Lao I had met (apart from the returnees, Marie and Jaques) who openly expressed unease about NEM-ruled Lao. But there must be many like her, valuing their own culture and undazzled by Western civilization in its declining years.

In fact Mrs Shayamang was aged thirty-five and had three daughters of ten, seven and two. Her husband reproached her when a third girl arrived, his disappointment was extreme and she felt guilty; I advised her to tell him that the father determines the sex of the child. However, the third is now loved no less than the others, as I could see when Mr Shayamang appeared on his Honda with the 'disappointment' in front of him on a toddler saddle and the others behind. The Shayamangs were both born in Vientiane and had recently moved to Tha Khaek to work for an oxygen company. Mrs Shayamang was earning 55,000 kip a month, her husband – less qualified – 45,000 (what three expats would spend in one evening on a two-course meal in a mid-range Vientiane restaurant).

By design I had arrived in Tha Khaek in time for the annual Wat Sikhotabun festival on the night of the full moon of the third lunar month. But Jaques had dissuaded me from participating. 'That wat is a very sacred site, sacred since the tenth century when King Nanthasen of Sii Khotabun built a wat there. Now its festival has got so run-down it's what Christians would call a sacrilege. I went last year and left after fifteen minutes, it's all commercialized, a pop music festival and junk market and fun fair. All our Buddhist festivals are fun, I'm not against the fun input, but this is the wrong conjunction. It'd be OK if it wasn't where it is when it is. That place, on this night, should have another atmosphere. OK, so you might enjoy it, observing the natives at play – but I doubt that. I guess you'd be upset same way I was.'

Early on the morning after the festival I cycled to Wat Sikhotabun, five miles south of Tha Khaek. Acres of gleaming green artificially fertilized paddyfields were overlooked by a long *ban* of tin-roofed houses. 'Bucolic Laos at its best,' said my guidebook, going seriously OTT about a litter-strewn track through an agricultural suburb exposed to some dire pop group on Thai breakfast-time TV. It seems strange that the Lao, so soft-spoken in conversation, should turn the volume so high on their TV sets. But maybe an excess of decibels is part of the thrilling novelty.

On arrival at the 'very sacred site' I felt grateful to Jaques. The wat's handsome entrance archway was defaced by an enormous banner advertising Beerlao. Between several brightly striped marquees stretched other banners, advertising Pepsi and shampoo and a new Thai soap powder that had just come on the market. At 8 a.m. the place was a hive of dismantling activity – thousands of plastic chairs being loaded on to trucks by novices, giant sound systems and stereo equipment of every sort being packed in crates and heaved on to other trucks for ferrying back to Nakhon Phanom, traders' stalls being taken apart and shoved into jumbos (big tuk-tuks) or pick-up trucks with Thai registrations. I remembered Jaques's comment that thousands of Thai attend the festival and encourage a brisk trade in 'narcotics'. Never have I seen such a concentration of litter – ankle deep over that five-acre field. Skeletal cows and calves mooched through it in search of edible bits: corn cobs, sugar cane leaves, banana fronds. The condition of the cattle around Tha Khaek was pitiable, a shocking contrast to the sleek herds seen elsewhere. I was soon to find out why.

Wat Sikhotabun stands on the edge of the Mekong embankment, high above the river, facing a pleasantly green stretch of Thailand. The steep slope is no longer grassy but concreted over and used as a litter dump. King Chao Anou built this wat in the nineteenth century; it was restored in the 1950s and enlarged in the 1970s when the monks' quarters were much extended to form what closely resembles a row of whitewashed stables. From a distance the *that* looks quite elegant; seen close up, less so. The *sim*'s interior was bare but for the Lord Buddha gazing down at a mountain of tawdry tinselly offerings and bowls of rice and pieces of fruit and sticks of incense. One monk sat in a corner intently counting money – a lot of money. On the edge of the compound, under an ancient bodhi tree (planted in the tenth century?) a pile of rocks supports a giant statue of the Lord Buddha, sheltered by a tin roof. This, to me, was Wat Sikhotabun's most sacred spot.

On the way back I overtook one of Tha Khaek's most enchanting sights, a miniature horse drawing a cart loaded with two massive earthenware water jars. These extraordinary animals, no bigger than donkeys, are unmistakably horses – not ponies. They are bred locally but no one could tell me anything about their origin. The jars hold 1,000 litres of water, purified with limestone, for domestic use and watering small kitchen gardens. They were introduced by the LWU who have trained groups to make them, each group providing jars for ten families. The LWU runs eighteen units where the moulds and equipment are kept.

At Tha Khaek's southern edge, the Bolisat Phattanakhet Phu Doi (the army-supported developers) have made quite a mark. Here stands an enormous new dry goods market with a three-tiered roof and an accompanying car park – in anticipation of the happy day when a bridge is built. Nearby, a terrace of twelve breeze-block shops remained unused though obviously this development had long since been completed. Also nearby was a pavilion restaurant – tin roof, no walls – furnished with coffee machines and fridges run off a generator, and serving imitation McDonald's burgers and chips and instant soup. It was filthy and smelly, the plastic tables unwiped, the fumes from the cooking oil rancid. I ordered a coffee and noted with satisfaction that business was not brisk. This seemed to be the place where rather self-consciously Westernized (or Thai-ized) young locals gathered; at noon heavy metal tapes were shaking the plank floor and youths wearing jeans and baseball caps groped girls very willing to be groped – a distressing deviation from Laotian mores. Here was the sort of cultural contamination the LPRP leaders dreaded (and must still deplore) yet did not know how to avoid. It comes with NEM; if you submit to outside investors, lenders, donors, consultants, you have surrendered your heritage – sold it for a mess of dollars.

Next stop, a cemetery. I collect graveyards and this looked a rare specimen – occupied by non-Lao bones, covering several sloping acres. On the hill above gleamed the colossal round tanks of a Shell petrol depot; below sprawled a timber yard and saw-mills. The nineteenth-century pre-colonial tombs were all Chinese: substantial stone houses, skilfully carved, memorials to rich merchants but now torn asunder by the power of trees – growing through floors, walls, roofs. Most of the graves were Vietnamese, also telling of wealth, some of the more recent quite bizarre – like large concrete dog kennels, painted dark blue with white roofs and white fretwork along the sides. Other newish family vaults resembled rows of Nissen huts, striped pink and yellow, with photographs of the deceased inset on a gable end. French bones lie in a separate section, the graves marked only by small head-stones or crosses half submerged in weeds.

Two p.m. is not Tha Khaek's liveliest hour. Most people are asleep, lying on sofas or mats in their shophouses, and the few who are awake look as though they wish they weren't. When a youth had served me a Beerlao at my favourite eat-drink shop, near the Mekong, he lay within the room and immediately slept. The street was deserted and still. Then a goose and gander wandered past, looking self-important as is their wont and making aggressive noises for no particular reason, causing two cats dozing on a shop step to raise their heads. I watched a half-feathered pullet fly on to the cook's pavement table and help herself to raw noodles from a basin beside the simmering cauldron of chicken soup to which noodles are added when ordered. Two minutes earlier the same pullet had been sipping daintily from the green-scummed water in the drainage channel, her naked bum pointed skywards – giving the morbid impression that she had already been plucked to go in the cauldron. But of course those noodles would be ster-ilized by the boiling soup. Oddly, on the hot Mekong plain people seemed less aware of 'food hygiene' than in the cool highlands. When I remarked on this later, Marie said it was an often observed fact, explained by the Pathet Lao's health education campaign in the liberated zone.

I spent the next two days cycling on level gravel roads through the cave-rich karst mountains east of Tha Khaek. A few miles beyond the town, slowly smouldering hillocks of sawdust mark the formidably large headquarters of the Great Lao International Timber Company. On one melancholy expanse loggers were drawing off the last of the trimmed corpses in half a dozen trucks, the bulldozers and cranes lurching after them. Most of the forest around Tha Khaek has been felled comparatively recently and the phrase 'a degraded area' is sickeningly apt. Slashing and burning, though sad to see, doesn't leave a landscape utterly ravaged. Farmers use axes and hoes and fire; the earth is not compacted by gigantic machines and mangled by their monstrous tyre marks.

I was puzzled at first by a series of nine rectangular roadside pits, some five feet deep and eighty yards by forty, each with its English label – 'Pond No. 1', and so on. Could this be some grandiose government-cum-NGO fish-breeding project gone wrong? But Nos. 8 and 9 were filled with water and in each floated ten mighty tree trunks, being sprayed with rotating irrigation hoses driven by a noisy generator.

Karst mountains have no foothills and suddenly I was pedalling between stark, separate, sheer peaks, their shapes and arrangements unconventional, their precipices richly forested. Here is beauty awesome and unique – to do with contrasts and juxtapositions, the same group of peaks and corrugations presenting different patterns of grandeur from different angles. And the wayside trees matched the rest, growing to heights I couldn't measure with the eye – but Hare, when parked beneath them, looked like a Dinky toy.

Paradise Cliff (so named by the French) rises sheer for 900 feet from the bank of a swift sparkling stream. Here I explored by torchlight a cave big enough to hold a cathedral. (All Tha Khaek's caves are spider-free owing to their dense population of bats of various species – visible high overhead, depending from the rugged ceiling.) In another cave – its entrance twenty-five yards wide and over 100 feet high – a statue of the Lord Buddha is accompanied by an extraordinary work of erosion, a stone protuberance eerily resembling an elephant's head. In a third cave, multi-storeyed ladders lead from one level to the next. After that the Foot rebelled so I stayed in the saddle – or sat around rejoicing to be in such a wondrous place.

Rejoicing, too, to be able to walk anywhere without caution, to have an uncratered landscape around me – and not to be harrowed daily by UXO tragedies. Here in the Lao Lum heartland, one is very aware of Laos still being an un-united (rather than disunited) country. The varying fortunes of the different provinces during the long war widened historical gulfs. For years Xam Nua, Xieng Khouang and the Ho Chi Minh Trail provinces endured physical and emotional hell while the Mekong plain merely suffered the inconvenience of mass migrations and (unofficial) American occupation.

Between the mountains several isolated houses, rarely seen in the highlands, stood near patches of paddyland and in the few very small *bans* people smiled at me wonderingly. Cattle browsed in the bush and I paused to watch a roadside contest between a mature humped bull and a young male, both lusting after a bulling cow; she, like all her species, was bisexual and almost knocked her chosen female partner into a culvert while the males jousted. Several times they formally locked horns – the junior's were only half grown – a curiously ritualistic encounter lasting about ten minutes. Then victory was conceded to the senior who chased his coy prey into the bushes. But alas! she favoured the toy-boy and came racing back to him. Whereupon the senior snorted loudly, lowered his head, pawed the ground – and charged. Exit toy-boy, last seen galloping through the bush with his tail in the air. Those are the little side-shows missed by people travelling in motor vehicles.

The Mekong dawns are even more liable than the sunsets to inspire purple prose so I shall say nothing about the skyscape when I set off for Mrs S——'s *ban* at 6.15. On the way, a new Tourist Authority sign urged me (in English and French) to admire Nasaad, one kilometre up a track that tunnelled through fragrant bushes and giant bamboo. Even in the dry season Nasaad water-fall is impressive – fifty yards wide, cascading down a 140 foot cliff on a forested mountain as yet unlogged. Not long ago this must have been a magical place; now the Tourist Authority, as loutish as its counterparts elsewhere, has provided a concrete picnic site and viewing platform. Many other vandalisms are sure to be perpetrated in preparation for the much talked of 'Visit Laos Year 1999!'

It had rained heavily during the night and the air was fresh and cool, not at all what one expects in February on the plain. In the middle of an extended *ban*, lining the road for half a mile, a big brick kiln was being fired; from every compound livestock went wandering off to forage along the verges and in the scrub. Several new houses blended the traditional design with 'Western' materials and colours – a not unattractive experiment though certainly much less comfortable, in the hot season, than wooden homes.

In an area of old secondary growth – tall trees and thick bush – the road became an almost impassable track; deep sticky mud twice jammed Hare's wheels as I waded through wide lakes of red water. (I'm told the locals remove mudguards in the rainy season.) Having consulted Mrs Bounyong's essential sketch map, I turned right on a ridgetop and descended steeply to cross an irrigation channel. Where the track became a bamboo-shaded footpath my destination could be seen, thatched or tin roofs rising above young trees. Migrants founded this *ban* about a century ago when the French army's 'pacification' of the hilly region to the east made things unpeaceful.

Mrs S—— looked slightly alarmed as I dismounted, muddy and sweaty, by her ladder; she was weaving in the underspace. Then she read Mrs Bounyong's letter and laughed and embraced me – a non-Lao style of welcome, but I remembered that she had worked with a British NGO. 'You are like my English friends,' she said. 'They were brave ladies always travelling around alone, no fear. I'm sorry my husband is away in Hanoi, at a wedding. He would like to talk to you about our difficulties here, he talks good English.'

Upladder, the long airy living-room was simply furnished: table and chairs, a big cupboard, a small TV set, a carved wooden couch displaying some of Mrs S——'s exquisitely woven cushion covers. Full-page advertisements from *Time* magazine, and WHO AIDS-education posters, decorated two walls.

Mrs S—— poured herbal tea from a thermos and said, 'Soon AIDS will be a bad problem. But we like not to think about it, we don't count our deaths – we've no way to make counts. Still, we see young people dying, boys and girls working in Thailand bring it home.'

I soon understood why Mrs Bounyong had introduced me to her friend, a woman uninhibited about discussing the local machinations of NEM.

We strolled around the *ban*, occasionally glimpsing the nearby Mekong through an abundance of greenery. Twenty-eight hand-pumps are shared by 105 households and around every home grow trees, shrubs, flowers, vegetables, herbs. In 1992, as the LWU leader, Mrs S—— organized the subsidizing of these pumps on condition each household contributed towards the total cost of the project. Then she took a group of villagers to Savannakhét, about 100 miles south, where they were trained to find underground water, dig 30-foot borewells with poles and install the pumps. Since then more than 300 handpumps have been provided, through similar self-help projects, in three districts around Tha Khaek.

Compared to highland *bans*, I noticed here a more obvious (though not extreme) disparity of wealth. Some newish homes had enclosed their underspaces and replaced ladders with cement steps. More than a few had small black-and-white TV sets, several families owned rather battered Hondas and bicycles were common. Nobody worked at anything other than farming, except Mr S——, the only Vietnamese resident, who invested in a rice-mill when electricity came to the area. I remarked on the youth of some mothers (their grown-up children looking like their siblings) and Mrs S—— explained that families without sons, in need of male muscle-power, encourage their fourteen- or fifteen-year-old daughters to find a husband quickly.

On balance, Lao Lum men and women share the household's physical work equally – but not the mental work. Women manage both the domestic and the local economy, making all decisions about growing crops, selling them, building houses, trading livestock, schooling children – and conceiving babies. Yet the new breed of urban government official (and too many foreign NGOs) treat wives as their husbands' subordinates.

During the next two days I learned a lot, all of it bad for my blood pressure. In March 1993, knowing electricity was to reach the area six months later, the Provincial Agriculture and Forestry Service Office installed two powerful lift pumps, to bring water up from the Mekong. These, donated by an American church group and AusAID, enabled villagers to grow rice in the dry season. Mrs S—— then organized the clearing by voluntary labour of an old canal first dug in 1968 – but four years later she turned against this 'development'. Few women, she said, are interested in a second crop; most families grow ample wet-season rice for their own use and earn enough cash from their spring onion and tobacco crops and from weaving. To irrigate a second crop, poor families have to borrow heavily, which makes no sense. And when the stubble is ploughed immediately after harvesting, where are the cattle to graze? The forest cannot sustain them in the dry season. 'And why,' asked Mrs S——, 'must we waste free fertilizer from animals and spend on sacks from a depot? And on big back-tanks of poison to spray pests! We have no need of such things for wet-season rice, we know well how to control those pests.' Also, a hidden risk is involved in double-cropping. It makes such heavy demands on a family's workforce that some parents are tempted to dispatch their daughters to Thailand to earn the cash to pay wage labourers. 'And you know,' said Mrs S——, 'how girls earn money in Thailand.' Laos has no tradition of hiring wage labour and the paying of relatives or friends has always been rare – and seen, when it happened, in the context of mutual help rather than as an employer/employee relationship. 'That was a good way to live,' said Mrs S——, 'and we see no need to change it. But now men say we should have formal structures about wages and hours worked and so on – why? As my English friends used to say, "If it works, why fix it?" All the time now those men from Vientiane must interfere.'

When this 300 hectare irrigation scheme was being planned, to 'benefit' several *bans*, the local communities were not consulted or even informed – until the irrigation officers needed free labour. (Now the canal has to be maintained only by those who irrigate a second crop.) Incredibly, this internationally backed 'development' made no provision for the improvement of domestic water supplies. The total cost was 382.4 million kip (at 700 kip to the dollar), yet families are still drawing water from hand-dug wells if they are lucky, from the Mekong if they are not. This outrage is calmly explained away by the Vientiane bureaucrats: 'The Department of Irrigation can't meddle with drinking water supplies, the Health Ministry is responsible for that.' Which echoes the sort of answer given by Irish government departments when their intelligence/probity/humanity is questioned. I could picture the bureaucrats, and their foreign advisers, sitting behind their desks 'thinking big' in total ignorance of the realities of Lao Lum peasant life on the Mekong plain.

Perhaps the government has multiple motives for encouraging double cropping but the land tax, based on annual rice yields per hectare, is the most obvious. Since 1994 this has had to be paid in cash instead of rice and according to the Finance Minister, Saysomphone Phomvihane, the 1996–7 land taxes came to 2.4 billion kip. Also in 1994, the electricity companies demanded cash instead of rice. Soon various new irrigation schemes had caused

such huge over-production that the rice price dropped spectacularly, forcing families to sell a large proportion of their crop to pay
land taxes and irrigation/electricity bills and leaving those who
had grown only wet-season rice in a very bad way.

The traditional Lao farming methods – and attitudes – are of
course anathema to agribusinessmen who regard both farmers
and their land as part of a 'factory' which it is the duty of irrigation engineers and other 'experts' to make more productive.
According to 'development strategists', the fertile Mekong plain,
if lavishly irrigated, artificially fertilized and chemically de-pested,
will produce an abundance of rice for those highland folk now
going hungry because swidden farming must be abandoned.
Which crazed gang of macro-economists came up with this out-
standing example of their profession's ineptitude? Leaving aside
the environmental damage, how is it proposed to transport that
abundance to the hungry hill folk? And how are they to acquire
the cash to pay for it? Air America Inc. is no longer around to
make rice drops, nor is the CIA still around to buy the rice.

Why are these economic advisers so hell-bent on wrecking a way
of life that provides sufficient food for people's needs? Is it
because such people live happily on the outer margins of the consumer society, contributing virtually nothing to 'economic
growth'? Do the macro-economists truly believe their craziness is
'helping the South to catch up'? It is charitable to assume they
cannot see how quickly their strategies destabilize and demoralize
communities hitherto content and in command of their own lives.

From her file, hanging on the wall in a woven bag, Mrs S——
produced a page from the *Vientiane Times*, 1–4 November 1997. It
reported the second annual conference on national land management, a 'modernization' project now undermining the age-old Lao
Lum custom of women inheriting fields, houses and livestock. Ian
Lloyd, a 'land titling consultant', informed the conference that:

> Before issuing land titling certificates we need a basic law to
> ensure activities are effective. Protecting land title is the basic
> premise which will provide the foundation for other laws, on
> business, mortgages, finance, investment, land rental, the sale
> of land and how land is used . . . Land titling and land trans-
> fer are the main goals for ensuring land is used efficiently.

Mr Kham Ouane Boupha, Vice-Minister of Agriculture and Forestry, explained:

> We need to classify land for agriculture, industry, communication, culture, business, and other areas. After issuing land titles we have to promote commercial production alongside forestry conservation. The land law will be passed in 1999, it will take so long to finish because it needs to cater for everyone including those who have more land than allowed and will have to give some of it up.

Mr Siene Saphangthong, Acting Minister of Agriculture and Forestry, announced:

> The government has formulated rules on land management and allocation to eliminate slash-and-burn agriculture and encourage people to take up fixed occupations. Land will be allocated to the many ethnic groups for effective management and use under the guidance of macro-level management bodies.

This 'land titling' project began on 1 June 1997 and is to be completed in 2004 – lots of scope there for consultants. Private companies, often Vietnamese, carry out these surveys and each family has to pay for having its land measured. The fields are then registered in the name of the 'head of the household' – the husband, unless a woman is widowed. Only if a wife insists on her customary rights is she given the land title. 'And not many insist,' said Mrs S—— sadly. 'They don't think much about this new way, they don't understand it.' However, Mrs Bounyong had told me that in urban areas, where the divorce rate is increasing, women do see the importance of having their property correctly registered.

Consider Ian Lloyd's gobbledegook: 'Land titling and land transfer are the main goals for ensuring land is used efficiently.' 'Used efficiently' from whose point of view? Lao farmers are immensely knowledgeable as cultivators and have always used land efficiently, producing enough food, century after century, to rear healthy families. Mr Kham Ouane Boupha provides an answer: 'we have to promote commercial production'. And what about 'those who have more land than allowed and will have to give some of it up'? Allowed by whom? This smells like a familiar food industry ploy, confining the peasants' land use to the absolute minimum. Will compensation be paid for what has to be given up? Or will everyone be treated like those hill tribes forcibly removed to make way for dam-builders?

As for Mr Siene Saphangthong's encouraging people 'to take up fixed occupations' – *what* fixed occupations? At the end of the twentieth century it is admitted that for millions in all countries there will never again be permanent jobs. Lao (and other) subsistence farmers are lucky. Contrast their way of life – self-sustaining, purposeful, every individual needed by his/her community, every individual skilled and with scope for creativity as a craftsman – contrast that with the empty, passive, hopeless, dependent lives of the urban unemployed, superfluous and denigrated and now being described, ominously, as an 'under-class'.

Mr Siene's announcement that 'Land will be allocated . . . for effective management and use under the guidance of macro-level management bodies' would be comical were it not so threatening. Who will be running those macro-level management bodies? Is it planned to turn the independent Lao peasantry into an ill-paid labour force tied to 'commercial production'? In Lao eyes, how will this system differ from the collectivization attempted by the LPRP when first it came to power? Is there any reason to suppose Lao farmers will be more amenable to diktats from a macro-level management body than they were to the diktats of the Party? In the late 1970s the Lao were in control of their own country and farmers were allowed to reject collectivization without conflict. At the dawn of the twenty-first century someone else will be in control and corporate investors may demand, as they do in so many vassal countries, the use of the state's security forces to 'impose discipline'.

The modernizing of 'backward' countries like Lao is in no sense a benevolent enterprise: it is undertaken to enrich the developers and turn everyone into either a consumer or an ill-paid labourer. That may seem too obvious to need saying, yet an astonishing number of well-meaning folk remain convinced that 'we' are helping when we initiate and implement 'modernization'. Our faith that the West's way of doing things is the best way has been so firmly implanted that even now, when the evidence that this is not so has piled up on every continent (including the Antarctic), we find it hard to question our own superiority. However, as Zygmunt Bauman has recently written, 'Questioning the ostensibly unquestionable premises of our way of life is arguably the most urgent of the services we owe our fellow humans and ourselves.'

When I discussed all this with Marie she commented astringently on the ideas (if one can call them that) fuelling the NEM juggernaut. 'The government,' she said, 'have bought the whole modernization package and one of its vital ingredients is patriarchy. The globalizers' world is a man's world. Even if some of the consultancy gang are biologically female their mindset is male – has to be, or they wouldn't be up there earning $500 a day fees! But how are our Lao men going to fare when their capable women are shouldered out of the way? They're not bred to make decisions or take responsibility on their own, in a male-controlled environment. But will they be able to admit that to all the officials who'll be taking charge of their *bans*? Won't they want to seem modern and go along with the new ways? Which will suit the officials fine – no constructive opposition, no women around pointing out their mistakes. And the black joke is the women will still be the most productive earners, paying all the bills . . .'

Back in Tha Khaek, I met a *falang* – the only one seen in that town. He was wandering around looking rather mournful and seemed to want to talk so we had a few Beerlaos on the embankment. Thirty years ago he had worked with the International Voluntary Service in Khammuan province, helping to resettle survivors from the Ho Chi Minh Trail region in roadside *bans* along Route 13. 'We didn't know then we were part of a big CIA plot, can you believe that? But it's true, we were kids and keen to help these poor guys bombed out of their homes by Vietcong bastards. They couldn't speak any language to tell us who was really bombing them – anyway I guess they didn't know! Our work was a real important part of the plot, for the image of good kind Americans sending nice young men to help. It was years before I got things sorted out in my head and got mad at the way we were used.'

Darcy had come to Tha Khaek, alone, on an impulse, to mark

the thirtieth anniversary of his arrival in Laos. 'I reckoned to find those villages all gone – folks back home in their mountains. It kinda sickens me the UXO and chemical residues are keeping so many down here – no way can they go home. Back in the States we don't get much information about how things are other places. It's real strange to be back – town's changed a lot, used to be all go with discos and casinos. In LA my job's in the radiology department of a big hospital and there's times I look back and can't believe it – that I led such a primitive life here!'

During my time in Laos the cost of living for *falangs* dropped almost daily as the kip declined. Though Laos is not even a tiger cub, its currency is tied to the Thai baht and it seems can't be un-Thai'd. In July 1997 the exchange rate was 900 kip to the dollar, when I first changed on 6 December it was 1,700, on 17 December 2,210 – two months later, in Tha Khaek, 4,100.

At 11 a.m. there was no other customer in the small bank – recently opened, all shiny tiles and plastic counters and chairs. A Thai soap opera – the TV perched on a tall filing cabinet – was enthralling the young staff of seven. Three apparently unarmed soldiers sat outside under a thatched shade, playing Snakes and Ladders. A Visa card sign decorated the door but no one inside had ever heard of such a thing, never mind knowing how it works. The 1,000 kip notes were brand new and carelessly counted; I received 5,000 too many and had to return that afternoon, interrupting a jolly staff coffee party. The careless young man, overwhelmed by gratitude, insisted on my joining the party and rushed across the road to fetch an extra cup from an eat-drink shop.

As the sun was setting beyond the Mekong I enjoyed a last supper-cum-English-class with my four interpreters. We each had a big bowl of noodle soup containing bean sprouts and round meaty objects that might have been something's eyeballs (or the other sort of balls if the something was small) and a salad of lettuce, raw runner beans and mint on the stalk. The bill for five came to £1.25.

12

Bicycle as Bicycle

Regretfully I left Tha Khaek – that friendliest of towns – while a faint pinkness suffused the eastern horizon and Venus faded. My relationship with Venus is special; so often, on different continents, she has shone alone in the dawn sky as another day's journey has begun.

The newly modernized Route 13, which bypasses Tha Khaek, cost more than money. A few miles north of the town, road engineers demolished part of the Sikhottabong wall, an awesomely magnificent natural phenomenon, several hundred metres long and more than fifty metres high. It looks man-made; immediately one thinks of the Pyramids and Inca walls. That erosion could have created it is very extraordinary – almost incredible. The local legend – it was built by order of the gods, using the forced labour of an ancient people – seems equally likely. Erosion must have spent millions of years on the job but it took the engineers less than an hour to dynamite one corner – and had Route 13's widening required total demolition it would by now have vanished. I don't know what, if anything, the experts say; no guidebook refers to Sikhottabong. However, my young Tha Khaek friends told me that the rectangular stones of which it is formed are on average 150 metres long, ten metres wide and fifteen metres high.

For sixty miles Route 13 ran level – or undulated mildly – through a wide, sparsely inhabited landscape quite recently stripped of its forest. By the wayside lay several groups of giant tree roots, bleached and trimmed and grotesquely beautiful, all neatly numbered with white paint, awaiting transport. These sell well in the Rich World as exotic 'garden features'. The symbolism was painful: forests being uprooted, Lao culture being uprooted.

In the few small dreary *bans en route* live some of the Hmong (and other minorities) displaced from the Annamites to the east by the Secret War – or, latterly, by dam-building consortia. These unfortunates either farm the infertile land 'freed' by loggers, or slash and burn amidst the occasional stretches of secondary growth. Surprisingly, I heard many more birds than in the high forests, perhaps because the 'relocated' have been deprived of their muskets. One young man, walking along the verge, tried to stone a cock pheasant, missed, then grinned at me ruefully. Pheasants were numerous and several electric-blue crow-sized birds flashed through the foliage. A local abundance of snakes was suggested by five traffic victims, between one and two feet long.

In the biggest *ban* I paused to watch a jolly Hmong wedding party 'invading' the bride's home to carry out a pretend 'abduction'. Soon an elderly man approached me, waving a rice basket in the air and followed by a young woman clutching a bottle in one hand and a liqueur glass in the other. Both were poorly dressed, slightly drunk and rather aggressive. The man pinned a tiny plastic flower to my left sleeve while demanding money; he took the lid off his basket to show it half full of kip. When I had contributed the girl unsmilingly poured me a glass of *lau-lao* and urged me to toss it back quickly – the pair were in a hurry to get on with their fund-raising.

Until eightish the air remained cool and throughout the forenoon a strong cross-wind prevented heat stress. That was a treacherously misleading wind. At noon, finding myself only twenty miles from my destination – Nem Thone – I made a silly mistake and pedalled on, not realizing that by the end of February the midday sun is dangerous at Mekong level. Before long I was feeling dizzy and queasy and the next two hours were spent under one of the rare surviving roadside trees, contemplating the complexity of its lianas and tangled vines and the various parasitic growths on the branches and trunk. No wonder ecologists (and others) become frenzied when fighting for the preservation of forests. That one tree contained a whole interconnected world, populated by a dozen species of insect– but such worlds cannot long survive, once the host tree has been isolated.

Continuing slowly, I diagnosed incipient heat stroke – a diagnosis confirmed by my not wanting a Beerlao on arrival in Nem Thone. Instead I drank four litres of water – the same colour as the local chicken soup – in the *ban*'s first eat-drink shop.

Nem Thone is a run-down trading centre rather than a *ban*. Its straggle of eat-drink shophouses, selling a limited range of identical goods and serving foul food, lines Route 13 for a few hundred yards. The mixed population – Lao Lum, Hmong, Vietnamese – has been hard hit by the road's 'upgrading'; previously it took days to motor from Vientiane to Savannakhét, now it takes hours and no one needs to stop in Nem Thone. This perhaps explains the dispirited atmosphere; several premises are big enough to cater for a busload.

Most passing drivers behaved barbarously. New shiny limousines with tinted windows, new Toyota pick-ups, new government department minibuses or four-wheel drives raced through at 70 or 80 m.p.h, arrogantly blowing their horns. This hazard being as yet infrequent heightened the danger for those toddlers, goats, dogs, turkeys and ducks who still regarded the middle of the road as their territory, not appreciating that an EU-style highway leaves them no rights. For me this summed up 'developing' Laos: the Haves intoxicated by their new vehicles and a new road on which to exercise them, the Have-nots and their precious livestock being treated as expendable.

In Nem Thone's two-roomed 'Gest Hoose' – opened four months previously – I was, according to the register, the eleventh 'gest' and the first *falang*. Evidently the rather grumpy Vietnamese proprietor hoped to capture backpackers but misunderstood their minimum requirements. (Anyway, who but a cyclist would choose to stop overnight in Nem Thone?) The tin-roofed windowless hut, built of wood scavenged from loggers, was a stifling inferno. My room had a plank bed without sheets, a torn mosquito net, an earth floor strewn with the last occupant's litter. When I firmly requested washing water a handpump had to be primed with cloudy brown water drawn from a very deep, almost dry well. The loo – shared with two neighbouring families – was some forty yards away, down a grassy slope scattered with chunks of concrete from a nearby building site where a little wooden house was being erected on 'modern' stilts.

Nem Thone's shops offered no portable sustenance for the

morrow: no nuts, no bananas, no hard-boiled eggs, no dried buffalo hide, only countless packets of imported junk foods, hanging from shop fronts. On the Mekong plain the consumption of this extremely profitable rubbish is seriously worrying and all generations are addicts; elderly folk who elsewhere in Laos would be carrying rice baskets here carry a selection of garishly coloured packets in transparent plastic bags. The cold drink craze has also taken off – yet another American bad habit – despite icy drinks being so unhealthy in hot climates. (As the Indians taught me many years ago, scalding tea is the most cooling drink when one's body is overheated.) Even in non-electrified Nem Thone fizzy drinks and Beerlao are cooled in large metal iceboxes standing on beer crates outside every little eat-drink shop. At intervals the ice is renewed; big chunks – delivered every morning by truck – are kept in deep pits.

I studied the local supper menus by lifting the lids off pots, pans and basins and finally chose steamed rice, fish soup and shredded raw cabbage. As all cooking is done before noon the rice was cold and hard and the soup lukewarm. Moreover, the salad had been dressed with that repulsive decayed fish sauce. No one can accuse me of being a gourmet but I gave up half-way through.

While trying to eat, I observed something rare in Laos – a public family row. On the bench beside me a young mother was cleaning out her docile toddler's ears with loo paper wrapped around matchsticks. Then father-in-law came on the scene, disapproved of this activity and reprimanded her sharply – though not of course loudly. She persisted, obviously feeling that she was doing the right thing; her treatment of the little fellow was gentle and loving and he was making no complaints, standing with his head trustingly laid sideways on her lap. Grandad then called in rein-forcements: two older women, also with toddlers, and his wife. Eloquently he condemned his daughter-in-law, but no one else seemed willing to take a definite stance, on one side or the other – a very Lao reaction. However, the young mother, having lost face, was deeply distressed. Picking up her son she moved to sit apart on a low stool, staring fixedly at the sky, her face tilted upwards, barely controlling her tears. This was not a happy family. When the young husband arrived he scowled at his wife and made to take the toddler, who screamed and clung to his mother – thus

Father lost face. Seizing the child quite roughly he disappeared up the ladder to the living quarters above the shop – the little chap now silent. Granny then went to squat beside her daughter-in-law and murmured something that brought a sudden smile to the young woman's face. Grandad, looking sulky, retreated to the back of the shop and poured himself a glass of *lau-lao*. Meanwhile, to my relief, the toddler could be heard laughing.

Outside the Gest Hoose I wrote my diary. A solitary forest giant towered above the shack-shop opposite, its myriad mighty branches engraved blackly on a soft apricot sunset sky. Along the Mekong one sees many such lone survivors – trees in some way defective, from the loggers' point of view.

Soon after 8.00 I was asleep – only to be awakened three hours later by a truck driver dealing with a major crisis a few yards from where I lay. It took me some moments to realize what was going on; one isn't at one's most alert when roused out of a deep sleep by violent metallic noises. It seemed the entire vehicle had to be taken apart and put together again. I lit three tiny candles and read until 1.50 when at last, after many false starts, the unfortunate trucker was able to drive away.

After a night of heavy dew the fields looked rained on, the air was cool and the sky so hazy that the sun rose as a blurred orange globe – poised, for one memorable moment, above a gracefully drooping stand of giant bamboo.

Between Nem Thone and Pak Xan most of the small wayside *bans* are long-established Lao Lum settlements, thatched houses on stilts overlooking paddyfields. Some (too few) of the day's fifty-five miles ran through primary forest. Over one glorious eight-mile stretch I had a steep high ridge on my left and, on my right, the wide jade-green Nam Gnouang, its banks all gleaming golden sandhills, some covered in pale green shrubbery. Then the river turned abruptly to join the Mekong and was spanned by a long, ugly, Soviet-donated bridge. Half-way across I stopped (here the wind was gale force) and gazed upstream towards the dusk-blue foothills of the Annamites. Then, from the other parapet, I looked downstream and marked how the vivid waters of the Nam Gnouang contrasted with the murky brown Mekong, flowing powerfully below the flatness of Thailand.

My guidebook comments, 'There is almost no reason to stop in

Pak Xan, a provincial capital without any attitude.' I disagree; the capital of Bolikhamsai province does have an attitude, if not of the sort likely to attract tourists. For one thing, it is a military base and I saw an unprecedented number of armed soldiers patrolling the jerry-built main street or lolling about at junctions. This is the town I was not allowed to cycle to from Phonsavanh because of its 'unsettled hinterland'. In 1979 it was identified as the headquarters of the Thai Isan Liberation Party, led by two Thai ex-MPs and dedicated to the overthrow of the LPRP government. The locals belong to a Thai tribe, the Phuan, and many are Christian – which does not endear them to the Lao government. In 1992 a bus bomb, allegedly aimed at the military, killed several Lao civilians and until recently *falangs* were advised to avoid Pak Xan and escorted out of the town if they lingered. This may explain people's reluctance to help me find Mr Osakhanh's house – he being Mrs Bounyong's nephew, an English-speaker employed by the Ministry of Agriculture and Forestry. Eventually, by chance, Mr Osakhanh found me; his aunt had warned him that a two-wheeled visitor was imminent and on seeing me wandering and wondering he made the obvious deduction.

The Osakhanhs' pleasant dwelling – Lao Lum crossed with French colonial – overlooks the Nam Xan's union with the Mekong, far from the grotty town centre. Here tall palms, mature banana groves and gay flowering shrubs – flowering even in winter – surround each home. In the shade of a deep veranda sat the pregnant Mrs Osakhanh, weaving on an enormous loom. She also spoke English; the couple had met while co-workers on a Lao–Swedish Forestry Co-operation project.

Later, when we were alone, Mrs Osakhanh confided how much she was dreading the birth of her first baby. It was due in April, the hottest season, and then she would have to endure staying in bed for a month, lying twenty-four hours a day over a basin of burning charcoal. Not to do so would be to invite bad luck – including lactation failure – by offending the relevant *phi*. A few months previously a neighbour had defied this custom after her second baby and the infant, though born healthy, had since gone from one infection to another, with frequent fevers. His mother's angering of the *phi* was being blamed and the father, who only believes in forest cures, was further upset by the baby's being stuffed with Western medicines. 'I don't believe in charcoal,' said Mrs Osakhanh, 'but still I must respect the *phi*.'

Charcoal apart, there is much to recommend Lao birthing and post-natal customs. The details vary from tribe to tribe but in general husbands help to deliver the baby, occasionally assisted by a mother or mother-in-law. Having cut the cord with a boiled bamboo knife the husband ties it with a boiled cotton thread, then washes mother and baby with boiled water. During *You Kam* – the first month – he must care for both, while relatives look after older children if need be. He does all the household chores and cooking, paying close attention to food taboos. Chillies, papaya and eggs are believed to impede the shrinking of the womb, fish and chicken should be eaten twice a day and herbal tea drunk every hour to stimulate lactation. (A blend of twenty or more forest herbs goes into those special teas.) 'It makes trouble,' said Mrs Osakhanh, 'when foreign bosses don't understand why men with new babies can't go out working in offices.'

As a hectic red-gold sunset shimmered and quivered on the Mekong we dined under a palm tree – sticky rice, plump grilled fish only an hour out of the Nam Xan, and a salad of lettuce, spring onions and parsley from the family's riverside plot. To my hostess's delight I ate immoderately, having been on rather short commons since leaving Tha Khaek.

By then I had realized that Mr Osakhanh was an unhappy young man – understandably so. He worked as a conservation officer on a monthly salary of US$30 (at the current rate of exchange) and his job satisfaction was nil. We talked until midnight and what I learned gave me a sleepless night. Because the Osakhanhs have since migrated to the West, I am free to quote my host; sadly, he won't be returning to Laos.

In 1993 some 2,300 square miles of Khammuan and Bolikhamsai provinces were officially designated a National Biodiversity Conservation Area (NBCA). (The Lao government delights in these pompous labels provided by the 'international community's' gaggle of transient consultants and resident advisers.) Most of that area was then accessible only on foot and its new status had been partly inspired by the discovery thereabouts, in 1992, of the hitherto unknown saola about which zoologists are still arguing. Does this antelope-like creature, with long thin horns curving backwards, belong to the goat-related *Caprinae* or to the *Bovinae* sub-family? That debate, however, did not bother Mr Osakhanh; his concern was to save the saola from extinction. And he was no less concerned about the dozen or so other globally endangered species living in this region. He had joined the Ministry in 1995 because his job description included 'reporting illegal intrusions' but soon it was made plain that he should not notice certain intrusions . . .

Enter the Lao villain of the piece, the Highland Regions Development Corporation – in Lao, Bolisat Phattana Khet Phoudoi (BPKP). I have mentioned observing an army-managed state corporation logging in Xieng Khuang province and the BPKP is another of those. During the decade after its establishment in 1984 its sale of primary forest Annamite timber to foreign buyers earned US$105 million, 40 per cent of Laos's total export earnings. In 1995 the sale of Khammuan province's timber put $12 million into the government's coffers – yet the provincial forestry department's budget was exactly $700.

A mixture of rage and grief brought tears to Mr Osakhanh's eyes as he recounted the fate of Mai Lang-Leng. This extremely rare Lao species of fragrant cypress was recently identified by British botanists as *Fokienia hodginsii* and now survives only in NBCAs on the remotest Annamite ridges separating Laos and Vietnam. (During the 1980s all those growing on the Vietnamese side were felled.) In 1996 Mr Osakhanh discovered that the vast majority of Laos's Mai Lang-Leng had been numbered and marked for felling by the BPKP. But he could do nothing to save them; each tree was valued at $100,000. They grew in ancient groves, scattered along high, well-drained ridges, and on the nearest level ridgetop other mighty trees were felled to make space for the BPKP's enormous Russian helicopters. These winched the Mai Lang-Leng to the nearest road, newly bulldozed through 'protected' NBCA forests. Trucks then took them quickly across the border to the Vietnamese port of Vinh from where they were shipped to South Korea and Japan – for use as temple beams, or to make coffins for the *rich* rich.

Mr Osakhanh saw the setting up of NBCAs as a smokescreen behind which the BPKP could collaborate with multinational dam-building consortia and 'timber barons' from Hong Kong, Taiwan,

Malaysia and Japan; such collaborations enable the military to pillage areas beyond reach of their own comparatively limited technology. To obtain all the desired concessions, 'outside investors' need only throw a handful of peanuts (by corporate standards) to a few Lao government ministers.

Mr Osakhanh's grandfather, a friend of Ho Chi Minh, was a Pathet Lao leader who for many years fought and suffered – 'and he had ideals'. His grandson made the depressing point that the dying off of that generation is leaving Laos increasingly vulnerable to exploitation I thought it tragic that he was planning to emigrate, when his country so desperately needs young people of vision, integrity and intelligence. Yet were he to remain in Laos he could achieve nothing. 'And I might have an accident,' he observed. 'People not welcome in NBCAS often have accidents. That's how the corporate cookie crumbles.' In the West he hoped to work for a conservation NGO independent of corporate funding and to publicize the dams controversy. Next morning, as I was leaving, he gave me a 'Discussion Paper' by Stuart Chape, published in 1996 by the World Conservation Union and dauntingly entitled *Biodiversity Conservation, Protected Areas and the Development Imperative in Lao PDR: Forging the Links.* Of that chilling document, more anon.

This was another cool morning and the mist lingered for hours – one of those mobile silvery mists that make landscapes seem magical, as though some elemental fairy wand were being waved. Here were stern mountains, nearby on my right, contrasting with the bland Mekong plain on my left. I had hoped to reach Lao Pako by sunset (Marie and I were to meet there) but after sixty-five miles the afternoon sun defeated me. Instead I spent the night in a friendly little riverside *ban* a few miles off Route 13 where the primary school teacher eagerly offered hospitality – then gathered his forty-three pupils for an impromptu English lesson.

Setting off at 5.45 I got the full benefit of a spectacular sunrise, unusually prolonged – high cloud-banks displaying every shade of pinkness and redness above a clear blue-green horizon.

For me Lao Pako was an unlikely destination, an 'ecotourism lodge'. But Marie had assured me that it lacked electricity and hot water, could not be reached by motor vehicle and was a tranquil, pop-music-free zone: the management forbids TVs, transistors and tape-recorders. In 1990 the site was leased from the government for fifty years by Burapha Development Consultants Ltd, a German/Austrian/Swedish/Finnish consortium which planned to grow bluegums but soon switched to ecotourism.

Fifteen miles from Vientiane I turned off Route 13 to follow a narrow road in the process of being crudely 'upgraded'; with every turn of the pedals indelible spots of bitumen splattered my shoes. This road, well signposted by Burapha, zigzagged across country for some ten miles, passing two large *bans* with a few Western-style bungalows around their edges. Then it ended in a fishermen's *ban* on the left bank of the Nam Ngum; from here most visitors hire a canoe to Lao Pako.

I preferred the sandy track that ran parallel to a concrete irrigation channel (Italian aid) with a sophisticated system of locks; beyond the fast-flowing water stretched miles of commercial sugar cane, securely fenced. Not long ago the locals grew their own rice on this land; now they are wage-labourers. Next came a bumpy footpath winding through woodland until Lao Pako's boundary blocked the way: a high wire fence, a massive wooden gate, a neat notice in Lao and English saying, 'You may come through this gate but please close it.' As the construction in question resembled a fortification rather than a gate, all my efforts to open it failed. It seemed I was stymied – one person could not lift Hare over – but in such situations Fate rarely lets me down. A wood-collecting Hmong boy appeared – aged perhaps twelve – and I shouted and beckoned. Slowly he approached, looking sullen, and indicated that I must not continue; his manner suggested an understandable dislike of ecotourists, for whose benefit so much land has been enclosed. Pointing to the notice, I assumed a worried expression and requested assistance. Reluctantly the boy laid down his load and helped me heave Hare over, then quickly disappeared into the bushes. I walked the rest of the way on a hilly footpath; all around was original vegetation of the sort known as 'dry monsoonal forest', the trees small to medium sized, interspersed with wild banana and bamboo.

Marie was breakfasting when I arrived. Standing to greet me she announced, 'I've a nice surprise for you!' Moments later the surprise appeared – Jaques, on his way back from Savannakhét. We spent the day together, strolling through the forest until noon, then swimming in the Nam Ngum, keeping close to the bank – the current is much stronger than it looks.

Despite my allergy to tourist resorts, I enjoyed Lao Pako. Only local materials were used in the construction of its four Lao Lum longhouses, with beds for twenty guests. During my three-day stay few other residents appeared, though several parties came from Vientiane for Sunday lunch; excellent Lao meals are cooked on bottled-gas stoves in the kitchen hut. The restaurant is a thatched platform high above a sweeping curve of the Nam Ngum; from the far bank rise steep forested hills and, looking upstream, one sees in the near distance low chunky blue mountains. A circular open-air bar, its thatch extending over the stools, serves imported luxury drinks as well as Beerlao. Those seriously in pursuit of solitude (or not wanting to spend more than 4,000 kip a night) can sleep far away in the forest in an isolated shelter, modelled on paddyfield watch-huts, with three rattan half-walls and no furniture. I chose the remotest of these; my bathroom was five minutes' walk away, a deep pool in a clear stream shaded by majestic 'survivors'.

There is something pleasantly eerie about the Lao Pako area. This came across to me, strongly, even before Marie mentioned that the place is locally regarded as 'a sort of *phi* headquarters', which explains why the lodge's site – an open level space, naturally treeless – had long remained unoccupied. When cultivating hereabouts, people often found ancient artefacts and in the winter of 1995–6 a Swedish-funded dig excavated forty-five complete jars, 270 kilos of potsherds, spindle whorls, iron arrowheads and knives, fragments of copper vessels, red ceramic plates and green glass, scrapers, stone axes and burnt animal bones. Carbon dating revealed that the site had been occupied, by the same cultural group, from the fourth to the sixth century AD. The dig – close to the guest dwellings – was then filled in. It is hoped to extend this archaeological exploration when more funding becomes available.

On the restaurant platform a frisky north wind tempered the afternoon heat while Marie, Jaques and I considered the Stuart Chape 'Discussion Paper'. This is a shocking example of the sort of pressures put by the 'international community' on the inexperienced governments of small, isolated countries – irresistible pressures, a bulldozer driven at an anthill. First, you 'place' the victim country on a scale of poverty related to Rich World values and conditions. We read:

> In the UNDP Human Development Report 1996, Lao PDR ranks 138 out of a total of 174 countries, with a Human Development Index (HDI) of 0.40, which compares with the average of 0.563 for all developing countries and 0.909 for industrial countries . . . Eighty per cent of the population of 4.6 million people is rural, with poor primary health care services, and limited access to safe water and sanitation. In the 1996 report, UNDP has introduced a 'new, multidimensional measure of human deprivation called the Capability Poverty Measure (CPM)'. The CPM considers the lack of three basic capabilities: to be well nourished and healthy (represented by the proportion of children under five who are underweight); healthy reproduction (indicated by the proportion of births unattended by trained health personnel); and the capability to be educated and knowledgeable (represented by female illiteracy) . . . Lao PDR has a CPM value of 54.6, ranking the country 80 out of 120 countries assessed on this basis. This ranking is established by the fact that 52% of births are unattended by trained health personnel, 54% of children under five are underweight and the female illiteracy rate is 57.9%. These figures reveal that almost half the population lives in poverty and lacks the minimum capabilities to achieve their human development potential.

Suddenly Jaques laughed aloud. 'Who do they think they're kidding?' He looked at me and asked, 'After travelling through some of our mountains, d'you believe the UNDP has the foggiest notion how many births are unattended or how many women illiterate?'

We read on:

> Lao PDR's low HDI is a reflection of a number of factors relating to the national economy and recent history. [There is]

limited infrastructure development, especially with respect to roads and other services. Much of the predominantly rural population remained effectively isolated from the main urban centres and could not break out of dependence on subsistence agriculture. However, in 1986 the Government announced the 'New Economic Mechanism' . . . and there has since been good macroeconomic performance in terms of such factors as GDP growth and reduction in inflation. [But] the reform process has revealed serious obstacles to a sustainable growth path. Firstly, the low level of domestic resource mobilization is a major constraint to economic development; it points to the need for sustained external assistance. Secondly, the country's development strategy is seriously hindered by a small production/export base, with export earnings depending mainly on electricity, agriculture, timber and wood products. Thirdly, Lao PDR has increasingly been faced with acute absorptive capacity problems, resulting from the underdeveloped macroeconomic institutions and serious shortage of skilled manpower. Fourthly, the early fruits of economic development have not been spread evenly to regions outside the urban centres; absolute poverty is still widespread in rural and remote areas . . . Considerable external support will continue to be needed for future development.

Marie's face was flushed with anger, making her look oddly like one of those 'deprived' rosy-cheeked women one sees in mountain *bans*. 'It's all so obvious!' she said. 'Droves of overpaid men in offices dream up these ludicrous HDIs and CPMs, compute reams of pseudo-findings, present them to the government and offer financial aid and expert advice. Who in authority is likely to argue with them? Simply "ranking" a country so far down the scale undermines a people's self-respect and self-confidence. And the carrot of financial aid is always tasty.'

Jaques added, 'Most Westerners – literate, with access to information – haven't a clue how the development industry operates. So it's no surprise the Lao don't argue when told they need "considerable external support" for the foreseeable future.'

Doggedly we read on:

As well as its growing strategic economic position in the region, Lao PDR also has major strategic importance as a result of its abundant natural resources – in particular its water and forest resources which have been, and will continue to be, the keystones of its economic development and which are increasingly attractive to its resource-depleted neighbours. Within the mainland Southeast Asia region the only other countries with comparable natural resource bases are Cambodia and Myanmar. Lao PDR has the advantages of location, and a stable political and commercial environment. However, Lao PDR is currently one of the least developed countries in the world. The country is faced with a great paradox. Despite its abundant natural resources, human development indicators remain among the lowest in the world, and its limited skilled human resource capacities constrain a 'home grown' approach to providing rapid solutions to urgent national development issues. The most obvious alternative, over the short to medium term at least, is to rely on foreign investment and exploitation of natural resource assets . . . The Government has taken the enlightened step of legally establishing a comprehensive and representative system of protected areas. It has also signed the Convention on Biological Diversity . . . Herein lies another paradox. After taking such a major initiative in declaring more than 12% of the land area for conservation . . . the Government is now coming under intense criticism from international lobby groups for its plans to link hydropower development to designated conservation areas . . . If the international community – donors, NGOs, bilateral partners, international banks and so on – is serious about providing effective assistance to the country then there needs to be a collective readjusting of perspectives in terms of 'what is best for Lao PDR'. While there may be issues of concern relating to current approaches to development, there are issues of equal concern in relation to the application of external conservation models and their relevance to the situation in Lao PDR . . . The investment contribution being made by the international community in biodiversity conservation needs to be provided on the clear understanding that the conceptual bases and methodologies of such conservation will be suited to the particular constraints and opportunities of the Lao situation. That is, the constraints imposed by severe underdevelopment and the need to address these as a matter of urgency; and the opportunities provided by high biodiversity values, unique landscapes and the need to work with local people in the development of effective management regimes. This may require acceptance by investors of linkages and trade-offs between development and conservation which may no longer be acceptable in their home countries (such as the use of protected areas as catchments for hydropower dams), but are nonetheless relevant – if not imperative – in the Lao context.

Marie slapped the book shut and feigned throwing it into the Nam Ngum. 'What a cunning thug!' she muttered through clenched teeth.

Jaques winced. 'Don't condemn him – it could be he's sincere.' Then he repeated what he had said to me in the bus. 'Those guys, mostly they're not bad – only ignorant.'

When I had fetched three hard-earned Beerlaos we debated that point.

Marie said to Jaques, 'What d'you mean by "ignorant"? Most of us associate ignorance with stupidity and you socialize with those types, you know they're not stupid. At best they choose not to be informed about the consequences of their decisions. And the arms manufacturers, tobacco companies and purveyors of infant formulas can't possibly be unaware that they are the direct cause of death, injury and disease.'

I had to agree with Marie though I would have preferred to agree with Jaques. Many corporate predators have had distinguished academic careers, are admired for their aesthetic sensibility, behave honourably and graciously in relation to their own sort – yet are insensitive, unscrupulous and destructive in their treatment, by remote control, of other peoples. Behind this contradiction Marie discerned racism – wrongly, in my view. A century ago the sort of men now exploiting distant victims were engaged in exploiting their compatriots. During England's Industrial Revolution the ordinary person's standard of living was ruthlessly lowered as rural workers were forced to migrate to the new urban slums, a process now being replicated in the Poor World, often in the guise of 'development aid'.

Then Jaques said, 'I mean ignorance in the Buddhist sense. Nothing to do with stupidity or academic brilliance or scientific know-how. Ignorance of our own nature and our connectedness to the rest of the world. The illusion that we can achieve happiness by asserting ourselves, as separate individuals – always controlling events and environments. Which leads to self-deception about true motives, the way Stuart Chape and his colleagues have to deceive themselves.'

'I think we need more beer,' said Marie.

The 'development and biodiversity conservation' conglomerate for whose benefit Stuart Chape wrote his 'Discussion Paper' includes the Swedish and Dutch governments, the World Bank, the EU, the UN Development Programme, the UN Environment Programme, the Wildlife Conservation Society and the Lao government. By now this conglomerate is extremely sensitive about the catastrophic social consequences of dam-building – the 'involuntary' (i.e. forced) resettlement of isolated communities. In Thailand, during the past forty years, the World Bank has funded so many dams that more than 150,000 villagers have been displaced to make way for the vast reservoirs that submerged their homes, fields and forests. World Bank officials claim that financial compensation (always meagre, sometimes not received), and resettlement sites and 'development' opportunities, leave the displaced 'better off than before'. The displaced do not agree.

In Laos, at the beginning of 1998, twenty-eight mega-dams were being constructed or planned. The Huay Ho dam, a joint venture between a Thai company, a South Korean corporation and the Lao state electricity company, had displaced 400 people. The Xekaman I dam, planned by an Australian/Malaysian/Thai consortium, threatened 2,220 people. The Nam Theun II dam – the most controversial of all, backed by Electricité de France, three Thai companies, Australia's Transfield and the Lao government – would displace more than 5,000 people. In June 1997 a UNDP report, *Basic Needs for Resettled Communities in the Lao PDR*, commented: 'Relocations caused by hydropower projects on the one hand appear to be of an involuntary nature: it is a case of absolute necessity and the villagers have no choice but to accept it. On the other hand the developers, generally foreigners, are the ones to assess and the ones in charge, and therefore in a way an international responsibility is involved.'

In September 1997 an Asian Development Bank report, *Sekong Sesan and Nam Theun River Basins Hydropower Study*, noted: 'The resettled Nya Heun people at Ban Chat San Unit 8 are suffering from severe malnutrition. Only 7kg of milled rice per adult was distributed in July and no rations were provided during August and September. We were told villagers had resorted to travelling to the market at Paksong to borrow money from money lenders at high rates of interest in order to purchase rice. Others travelled great distances to find creeks that had fish in them. This situation is a human rights emergency that needs immediate attention at a high level in Vientiane.' (Marie informed me that the situation received no attention at any official level.) The report continued: 'The cultural identity of an ethnic group may be linked to residence within a particular agroecosystem. Thus, for example, ethnic groups in southern Laos may suffer an irreversible loss to their textile tradition if they lose access to the forest and village resources that provide the dyes and the raw silk.'

Marie replaced these reports (and several others) in her briefcase and said, 'Mountain people who've always lived outside the cash economy just can't be humanely resettled down in an alien place where their knowledge and skills are irrelevant. There were only 1,200 families in the Nya Heun tribe, living in thirty groups. Now they're dying out, not only from malnutrition and malaria but from broken hearts. I know, I've visited them in that dreadful Unit 8 and looked into their eyes and seen no will to live. But who cares? The dam-builders don't, the government doesn't. The UN a few years ago passed two pious wordy Resolutions condemning forced evictions world wide – but as usual it takes no action. Can you imagine a UN High Commissioner for Human Rights standing up to the vested interests represented by Stuart Chape?'

We talked then about de-skilling, an insidious and fast-spreading form of impoverishment. I recalled observing the process in my own home town – which, but for its cathedral and illustrious past, might more accurately be described as a village. Fifty years ago Lismore supported tailors, shoemakers, seamstresses, basket-weavers, blacksmiths, bakers, butter-makers, poultry-keepers – all fully employed. When modernization rendered such local talent superfluous the children and grandchildren of those skilled workers found alternative employment in distant places. But for the majority of the de-skilled in a country like Laos that option is not there – and never will be. De-skilled peasants, without access to the level of education that enables people to adapt to the modern world, are doomed – reduced to scrabbling around on the fringes of the consumer society, trying to earn cash to buy mass-produced substitutes for what they used to make, with pride, out of the natural materials around them. In Laos this consequence of 'development' seems especially saddening, given the artistry applied to everyday objects and structures: garments, furniture, rice baskets, winnowing trays, fences, balconies, woven house walls, thatched roofs.

Jaques remarked, 'Most people, listening to you two, would say you were being arrogant. There's more hard work in weaving a wall than in building with concrete blocks. And using tin sheeting is easier than collecting and binding grass sections. And it's quicker to buy a plastic chair than to carve one.'

That reminded me of a reviewer of *The Ukimwi Road* who countered my criticisms of the aid industry by arguing that 'it is arrogant to deny Africans the right to try to attain some of the West's advantages'. A kindly argument – but unconvincing for lack of proof that Western interventions have benefited the majority throughout the Poor World. 'Arrogant' and 'simplistic' are favourite big sticks with which to beat those who dare to challenge 'progress'. But I have been too long on the road to fear such sticks. Thirty-five years ago I was accused of being 'simplistic' when I campaigned against the new agribusiness then replacing farming in Ireland. I was scoffed at as an ill-informed romantic, looking backwards through rose-tinted spectacles, refusing to recognize global needs. Agribusiness, requiring the replacement of men by machines, the cruelty of factory farming and the use of deadly chemicals, was allegedly essential to feed a rapidly increasing world population. Since then, we have seen many millions of tons of surplus food being destroyed to keep prices high and millions of dollars/marks/pounds being paid out to farmers who refrain from cultivating their land. Yet now exactly the same argument is in use to justify the genetic modification of food plants.

On my last evening in Lao Pako I had one too many beers with new friends, an exceptionally congenial Swedish couple. When Mr Bylen stood me a seventh I thought it impolite to refuse though the sixth had felt like enough. Eventually, in merry mood, I tottered off into the forest carrying a mini-lamp which soon expired. By an unfortunate (or incompetent) coincidence my pencil torch did likewise a moment later and somewhere I took a wrong turning – as I tend to do, even in daylight when sober. It was a moonless night and no starlight could penetrate the foliage: the darkness was total. Uncertainly I stumbled over tangled tree roots and into inexplicable shallow holes, then attempted to retrace my steps. I was not drunk enough to be reckless; when I seemed to be getting into denser forest, on a rougher path, I decided to stop and sleep on a root-free space. Luckily there was no dew (an ominous sign, as I realized next day when the temperature soared into the nineties) and I slept soundly, using my journal bag as pillow.

I woke before dawn – without a hangover, which says much for Beerlao – and uncurled myself and stretched (feeling rather like a cat) and lay listening to the first bird and insect noises and the faraway crowing of cocks.

Awaiting the sunrise, I wondered about ecotourism. It sounds less malign than mass tourism but around Lao Pako how do the locals feel when foreigners lease their land, ban hunting and wood cutting and erect a high wire fence? Already this area has been degraded – so why impose such restrictions on people who will perforce ignore them but are made to feel like quasi-criminals by their existence? Daily I saw young men roaming around with home-made guns, seeking protein and looking alarmed when they realized I had noticed them. And during my forest walks I observed that several trees, including a mahogany, had recently been felled with axes. Much is made of the Lao Pako lodge providing jobs for twelve villagers – but if the rest have to hunt and collect firewood furtively . . . ? Also, the expat manager did not respect his staff. On the previous morning I had witnessed him loudly and at some length insulting the young man behind the bar – in front of three other staff members and four *falangs*. He reminded me of a 'Rhodie' reprimanding an errant black – a 'munt'. In Laos, where such behaviour causes deep humiliation, and the ordinary people are so consistently courteous, expats of this type should be deported.

Unless those running a project are genuinely committed to conservation, methinks ecotourism is a mere gimmick to attract those jaded by conventional tourism. Marie had told me of plans, which she was challenging, to establish an 'ecopark' nearby, a few miles upstream. This would mean forcibly 'relocating' two small *bans*, building a multi-storey hotel and entertainment complex, then persuading people that here they could have a thrilling encounter with Nature on the bank of the Nam Ngum surrounded by 'virgin forest'. The cynicism of such developers is peculiarly sickening; they take advantage of those who vaguely want to be 'ecologically sound' but can know nothing of the complexities involved.

In Vientiane, when I paid a farewell visit to Mrs Bounyong, she told me about a bird sanctuary established some eight years previously by villagers who linked a drastic drop in the local fish population to a lack of those birds whose droppings nourish fish. (The birds had of course been eaten.) A specially created lake and a headman's 'preservation order' had the desired effect; hundreds of herons and bitterns settled nearby and the fish increased and multiplied and filled the lake. It is drained every March, when the fish are sun-dried and divided between the *ban*'s ninety families. In 1996, a foreign eco-NGO got wind of this enterprise and were astonished that illiterate villagers had proved capable, *sans* outside advice, of diagnosing what was wrong and retrieving the situation. Then they were affronted by the villagers' polite but firm refusal to allow them to set up ornithologists' observation platforms – another ecotourism project, to raise funds for that NGO. As Marie had observed in another context, Lao peasants could teach their government ministers a thing or two about rejecting foreign meddling. Sadly, a forest fire had recently broken out near this *ban* (Chinese loggers were blamed) and as some 300 men struggled to fight the flames a tiger appeared – less than forty miles from Vientiane. Mrs Bounyong feared that the misfortunate animal, deprived by the blaze of his natural prey, might soon kill a buffalo or a person and therefore be himself killed. Or the Chinese loggers might shoot him for his body parts.

It took me three hours to cover the thirty miles from Lao Pako to Vientiane; I arrived at 9.30, as the heat was becoming intolerable. (That week's high temperatures were described by Sheila as 'freakish, not expected until the end of March'.) On Route 13 I overtook all other cyclists, including a young man on a racing bicycle; the Lao are notable for strength and stamina rather than speed. However, as cyclists they achieve remarkable feats of balance. I passed one woman holding a parasol in her left hand and having her minute baby – not in a sling – tucked under her left arm while heavy wicker pannier bags of vegetables hung from a bamboo pole tied to the carrier.

In Lao Pako I had overheard a UN family planning consultant defining the Lao addiction to babies as a 'major problem'. Certainly the fifth or sixth (or tenth) infant gives as much joy to both parents as the first – and to its older siblings, who swamp the junior member with affectionate attention. Soon after my return home there was a media debate about the right of parents to administer corporal punishment to their children. Any Lao would have been scandalized, seeing the use of physical violence to discipline children as utterly depraved and barbaric.

Vientiane's streets were in an even more parlous state than before. A thick blanket of dust enveloped everything and everyone; all age groups were afflicted by rasping coughs. Deep, wide trenches had been dug throughout the city centre, colossal drainage pipes lay all over the place in segments – many broken – and high ridges of excavated earth blocked the traffic. I tried to picture the scene when the rains started in May but my imagination boggled. The Vietnamese companies involved were proving criminally inefficient in their failure to co-ordinate their activities. Also, the relative sizes of kick-backs for the road-construction team and the water and sewage teams were a source of delaying dissension. My expat informant, who was overseeing a foreign-funded irrigation project, grumbled that the Lao are not really interested in 'development' and often say, 'It was OK before . . .' He went on: 'At first they can seem full of enthusiasm for a new idea but they lose interest when the need for hard work and organization hits them. They've just not got the mindset for being developed. We're only wasting money on them.'

The day of my departure was overcast and not too hot, as though the weather *phi* had registered my low spirits and decided to be kind. I so much wanted not to leave Laos that I left four hours earlier than necessary. The first empty tuk-tuk to come past Sheila's house was rather battered but driven by a young man with an enchanting smile – Mr Soubanh – who leaped out to help me with my luggage. By this stage I was not travelling light, having acquired an inordinate number of books, pamphlets, reports and diverse documents.

Within moments the tuk-tuk had suffered the first of three breakdowns. Each mishap required Mr Soubanh to grovel beneath the engine for ten or fifteen minutes, doing esoteric things with his bare hands. He then reappeared, grinning reassuringly, covered in red dust and black oil, and on we chugged at less than my cycling speed. It never occurred to Mr Soubanh that I might need to get to Nong Khai at a certain hour and this seemed a fitting way to leave Laos: slowly and inefficiently, in the company of an endearing young man who coped serenely with his machine's idiosyncrasies and had no sense of time.

Often in the past I had regretted the end of an enjoyable journey but never before had I felt so sad when leaving a country – and this despite an imminent reunion with two granddaughters. It took me a little time – so strong was this emotion – to recognize its real source. On the way to the border it had felt purely personal: I was sad to be leaving the most lovable and in many ways the most civilized people I have ever travelled among. Later, on the overnight train to Bangkok, I realized that at the deepest level I was grieving because were I to return in a few years I would not find the same Laos – not even in the mountains.

Afterwords

To the indigenous peoples of North and South America, Columbus's discovery was a historic disaster leading to the loss of their traditional freedoms and livelihoods, the devastation of their lands and the destruction of their cultures. That story continues today . . . for other non-European peoples all over the planet. For them Columbus's discovery in 1492, and Vasco da Gama's sailing to India in 1498, signify the beginning of half a millennium of European world domination – at first Christian and latterly secular.

James Robertson, 1990

Marie wrote to me in July 1998.

Dear Dervla,

At last the 'Asian crisis' has reached Laos, maybe a long-term good thing. Quite a few predators have taken fright and pulled out including Phu Bia Mining, Mansfield, Svenska, Sweco. Best of all, Nam Theun II dam is looking less attractive with some Thai investors selling some of their shares, though our government is still pushing for it. But Thailand won't be buying as much electricity as planned before and won't be paying such a high price, so conditions for the World Bank loan will be harder. Forget biodiversity, just from the economic angle Nam Theun II now looks stupid.

But this recession is a short-term bad thing. When you left four months ago the kip was 4,100 to the dollar, now it's 5,400. Meat costs four times more than six months ago, rice has gone from 450 a kilo to 1,600. Many Vientiane families are hungry, government employees worst hit. Before, most city families were self-sufficient in food, growing rice and veg. on the plain around, keeping poultry and fish-ponds near their homes. That's changed, very quickly, with more and more common land leased out by the government for commercial farming. Lao people working with international NGOs on a dollar wage are not so desperate even if they're paid in kip. But my friends running small businesses can't buy imported raw materials or spare parts and have sacked most workers. Two Lao Aviation planes were seized because the company couldn't pay the leasing rates. So we have no more flights to Bangkok and domestic flights are much reduced and *falangs* advised to avoid them. In May the morning flight to Phonsavanh crashed, some spare part had been improvised. Lao friends of mine going to an environmental conference in Bokeo province were advised by the Prime Minister's office not to take the scheduled flight but go by road via Thailand – a two-day journey! It's said the Lao Tourism Authority is rethinking its plans for 1999 – supposed to be the 'Visit Laos Year'! If so, that would be another good long-term outcome. Here expats have always forecast, 'If the Thai economy coughs the Lao economy will die of pneumonia.'

The city streets are in such a state I can't describe them, the construction teams seem to make no progress – why? There are many rumoured reasons but as usual no facts available. A few weeks ago the Lao Pako manager rode his motorbike into a big new hole six metres deep and unmarked – broke his shoulder and his head and lost his memory.

In May and June the Poo Khor Khain mountain, a so-called 'protected area' about 60 km from Vientiane, had extensive forest fires doing sickening damage. It was (still is) being logged by BPKP and repeatedly the workers' fag-ends set things alight. So what's new?!

I'm sorry Dervla this is all so grim but you wouldn't want me to write you fairy-tales.

In December 1998 Marie wrote again, enclosing a cutting from the *Vientiane Times*. I read the cutting first.

NAM THEUN II TAKES MAJOR STEP FORWARD

Completion of the proposed Nam Theun II hydropower project, which has been disputed for years between the developers and environmentalists, took a major step forward on November 16 when a 'Heads of Agreement' was signed between the government of the Lao PDR and the Nam Theun II Electricity Consortium (NTEC). Although negotiations regarding impacts of the giant dam, to inundate 450 square km, are still going on, many construction activities have already been carried out by NTEC. Its Director, M. Jean-Christophe Delvallet, said, 'The very large revenues of Nam Theun II for the government will without any doubt greatly benefit Laos, its economy and people.'

This project has been the subject of an extensive series of environmental, social, financial and economic assessments by the developers and many independent experts working on behalf of the Lao government and the World Bank. One of the project's very important consequences will be assured funding for thirty years of the management of the Conservation Area which forms the greater part of the project's catchment area. Adequate funding should preserve it from the stress of population pressures. Studies have estimated that the people to be resettled would enjoy new livelihoods and live in project-funded housing at over triple their present income levels.

The Lao government will receive about half of all project-related revenues in the first twenty-five years. Ownership of Nam Theum II will then be passed over, debt-free, to the Lao PDR with annual sales revenues of about US$250 million. These benefits will be used by the government to help construct poverty-alleviating infrastructure projects. However, problems still facing the developers and the government could conceivably alter some of the projections. The biggest problem is the current pricing negotiations with the main buyer of electricity, the Electricity Generating Authority of Thailand (EGAT). Officials say they are also waiting for World Bank support to act as financial supporter and guarantor of the project. Subject to gaining World Bank approval, construction could begin at the beginning of 1999.

Dear Dervla,

Do you remember the first draft I showed you of the 'Social Status' for Nam Theun II? The first two anthropologists appointed to do the job were too humanistic for everybody's liking and the final report has been doctored considerably and contradicts a lot of the research done. Dervla, these gentle nomadic people have literally been ethnically cleansed from the Nam Theun area – resettlement amounts to that. It is a terrible tragedy that none of the NGOs is addressing. And none of the reports are truthful and accurate. IUCN funds all these reports, then makes it very difficult for the general public to get hold of the sensitive ones. Yet they are all supposed to be Discussion Papers, like the one you had at Lao Pako, to stimulate honest debate. Last June fourteen Thai NGOs sent a letter to Thailand's Prime Minister urging their government not to buy power from Nam Theun II, which will force the relocation of more than 5,000 people from twenty-eight different ethnic groups. They said, 'Our ailing economy has resulted in a negative growth rate in electricity demand and large reserves of existing generation capacity, which becomes a burden on the investment costs for EGAT, and eventually on consumers. Nam Theun II is highly risky for Thailand and Laos. In the years since it was proposed, the dam's cost has risen from $800 million to $1.5 billion, while its expected returns have fallen from $250 million to $38 million.' All this was published in the *Bangkok Post*, it would never get into the *Vientiane Times*.

Unpleasant progress has been made on many other dam proposals. Massive road building projects are happening all over the country, often linked to those proposals. Now the Norwegian government is giving us a present of US$1.84 million to fund an economic, technical and environmental analysis for the Seset II dam project – only 12 miles north of Seset I! Four Norwegian consultant companies are competing for the feasibility study and I'm told the evaluation of their bids is under way. This is the first benefit the international community gets from all these dams, mountains of work for consultants charging a thousand dollars a day. The study is to be carried out between now and November '99 so we have time to campaign against Seset II. As we must do, we must never despair and give up and let them get on with it. That's what they want, they're very afraid of publicity so please discuss this in your book! Near the site proposed for Seset II a pair of Giant Ibis were spotted recently, the first sighting of these birds, anywhere, for over thirty years. Also White-winged Wood-duck babies were seen in that area, plus nesting Sarus Cranes and three rare species of stork, all globally threatened.

Although Laos is now the darling of the aid and development industries (as you say Rwanda was in the '70s and '80s), very few expats attend to any of the real issues. People on such high salaries and so disconnected from ordinary Laotians are useless. UNDP is a quagmire of corruption just because people earning that much are not prepared to risk their jobs by entering even the tiniest of controversies. They end up acting a part and saying nothing about anything. Meanwhile the government (which needs no encouragement) picks up from them on the latest development fashions of the day and copies them and also manipulates the UNDP to its own advantage.

Despite rumours of total economic collapse a big building boom goes on in Vientiane. Trees are being cut down everywhere and in a couple of months five-storey apartment blocks or silly vulgar mansions have taken their place. They have felled a lot of those ancient and magnificent trees along the Mekong, to make way for a wide concrete walkway by the riverfront. The process of hacking them down was horrific and from our house I could see and hear it. They were much too hard and wide for even the latest type of chain-saws. It took weeks of mangling at them, then their root networks were left like tortured remnants – they were political prisoners holding out to the very last! It has all been so sad, you would weep with me.

Crime in Vientiane has really gathered momentum. Very violent motorbike thieves patrol the night streets – so safe when you were here! They are all the sons of senior military personnel and government ministers, running riot, so there is nothing the police can do. Jaques got mugged last week and his motorbike stolen. This was not a particularly brutal attack but recently several Lao have been stabbed or shot dead when attempting to hold on to their motorbikes. Some stories have been exaggerated because this is all so very new and frightening for Lao people but the fact remains these crimes are happening and not being committed by the destitute poor but by arrogant and well-connected youth.

The rains never really came, there has been a drought in the midlands, people say the Indonesian smoke-blanket had a lot to do with it. If ever I have good news I'll send it at once!

15 January 1999

Dear Marie,

It's frightening that a country can be changed so quickly – what you say about crime in Vientiane, the Mekong embankment trees and so on. I've just come across John Pilger's definition of what you called 'the '90s' most irritating buzz-phrase'. He wrote in the *Irish Times*, 'The international community is not "international" at all; it is the Western establishment whose will is sometimes expressed through the Security Council, at other times through NATO, generally unilaterally. At all times it is dominated by the US. It is a new order with an old meaning: imperialism.' This definition should perhaps be expanded to include those Asian, African and South American predators who, in collusion with Rich World consortia, exploit the Poor World – their own peoples and natural resources.

Last week I met, through a mutual friend, a Swedish 'economic adviser' (Karl) who knows Laos well, speaks the language, claims to love the people, yet is passionately pro-dam and every sort of macro-development. My first impression was of someone glowing with kindness who saw helping Laos as his vocation; he seemed the antithesis of the typical band-wagoneering expat 'expert'. Believing in the absolute superiority of the contemporary Western way of life, he can conceive of no reason for not sharing our 'advantages' with the rest of the world. He spoke with missionary zeal of bringing 'academic centres of excellence' to Laos to enable the leadership to become 'politically mature' so that they could 'form a modern nation-state and get democracy off the ground'.

There followed some bare-knuckle stuff – the fact that we were total strangers, meeting on neutral ground in a Dublin hotel, freed our confrontation from any hostess/guest constraints. Why, Karl demanded, should interfering foreigners oppose any project, hydropower or otherwise, that the Lao government has decided it urgently needs? Why should paternalistic outsiders claim to know best and try to deny to others the goods and services they themselves enjoy? My attitude, he argued, was patronizing and racist, wanting to keep Lao peasants as quaint relics of times past, living in squalor as ignorant impoverished subsistence farmers. He can only see the rural Lao as 'primitive', not yet living in what he calls the 'real world' and unable to get there without our assistance. I see them as civilized, well-balanced people, immensely knowledge-able about their own environment – and what right have we to disrupt their small, sustainable, independent communities? In my exasperation I accused Karl of being a cultural imperialist which I now realize was too glib and unfair to him as an individual. James Robertson, in one of his several inspiring books on the need for radical change, sums up the Karl type:

> Owing to the pressures of professional groupthink and the over-riding imperatives of career survival and success, most mainstream practitioners in all walks of life – including politics and the communications media – become prisoners of the existing systems of organisation and perception in which they operate, and lose the capacity to do more than tinker with them.

Apart from 'professional groupthink' (splendid phrase!) what we are also confronting here is a total incomprehension of peoples who live by other standards, who differ from us on every level: spiritual, emotional, intellectual. Inevitably this leads to a gross lack of respect, a failure to appreciate the worth of those peoples' own traditions and wisdom and sensibilities. Karl could not see how profoundly insulting it is for outsiders to tell the Lao (or whoever) that their way of life is inferior and they must be remoulded in our image and likeness – which means making them as dependent on remote institutions beyond their control as we are. Neither could he see what James Robertson – amidst thousands of others – has pointed out: 'Already, the present human population is consuming and polluting more than the Earth can sustain. That all people could ever attain the high-consuming and high-polluting ways of life of today's rich countries, is a sheer impossibility. A change of direction to progress of a different kind is bound to come, either through purposeful endeavour or as the aftermath of global catastrophe.'

Most of us 'green radicals' merely wring our hands, gnash our teeth, foam at our mouths – and feel helpless. Yet we do have thinking leaders like James Robertson who offer practical alternatives to the present mad way of running the world. And more and more people are listening to them. *Nil desperandum!*

Glossary

ban village

BPKP Mountainous Region Development Company

bund low, narrow embankment separating paddyfields

falang foreigner

HDI Human Development Index

IMF International Monetary Fund, a specialized lending agency linked to the UN

IUCN the World Conservation Union

IVS International Voluntary Service

khene stringed musical instrument

kip Lao unit of currency

koti monks' living quarters in a wat

LPA Lao People's Army, formed in 1976 when the Lao People's Liberation Army (LPLA) was established after the founding of the Lao People's Democratic Republic

LPLA Official title of the Pathet Lao, formed in 1949 by Kaysone Phomvihan. Between 1962 and 1970 it consisted of more than 48,000 guerrillas

LPRP Lao People's Revolutionary Party, founded in 1955; became the ruling party in 1975 and remains in power running a one-party state

LWU Lao Women's Union

MAG Mines Advisory Group

muang administrative district and the central town

naga cobra diety

NBCA National Biodiversity Conservation Area

NEM New Economic Mechanism

NGO non-governmental organization

phi spirits worshipped by Lao animists

RLG Royal Lao Government, the ruling authority in Laos from 1947 until 1975

sim temple (Buddhist)

sin distinctive Lao skirt, intricately embroidered

swidden slash-and-burn agriculture

that Buddhist stupa

TNC transnational corporation

UNDP United Nations Development Programme, created in 1965, the world's main channel for multilateral technical and pre-investment assistance to 'undeveloped' countries. Other UN agencies do the fieldwork while UNDP sees to overall planning, financing and monitoring

UNICEF United Nations International Children's Emergency Fund

USAID United States Agency for International Development

UXO unexploded ordnance

wat Buddhist monastery-cum-temple-cum-school

WHO World Health Organization

WTO World Trade Organization

Bibliography

Butcher, Tom and Ellis, Dawn, *Laos*, Pallas Athene, London, 1993

Castle, Timothy N., *At War in the Shadow of Vietnam*, Columbia University Press, New York, 1993

Chape, Stuart, *Biodiversity Conservation, Protected Areas and the Development Imperative in Laos PDR: Forging the Links*, The World Conservation Union, 1996

Chomsky, Noam and Herman, Edward S., *After the Cataclysm*, Spokesman, Nottingham, 1979

Choulamany-Khamphoui, Outhake and Schenk-Sandbergen, Loes, *Women in Rice Fields and Offices: Irrigation in Laos*, Empowerment, Heiloo, the Netherlands, 1995

Claridge, Gordon, Thanongsi Sorangkhoun and Baird, Ian, *Community Fisheries in Lao PDR: A Survey of Techniques and Issues*, The World Conservation Union, 1997

Evans, Grant and Rowley, Kelvin, *Red Brotherhood at War: Vietnam, Cambodia and Laos since 1975*, Verso, London, 1984

Gosling, Betty, *Old Luang Prabang*, Oxford University Press, Oxford, 1996

Handicap International, *Living with UXO*, 1997

Hoskin, John and Hopkins, Allen W., *The Mekong*, Post Books, Bangkok, 1991

Ivarsson, Soren, Svensson, Thommy and Tonnesson, Stein, *The Quest for Balance in a Changing Laos*, Nordic Institute of Asian Studies, 1995

Lewis, Norman, *A Dragon Apparent*, Jonathan Cape, London, 1951

Library of Congress Federal Research Division, *Laos: A Country Study*, New York, 1994

Mansfield, Stephen, *Culture Shock! Laos*, Kuperard, London, 1997

Mayoury, Ngaosyvathn, *Lao Women: Yesterday and Today*, State Publishing Enterprise, Vientiane, Laos, 1995

McCoy, Alfred W., *The Politics of Heroin: CIA Complicity in the Global Drug Trade*, Lawrence Hill Books, New York, 1991

Stuart-Fox, Martin, *A History of Laos*, Cambridge University Press, Cambridge, 1997

Guidebooks

Bickersteth, Jane and Eliot, Joshua, *Laos Handbook*, Footprint Handbooks, 1997

Cummings, Joe, *Lonely Planet: Laos*, 1996

Jones, John R., *Guide to Laos & Cambodia*, Bradt Publications, 1995

Index

M